THE GREATER MEDIEVAL HISTORIANS:

An Interpretation and a Bibliography

Indrikis Sterns

University Press
of America™

TABLE OF CONTENTS

iii

iv

PREFACE

The aim of this work is to introduce the history student and the curious reader to the course of the development and progress of medieval historiography from its beginnings with the first Christian historians down to the period of the flourishing of the medieval chronicle. To achieve this end, the work is divided into three parts: Early Christian Historians, Historians of the Early Middle Ages, and Historians of the High Middle Ages. Each part, in turn, is divided into two sections: the interpretative introduction and the select bibliography. In the introductions to each part are discussed the greater historians and their major works of that period, and, if it seems desirable to explain and link the origins with a further progress of a developing trend, some historians of a lesser repute are included. In the next section of each part are bibliographies of all the works discussed in the interpretative introduction, listing first the best editions in their original language, followed by English translations, and, if available in English, by modern studies. If a historian's work in its original language is printed in one of the standard and most frequently used medieval source collections, such as the Patrologia Graeca, Patrologia Latina, Monumenta Germaniae Historica, Rolls Series, Recueil des historiens des croisades, this edition, not necessarily being the best text, is usually indicated.

As all publications of such nature are selective, subject to the author's choice and the specific needs of the field, so is this. However, it is hoped that the present work will partially fill the gap, so long felt by medievalists, in the history of medieval historiography. In particular this edition is meant for students who not only are interested in the development of history writing, but also want to locate chronicles in printed editions, in original language and English translation alike.

No one could put this work together by using only his private library and his own knowledge; assistance from without was always sought and appreciated. To all those who helped, the author's warmest thanks. Particular mention need be made of the useful collections at the Library of Princeton University and at the Library of the author's <u>alma mater</u> -- the University of Pennsylvania, and of the oblingingness of Mr. Michael Thornton, the librarian at Mary Immaculate Seminary, Northampton, Pa. Likewise, the author wishes to extend his sincere gratitute to Dr. Robert Thornburg who read the entire manuscript.

EARLY CHRISTIAN HISTORIANS
(to St. Augustine)

Modern historians usually date the beginning of the classical Roman Empire with the reign of Augustus (30 B.C.-14 A.D.); and once established, the Empire for four hundred years withstood all kinds of threats until it began to crumble in the late fourth century A.D. No one really disputes the fact that the major factor contributing to the disintegration of the Empire in the fifth century was the barbarian invasions, followed by the founding of several Germanic states on the ruins of Rome's territory in the West.

The reign of Augustus also witnessed the birth of Jesus Christ, whose teachings, formulated during the reign of Tiberius (14-37), spread westward during the imperial centuries, until in 392 Christianity was for the first time, with an imperial edict, declared the only legal religion in the Roman Empire. Christianity, and the domination of Germanic peoples of Western Europe, became the most intrinsic foundations of the following era in the history of mankind--the Middle Ages. Historians ascribe different dates to the end of the classical world and the beginning of the Middle Ages. The basic concept of religion during antiquity was that of paganism, while the only recognized religion in Europe and the Byzantine Empire during the Middle Ages was Christianity. Thus the years of infancy of Christianity marked by dissemination of the new religion, persecutions of its followers, recognition as one of the legal religions by Constantine in 312 and final victory in the early fifth century as the religion of the state ran concurrently with the classical period of the Roman Empire.

Significantly enough, the classical Roman historical school began with Caesar (ca. 100-44

B.C.), Sallust (86-ca. 35 B.C.) and Livy (59
B.C.-17 A.D.), continued for four centuries on
several levels and in different fields, and came
to an end with the first massive German intrusion
in the Empire.   In 378 A.D., after the battle of
Adrianople, the defeat of the imperial army set
in motion the Visigothic peoples and threw the
road wide open for their rambling through the
Balkans and Italy and the sacking of Rome in 410.
The last of the great classical historians, the
Romanized Greek Ammianus Marcellinus (ca. 300-ca.
400) ended his History with the battle of Adrianople and the death of Emperor Valens (364-378).
Fourteen years later Emperor Theodosius (379-395),
Valens' successor, declared Christianity the only
legal religion in the Empire.   Ammianus Marcellinus was spared from witnessing the barbarian
pillage of the eternal city and the suppression
of the worship of the Graeco-Roman gods.   However, his death in ca. 400 concluded the noble
line of Roman classical historians.

Though the Roman imperial historians differ
in many ways from each other, they, nevertheless,
had two very distinct experiences in common.
First, they all had seen nothing but Roman gran-
deur and the invincibility of the Roman army.
Barbarians, apart from being Rome's enemies, were
of little concern and played a minor role in
their works.   Secondly, all of the imperial historians were pagans who wrote histories from the
viewpoint of pagans and almost completely ignored
the growing force of Christianity.   True, some of
the classical historians occasionally mentioned
the Christians; Tacitus (ca. 55-ca. 117), for
example, wrote in book 15, chapter 22 of the
Annals about the persecutions under Nero.   However, none of Rome's historians became Christian
or discussed Christianity at any length; nor did
they comprehend Christianity from a Christian
standpoint.   These two tasks--to write histories
of the barbarian migrations and of the spread of
Christianity--were left entirely to Christian
pens.

The earliest of the Christian writers of importance was JUSTIN MARTYR (Justinus Martyr, ca. 100–ca. 165), also called Justin the Philosopher. Justin was born in Samaria[1] of pagan parents, was converted to Christianity at about the age of thirty-eight, and later opened a school of Christian learning in Rome, where he tried to convert men to Christianity by philosophical argument. He was martyred by Emperor Marcus Aurelius (161–180). Justin had written several works, but only three are extant: two Apologias against the Gentiles (Apologia prima and Apologia secunda pro Christianis) and the Dialogue with Trypho the Jew (Dialogus cum Tryphone Judaeo). To historians the Apologias are of great value, for they contain a description of Christian worship ritual from the second century A.D. Justin also defended the Christians against the Roman government's accusations of immorality and atheism as well as against Jewish writings which criticized Christianity. Justin also made references to the Gospels, thus indicating that these were used already in his day. Justin Martyr wrote in Greek and is regarded as one of the earliest Greek Fathers of the Church.

The earliest Latin Father of the Church of great importance was TERTULLIAN (Quintus Septimius Florens Tertullianus, ca. 155–ca. 230). He was born in Carthage, received a good education, for a while taught rhetoric, and in about 197 was converted to Christianity. Many of his writings are extant, but to historians the most important are two: To the Pagans (Ad nationes) and Apologia (Apologeticum). Tertullian, like Justin, defended Christianity against charges by Rome of disloyalty to the government. He also asserted the superiority of Christianity over philosophical and pagan religions.

Neither Justin Martyr nor Tertullian was a historian in the true sense of the word; they have only left valuable information about the early Church and the attitude of the Roman gov-

ernment toward the new religion. The first of
the ancients who attempted to write a historic
sketch of Christianity and to work out a new--
Christian--approach to history, was SEXTUS JULIUS
AFRICANUS (ca. 160-ca. 240). The Christians had
accepted the Jewish Bible as part of their sacred
writings, by this introducing in their sacred
history the peoples of the Old Testament. On the
other hand, the Christians were also conscious of
their residence in a secular state, in the Roman
Empire. Thus a problem arose: how to reconcile
the history of the ancient Hebrews and the gentiles[2] as described in the Old Testament and the
Christian era as documented in the New Testament
with their own age and with the secular history
of Rome. Sextus Julius Africanus, a resident of
Palestine and prefect of Emmaus-Nicopolis, wrote
between 212 and 221 a Chronography (Chronographia), also called the Chronicle (Chronica), in
five books in which he attempted to harmonize
classical and biblical chronology. Julius Africanus summarized Hebrew and pagan history from
Adam or the Creation, which he fixed 5500 years
before the birth of Christ, to 223 A.D., to the
third year of the reign of Emperor Elagabalus
(218-222).[3] His milestones for dating events
were the Creation, the Flood, and the Olympiads.
As his source Julius Africanus used the Bible
most extensively and to a lesser degree also the
histories of Herodotus, Thucydides, Polybius and
several other Greek historians whose works are
lost to us. Julius Africanus had computed the
Flood of Noah to 3238 B.C.; the entry of Abraham
into Palestine to 2223 B.C.; the Exodus to 1795
B.C.; the first Olympic games to 1020 years after
the Exodus, 775 B.C.; the first Roman consuls to
502 B.C.; the beginning of the Peloponnesian War
to 431 B.C.; the beginning of the Macedonian Empire to 328 B.C.; the death of Cleopatra (in 30
B.C.) to the eleventh year of the Roman Empire
and the fourth year of the 187th Olympiad, or
5422 years after the Creation, or 28 B.C.; the
death of Christ to 31 A.D. Julius Africanus also was convinced of the Second Coming, thus of

the end of the world, which he expected to happen in 500 A.D. Of Sextus Julius Africanus' Chronography only fragments are extant.

A contemporary of Sextus Julius Africanus was the great bishop of Carthage CYPRIAN (Thascus Caecilius Cyprianus, ca. 210-258). Cyprian was Tertullian's pupil. He was converted to Christianity as a fully matured man and quickly gained prominence in the Church. He was bishop during the first state-wide persecutions under Emperor Decius (249-251) and after the persecutions he had an important role in deciding the fate of the lapsed; he advocated receiving back into the Church those who had apostatized from the Christian Church during the persecutions. To defend them Cyprian wrote a treatise, The Lapsed (De lapsis). This work is a good account of the persecutions during the mid-third century. Also valuable as historical sources are Cyprian's Letters (Epistulae). Cyprian was martyred in 258 by Emperor Valerian (253-260).

The great persecutions of Christians occurred during the last years of the reign of Diocletian (284-305), and a contemporary Christian writer LACTANTIUS (Lucius Caelius Firmianus Lactantius, ca. 260-ca. 340) has left a good account of those events. Lactantius was educated in Carthage and later taught rhetoric in Nicomedia.[4] During the persecutions which he witnessed as a pagan, he was so moved by Christian heroism, that he decided to join the Christians. Later he was appointed by Emperor Constantine (306-337) as the tutor of his son Cryspus. Lactantius has written several works, but to Christian historiography the most important is The Death of the Persecutors (De mortibus persecutorum), a treatise about the great persecution emperors: Nero (54-68), Domitian (81-96), Decius and Diocletian. His work also reveals many facts of the social and economic situation within the Roman Empire under Diocletian as well as his administrative reforms.

The first of the Christian writers who composed a systematic history of Christianity was EUSEBIUS OF CAESAREA (ca. 260-ca. 340), frequently also called after his teacher Eusebius Pamphili. Eusebius was born in Palestine and spent almost all of his life in Caesarea,[5] where in about 314 he became the bishop. He had been imprisoned twice during the persecutions of Galerius (305-311) and Maximin (308-313), but for reasons which are not clear he had escaped death. Later Eusebius had become a friend, admirer, and confidant of Emperor Constantine, who valued his talent and loyalty highly: at the Council of Nicaea in 325 Eusebius was allowed by Constantine to present his Creed of Caesarea; in 331 Constantine wanted to make him bishop of Antioch (which offer Eusebius declined); in 335 Eusebius was entrusted with the chairmanship of the Synod of Jerusalem; and to Eusebius Constantine revealed his earlier vision of the cross in the sky before the battle at Milvian Bridge in 312.

Eusebius was a prolific writer: he composed forty-six works, of which many are lost entirely and others have survived only in fragments, but his three most important historical works, the Ecclesiastical History (Historia ecclesiastica), also known as the History of the Church, the Life of Constantine (De vita Constantini imperatoris libri quatuor), and the Chronicle (Chronicorum libri duo) are preserved. In the Chronicle Eusebius continued and revised Sextus Julius Africanus' method of harmonizing biblical and classical chronology. Eusebius' work is arranged in two parts or books, the "Chronicle" proper and the "Chronological Tables" or "Canon." In the former part, the "Chronicle," Eusebius attempted to establish a chronology of ancient peoples, their rulers and important events according to their own system of reckoning time. In the "Tables" Eusebius produced a tabulated concordance of chronologies of the most significant peoples in antiquity: the Assyrians, the Egyptians, the Hebrews, the Lydians, the Medes, the Persians, the

6.

Greeks, the Macedonians, and the Romans. As the basis for correlating dates of the various ancient peoples in the "Tables" Eusebius used the birth of Abraham, which he had calculated at 2015 B.C. With the first Olympic games, which according to Eusebius and Julius Africanus took place in 775 B.C.,[6] a permanent continuous four-year period for dating events was introduced. Another permanent column was introduced at 753 B.C. with the founding of Rome. Finally, the Nativity was computed 2015 years after the birth of Abraham, and correlated to the fourth year of the 194th Olympiad,[7] to the 751st year after the founding of Rome, and to the forty-second year of Augustus' reign. Events in Roman history, beginning with Julius Caesar's dictatorship, are also dated according to the regnal years of each emperor. In the first part of the <u>Chronicle</u> Eusebius has reconstructed the Roman consular register year by year and synchronized it to the Greek Olympiads. Eusebius' sources, next to Sextus Julius Africanus and the Bible, were ancient historians, writing in Greek: Berossus (3rd cent. B.C.), Alexander Polyhistor (3rd cent. B.C.), Manetho (3rd cent. B.C.), Diodorus of Sicily (1st cent. B.C.), Dionysius of Halicarnassus (1st cent. B.C.), Flavius Josephus (37-ca. 95). He also used Greek Olympic Tables, and several other historical works which are lost to us.

Eusebius of Caesarea, living in the eastern part of the Roman Empire where Greek civilization enjoyed the dominant role, wrote all his works in Greek. However, to make Eusebius' "Chronological Tables" accessible to the Latin speaking West, ST. JEROME (Sophronius Eusebius Hieronymus, ca. 347-ca. 420) translated the "Tables" (without the first part of the <u>Chronicle</u>) into Latin and continued them to 378 A.D., to the death of Emperor Valens (364-378). The "Chronological Tables," or "Canon," by Eusebius as expanded by St. Jerome then became the standard source of information during the Middle Ages for comparative universal chronology. They were later extended by several

7.

Christian chroniclers: to 459 by PROSPER OF
AQUITAINE (Prosper Tiro Aquitanus, ca. 400-460)
and to 627 by ISIDORE OF SEVILLE (Isidorus
Hispalensis, ca. 560-636). Even recently com-
puted chronologies about antiquity and the early
Middle Ages, though thoroughly revised and
greatly augmented, are essentially based on
Eusebius' "Chronological Tables."

Eusebius used the later part of the "Chronological Tables" as the basis for writing his
greatest historical work, the <u>Ecclesiastical</u>
<u>History</u>. It was completed in 325 in ten books
and is the first systematic and successful history of the Christian Church from the days of
Christ to the victory of Constantine over
Licinius (308-324) at Adrianople in 324. In the
first book Eusebius discusses Jesus Christ and
His contemporaries. In the following nine books
he describes the Church under the Roman emperors
from Tiberius to Constantine. Eusebius pays particular attention to the attitude of the Roman
government towards Christianity, to the establish-
ment of the office of the bishop and the apostolic
succession, to persecutions of Christians and
their martyrs, to the various early Christian controversies and to the formulation of orthodoxy,[8]
to early Christian apologetic writers and to the
fixing of the canon of the New Testament. However, above all, Eusebius tried to describe the
victorious though difficult road of Christianity
down to his own day, to the recognition of Christianity as a legal religion in the Roman Empire.

Eusebius is regarded as the most learned man
of his day. He had all the qualities for writing
a history of the Church: he had ample knowledge
of historical facts; he was well read in the
Scripture; he had immense interest in ecclesiastical questions; he was a laborious researcher in
libraries, a diligent reader of Christian authors,
and a careful observer of events of his own time.
However, he was not a great rhetorician or a

magnificent stylist; his narrative is rather businesslike, sometimes even monotonous, though never boring. Eusebius frequently has overburdened his narrative with facts, with quotations from the Scripture, with excerpts from earlier Christian authors, and with word by word reproductions of several important imperial decrees as well as letters of several influential Christian bishops. Some of the transcripts and excerpts are preserved only in Eusebius' work. Contrary to the practice of the ancient historians, Eusebius indicated his sources and authorities; therefore his Ecclesiastical History is an unusually well-documented work; it is even better footnoted than the histories of the classical authors. Consequently, Eusebius' Ecclesiastical History has become an indispensable treasure of facts and information to all modern historians interested in early Christianity. For his unique contribution to writing the first successful and scholarly history of the early Church, Eusebius is generally recognized as the "Father of Church History."

The third of Eusebius' historical works is the Life of Constantine. It is very much inferior as a source of factual information than the Ecclesiastical History; even in regard to reference of sources and documents this treatise lags far behind the History. Eusebius wrote the Life after the emperor's death, and in reality it could be regarded as a eulogy of a deceased friend. Nevertheless, the Life of Constantine contains some important facts about the deeds and thoughts of the emperor and particularly information about the Council of Nicaea in 325; therefore it is always consulted when the epoch of Constantine is reconstructed by modern scholars. However, the Life should be read and used with criticism and caution.

Though Eusebius is superior to the great pagan historians Thucydides, Polybius, and Tacitus in regard to revealing his authorities, he is, on the other hand, inferior to them in

9.

reasoning and the pursuit of rational explanations of causes and events. Eusebius believed in providence and direct divine intervention in shaping the human past; he believed in miracles and in the rightful punishment of Jews for their part in Jesus' crucifixion; but above all, he was biased in favor of Christians and Christianity. All of these characteristics, so noticeable in Ecclesiastical History, entered the works of later medieval chroniclers and became an integral part of medieval historiography.

However, that is not all of Eusebius' contribution to the development of Christian historiography. The early Christian apologists, such as Tertullian and Justin Martyr, wrote treatises in defense of Christianity, but strictly speaking, their works were not histories. Even Sextus Julius Africanus was not a historian in the precise sense of the word; he was a chronologist. Eusebius' Ecclesiastical History is a true investigation into the past of the Christian Church. The real factor, however, that separates Eusebius' Ecclesiastical History from the works of pagan historians is his approach to history. To Eusebius the central theme was no longer a history of one particular people, or of an empire, or of a comparatively short period of time in a nation's or tribe's past; Eusebius wrote a history of all the peoples who had embraced and followed the teachings of Jesus Christ. Whether a Christian was a Greek or a Roman, a Jew or an Egyptian, a free man or a slave, a rich government official or a soldier of the ranks, or even an emperor, made no difference to Eusebius' scrutiny. As long as they were Christians, they all became subjects to his investigation and description. In the works of ancient historians the central role was assigned to pagan kings and pagan gods. Eusebius is the first historian who moved to the foreground of history all the peoples who had acknowledged Jesus Christ as their only leader and God. Furthermore, Eusebius had studied as his prime theme Christians as members of the Church, not as subjects of the Roman Empire. Therefore Eusebius' <u>Ecclesiastical History</u> first of all is a universal history, for it deals with all people who have accepted the teachings of Jesus; and secondly, Eusebius' <u>History</u> is a sacred history, a history of the chosen people. Thus, Eusebius established a new approach to history, he founded a new philosophy of history, a Christian concept of history. This is his other major contribution to medieval historiography. Following Eusebius' tradition, all later European historians wrote their works only about Christians, with no differentiation as to their national origin or tongue they spoke. Pagans and non-Christians entered the works of medieval historians only as the enemy of the Faith with whom the Christians were waging long and bloody wars, or as heathens whom the Christians attempted to convert to the religion of Jesus Christ. Quite frequently medieval histories also became sacred histories, for they described the advance and expansion of Christianity, the past of a national or local church or of a monastery, or the lives and deeds of saints. Thus, with Eusebius' <u>Ecclesiastical History</u> began a new era in European historiography, the Christian era, which in about seventy-five years completely replaced pagan historiography. The last of the great pagan historians, Ammianus Marcellinus, died in ca. 400, and no one after him succeeded in writing a popular history from the pagan point of view.

Eusebius' <u>Ecclesiastical History</u> was translated into Latin in the early fifth century (402-403) by RUFINUS OF AQUILEIA (Rufinus Tyrannius, ca. 345-410). Eusebius' ten books Rufinus compressed into nine, and to this translation he added two books of his own (<u>Historiae ecclesiasticae libri duo</u>), in which he discussed events from the Council of Nicaea in 325 to the death of Emperor Theodosius (379-395) and the division of the Empire between his sons Honorius (395-423) and Arcadius (395-408) in 395. Rufinus' rendering of Eusebius' <u>History</u>, as supplemented by his continuation, became the standard work in the West for early church history throughout the Middle Ages.

Eusebius' Ecclesiastical History found continuators also in the East. Three Byzantine historians--SOCRATES (Socrates Scholasticus, ca. 380-ca. 450), SOZOMEN (Salaminius Hermias Sozomenus, ca. 400-ca. 450), and THEODORET OF CYRUS (Theodoretus Cyrensis, ca. 393-before 466)--continued Eusebius' work, each writing his own Ecclesiastical History. Socrates dealt with the years from 305 to 439; Sozomen covered the period from 323 to 423; and Theodoret from 324-429. They all wrote in Greek. Under the direction of King Theodoric the Great (471-526) first minister CASSIODORUS (Flavius Magnus Aurelius Cassiodorus Senator, ca. 487-ca. 583) these three church histories were condensed and translated into Latin by Cassiodorus' secretary Epiphanius, and Cassiodorus added to this compendium his own Chronicle (Chronica) from Abraham to 519 A.D. The new work, known as the Tripartite History (Historia ecclesiastica tripartita) became another popular handbook for church history during the Middle Ages.

As mentioned above, Eusebius outlined a new approach to history; he was the first who sketched the features of a Christian philosophy of history. However, the task of perfecting Christian views on history and the development of the traditional Christian philosophy of history during the Middle Ages had to wait for one hundred more years, till St. Augustine in 426 completed his greatest work, the City of God.

ST. AUGUSTINE OF HIPPO (Aurelius Augustinus, 354-430) was born on November 13, 354 in Thagaste, a small town approximately forty miles south of Hippo Regius,[9] in North Africa. His mother Monica was a devout Christian (thus St. Augustine was acquainted with Christianity from childhood); his father was not. After attending the local neighboring school at Madaura, then studying at Car-

thage for four years, Augustine in 375 began
teaching rhetoric, first in his native town, then
in Carthage. While in Carthage, Augustine became
acquainted with and even a follower of Manichaeism,[10] though with some doubts in his heart. In
383, still associated with Manichaeism, St. Augustine voyaged to Rome to teach rhetoric. In Italy
Augustine also became attracted by the teachings
of Neo-Platonists.[11] After a successful year as
a rhetorician in Rome, Augustine obtained a pro-
fessorship in rhetoric in Milan. There he listened to the sermons of St. Ambrose (ca. 340-
397), the Christian bishop of Milan. Under the
influence of his preaching, Augustine became more
and more critical of Manichaeanism and Neo-Platonism and finally, after extended hesitation, on
Holy Saturday,[12] 387 he was baptized into Christianity by St. Ambrose. Soon afterwards Augustine left Milan and via Rome and Ostia[13] in 388
returned to Thagaste, where he lived a monastic
life and devoted his time to the study of the
Scripture. In 391 St. Augustine went to Hippo,
where the local Christian bishop persuaded Augustine to take the holy orders.[14] In 396 he was
made assistant bishop of Hippo, and in the following year, after the death of the reigning
bishop, Augustine became the bishop of Hippo. He
held this office until his death of August 28, 430.

     St. Augustine's works are voluminous. Basi-
cally they deal with two problems: the formulation of the orthodox Christian doctrine and the
defense of Christianity against attacks from the
followers of Roman pagan religion. Several of
his writings also deal with the refutation of the
teachings of Manichaeans, Neo-Platonists, and
several Christian controversialists, such as
Arius, Donatus, and Pelagius.[15] In these works,
totaling nearly one hundred, the fundamental con-
ceptions of orthodox Christianity were ironed out,
and they remained unchanged until the thirteenth
century, when St. Thomas Aquinas (1225-1274) in
part reshaped some of St. Augustine's maxims.

For historians, however, more important than Augustine's doctrinal views is his Christian philosophy of history. St. Augustine's attitude towards history is not explained in one single work; it should be gathered from various writings. However, two works excel among others--his autobiography, Confessions (Confessiones), written between 397 and 401, and above all, the City of God (De civitate Dei), a work in twenty-two books, written between 413 and 426 in defense of Christianity, which was under attack because of the sack of Rome in 410 by the Christian Visigoths under their leader Alaric (ca. 370-410).

The City of God is an exposition of St. Augustine's philosophy of religion and Christianity, of man and society, of state and government, and of history. However, Augustine examined man and his place in society and history and his relation to state and government only from the viewpoint of religion and according to his attitude towards Christianity. Man's role in the past St. Augustine valued solely in the light of biblical history. That is to say, Augustine, though recognizing the existence of pagan secular states and empires and occasionally discussing some aspects of their history, treated the whole human past as a complex of events in the life of the descendants of Adam. Consequently, St. Augustine divided the entire course of the history of mankind into six ages or periods: "The first period, as the first day, was from Adam until Noah: the second, as the second day, from Noah unto Abraham: the third, as the third day, from Abraham unto David: the fourth, as the fourth day, from David unto the removal to Babylon: the fifth period, as the fifth day, from the removal to Babylon unto the preaching of John. The sixth day beginneth from the preaching of John, and lasteth unto end; and after the end of the sixth day, we reach our rest. The sixth day, therefore, is even now passing."[16] Thus, like his predecessors Sextus Julius Africanus and Eusebius of Caesarea, St. Augustine recognized

14.

the history of man as sacred history, for he began it with the creation of the first man, Adam,
and correlated it only to biblical history.
Furthermore, Augustine partly retained the chronological schemes of Julius Africanus and Eusebius; but on the other hand, he limited the whole
history of mankind between two milestones, between Adam and the Second Coming of Christ; and
this span in time he divided into six distinct
ages, after the six days of Creation.

Even then, Augustine did not leave the periodization of the human past with the grouping of
events according to the Scripture. He advanced
his own, specifically Christian approach to history by dividing all peoples of mankind into only
two large groups. About the progeny of Adam St.
Augustine has said: "Though there are very many
and great nations all over the earth, whose rites
and customs, speech, arms, and dress are distinguished by marked differences, yet there are no
more than two kinds of human society, which we
may justly call two cities, according to the
language of our Scriptures. The one consists of
those who wish to live after the flesh, the other
of those who wish to live after the spirit. . .17
The /second/ city is that of the just, the /first/
is that of the wicked. . .18 Jerusalem is the
city of the saints; Babylon of the wicked. . .
By Babylon is meant the city of this world . . .19
The city of Jerusalem is called Sion. . . Sion is
the city of God."20 The city of God, St. Augustine believed, was founded by God himself,21 and
its first inhabitants were the good or faithful
angels; they made up the heavenly city even before the creation of man, when God was still in
the process of separating light from darkness.22
Then, with the creation of Adam and Eve arose the
first sin, the human procreation of man; Adam be-
got his two firstborn sons, Cain and Abel: "Cain
was the first-born, and he belonged to the city
of man; after him was born Abel, who belonged to
the city of God."23 But Cain slew Abel, and with
this act of fratricide arose two loves--the love

15.

of God and the love of self--and the two loves
originated two different cities of sicieties:
"Two cities have been formed by two loves: the
earthly by the love of self, even to the contempt of God; the heavenly by the love of God,
even to the contempt of self."[24] Cain out of
self-love, built a city, while "Abel, being a
sojourner, built none. For the city of the
saints is above."[25] Augustine even amplified
this notion by saying that with human birth and
death, as with the human race as a whole, had
begun the historical course of the two cities:
"Adam was the father of both lines,--the father,
that is to say, both of the lines which belonged
to the earthly, and of that which belonged to the
heavenly city,--when Abel was slain, and by his
death exhibited a marvelous mystery, there were
henceforth two lines proceeding from two fathers,
Cain and Seth /third son of Adam/, and in those
sons of theirs, whom it behoved to register, the
tokens of these two cities began to appear more
distinctly."[26] Although these two cities or
societies thereafter continued to prosper concurrently as each gave its own color to human
history, they nevertheless took different roads
in shaping the human past; in fact, they lived in
enmity to each other, with different laws of religion.[27] The city of man concentrated its attention on foreign wars and domestic quarrels and
demanded victories as the goal for its aims, but
these victories either ended in death or were
mere respites from further war. Nevertheless,
Augustine recognized peace as the highest aim of
the city of man, for "it makes war in order to
attain to this peace." However, such a peace,
achieved by victory, is only a temporary peace
and joy, whereas in the city of God there will
be an ultimate victory of eternal, supreme and
untroubled peace.[28]

On earth the two societies live intermin-
gled, but they make up two forms of living, one
being its own presence, the other symbolic pre-
sentation of the heavenly city.[29] The former is

16.

the city of man or Babylon; the latter is the earthly Jerusalem.[30] The city of man throughout the world forms one community, but each individual in that community is guided by his own passion and pursues his own purpose. The earthly city does not live by faith, but seeks only an earthly peace, concord among men and obedience among citizens. The earthly Jerusalem, or that part of human society which is the shadow of the heavenly city, only sojourns or is on pilgrimage in this mortal life.[31]

The city of God, according to St. Augustine, was founded by Christ himself, being God, and when Augustine refers to the city of God, he means both, the earthly Jerusalem as well as the heavenly Jerusalem. But as the city of God moved along through ages, the earthly Jerusalem acquired a ruler, and the first king of the terrestrial city of God became David, and this city was made up of the true Israelites and of the gentiles who believed in Jesus Christ through patriarchs and prophets of the Old Testament before the Coming of Christ, before He became man through Mary.[32] Augustine was also fully aware that in the earthly Jerusalem, as in the earthly city of man, or Babylon, people marry and are begotten by carnal intercourse between males and females. Thus, to the earthly Jerusalem belong citizens from all nations and all tongues who recognize as its founder, leader, and king Jesus Christ, the one supreme and true God, Who pays no attention to diverse customs, laws, and traditions as long as His people strive after human peace. The highest preoccupation of the city of God during its existence in this world is the invocation of God; its citizens are Christians, the people of Christ.[33] Therefore to St. Augustine, as to Eusebius of Caesarea, the history of this earthly Jerusalem, or the Christian society on earth, was a universal history, for all nations are blessed and called to eternal life in the kingdom of heaven as fellow-heirs to Christ in the New Testament as well as in the Old Testament, for the

17.

city of God has accepted the Old and the New Testament as canonical.[34]

The question arises whether the terrestrial city of God, thus the people who live after the spirit, are conscious of their saintly community, whether they are organized in some kind of congregation or society. In St. Augustine's mind the Christian Church is representing the city of God on earth: "What is the city of God, but the Holy Church? For men who love one another and who love their God who dwelleth in them, constitute a city unto God."[35] Only the saintly make up the heavenly city on earth, for St. Augustine was well aware that amongst the members of the Church, or in a Christian congregation, there are those who neither are saints nor live by faith; even the heretics are among the members of the Church.[36]

According to St. Augustine's chronology the sixth age of mankind had started with the preaching of John the Baptist, and will last until the end; in other words, the sixth and last age of man is the period after Christ's first coming, the period of Christianity. Our own time, the present, then falls into the sixth age, and the present, Augustine believed, "has no duration." However, Augustine also held in esteem the Christian belief of Christ's second coming: "the present cannot possibly have duration."[37] Christ will reappear again on the Day of the Last Judgment when all the dead and the living will come before the Supreme Judge and He will separate the citizens of the heavenly city, or the faithful joined by the good angels, from the wicked and bad angels, from the citizens of the earthly city.[38] Thus, after the resurrection there will be again two eternal kingdoms, each with its own boundaries, the one Christ's, the other the devil's.[39] The former is the eternal, or heavenly Jerusalem, where at the end of the pilgrimage in this world, after resurrection no one will marry nor take wives, where no one will be born, because no one will die.[40] The citizens of the

18.

heavenly kingdom will attain eternal life: "In that city all the citizens shall be immortal, men now for the first time enjoying what the holy angels have never lost. And this shall be accomplished by God, the most almighty Founder of the city."[41] The citizens of the heavenly, eternal city of God will enjoy unending happiness, because they, through eternal life, will attain the supreme good, which is peace: "The end or supreme good of this city is either peace in eternal life or eternal life in peace."[42] And "the peace of the celestial city is the perfectly ordered and harmonious enjoyment of God, and of one another in God."[43] The ruler or the monarch of the heavenly Jerusalem will be Christ, the eternal king of the city of God.[44]

On the Domesday also the fate of the wicked, of the citizens of the earthly city, or city of man, will be decided, and their lot will be unending wretchedness; the punishment of the wicked will have no end; they will suffer eternal fire and endure perpetual misery. Moreover St. Augustine found their sufferings and wretchedness more pitiful because there will be no death to end their pain; it will be an eternal punishment and misery under the rule of the devil.[45] Thus, according to St. Augustine, after the Day of the Last Judgment there again will be two universal communities, two eternal cities, but now the citizens will be permanently separated from each other, and such an arrangement, then, will last forever.

About the city of man, or the earthly city, St. Augustine has said that in spite of its expansion throughout the world, it is a single community, for the bond of a common nature makes all humans one. That is to say, on earth the two cities, or the believers and the unbelievers, are linked together, for "we all are in that one man /Adam/, since we all are that one man, who fell into sin by the woman /Eve/ who was made from him before the sin."[46] Therefore men in this world

19.

as descendants of Adam, because of the original
sin, are corrupt by choice and condemned by justice, and beget corrupt and condemned children.[47]
However, the city of God hates the lovers of this
world, for in the earthly city of man one cannot
find justice: "True justice has no existence
save in that republic whose founder and ruler is
Christ."[48] Furthermore, the city of man seeks
the praise of men, and the rulers as well as the
ruled in the earthly city are dominated by the
lust of domination. But the desire to dominate
leads to chronic warfare: "This city is often
divided against itself by litigations, wars,
quarrels, and such victories as are either life-
destroying or short-lived. For each part of it
that arms against another part of it seeks to
triumph over the nations through itself in bond-
age of vice."[49] To bring order in this disorderly society of man, or in the earthly city, secular states and empires were founded. Such an
arrangement for maintenance of peace, law and order, to protect human lives and property is the
state, "a multitude of men, bound together by
some associating tie."[50] The secular state, or
the earthly city, was set up by God[51] to enforce
laws, manners, and institutions, in order to
maintain earthly peace; even the heavenly city
while sojourning on earth avails itself of this
peace and supports the laws and institutions of
the state.[52] Therefore, a state cannot be administered without justice, because without justice there can be no people held together by a
common tie, and when there is no people, there is
no state.[53] St. Augustine also held the belief
that secular states and rulers as set up by God
are established for the benefit of the whole of
mankind, and therefore their subjected people
should be obedient to them, their commands, laws
and justice.[54] Thus, the earthly city--or secular states, which in St. Augustine's mind are
one[55]--is established to maintain peace, justice
and law, and every human, whether a citizen of
the earthly city or of the heavenly city, while
sojourning in this world, has to live in a state

20.

under a ruler. The city of this world has and makes its own history.[56]

St. Augustine is somewhat uncertain in his mind as to when the earthly city came into existence. In the City of God, book 15, chapter 21, he says that it began with Adam; in chapter 5, with Cain's killing of Abel; but in book 16, chapter 10, Augustine writes: "From the time when they proudly built a tower to heaven, a symbol of godless exaltation, the city or society of the wicked becomes apparent. Whether it was only disguised before, or nonexistent; whether both cities remained after the flood,--the godly in the two sons of Noah who were blessed, and in their posterity, and the ungodly in the cursed son and his descendents, from whom sprang that mighty hunter against the Lord,--is not easily determined." In any case, in the mind of Augustine the secular state (men in the earthly city) has reached its prime already by the time of Abraham and his journey from Ur to Haran and Palestine, thus with the beginning of Hebrew history, or ca. 1950 B.C.: "During the same period /of Abraham/ there were three famous kingdoms of the nations, in which the city of the earth-born, that is, the society of men living according to man under the domination of the fallen angels, chiefly flourished, namely the three kingdoms of Sicyon /i.e., Greece/, Egypt, and Assyria. Of these, Assyria was much the most powerful and sublime. . . Its head was Babylon, an earth-born city, most fitly named, for it means confusion."[57]

Augustine devoted the greater part of books 16 to 18 to retracing the history of the city of man or secular states in antiquity and correlated that history to sacred[58] or biblical history, recounting the past, again like Eusebius of Caesarea, from Abraham to his own times, and then proceeded with a vision of the future down to the Second Coming. Book 18 deals mostly with the sixth age, the age of Christianity.

21.

Of the secular states, next to Assyria, St. Augustine regarded Rome as the most powerful empire, the former in the East, the latter in the West, and chronologically following Assyria. Like Eusebius, Augustine fixed the founding of Rome at the beginning of the reign of Hosea of Israel, thus ca. 750 B.C.; and Rome came into existence as a result of another fratricide, when Romulus slew Remus. Although Augustine was quick to draw parallels to Cain's slaying of Abel, he immediately pointed out that the quarrel between Remus and Romulus divided the city of man against itself, whereas Cain's slaying of Abel separated the heavenly city from the earthly city. Thus, the founding of Rome through the killing of Remus was fractricide within the earthly city, and therefore Augustine called Rome the daughter of Babylon, and the second Babylon--in the West.[59] However, Augustine was convinced that the rule of Rome has brought--by God's pleasure--law and enduring peace for the whole world and made the city of man into a single society, into a world community, though at a terrible cost--unending series of wars and tremendous slaughtering of men. Therefore the peace achieved by Rome is only an earthly peace, inferior to the heavenly peace in the city of God. The earthly city, or the secular states, will be destroyed again by God on the Day of the Last Judgment.[60]

Consequently, Augustine has rejected the idea of the recurrence or reappearance of history in periodic revolutions or cycles. To Augustine the human past began with the creation of Adam, reached its climax with the birth of Jesus Christ, and will continue its strait progress of building the city of God till the Resurrection. After Jesus' second coming, there will be no second death: "Once Christ died for our sins; and, rising from the dead, He dieth no more."[61]

However, St. Augustine not only defined the idea of two societies, of the two cities in the historical process of the human past, but also

22.

provided the dogmatic background for other characteristics of Christian history during the Middle Ages. The early Christian apologists, particularly Eusebius of Caesarea, had already touched some of them, of which the most significant was God's direct intervention, or God's omnipresence in shaping human affairs. St. Augustine made it clear that God forsakest nothing that he has made,[62] and that He is the highest cause of everything that happens in this world:[63] "Of one thing we are certain. . . that except by God's will nothing can happen to any one. . . The Cretor makes what use He pleases of all His creatures."[64] God is present everywhere by His power of His majesty,[65] and no one can escape His presence.[66] God not only is the ultimate cause for whatever happens, but He also has foreknowledge of everything that will happen, and God's foreknowledge is infallible: "God can never be believed to have left the kingdomes of men, their dominations and servitudes, outside of the law of His providence."[67]

When St. Augustine wrote the City of God, Christianity had already been legalized for a whole century. Nevertheless, he still drew much spiritual strength and examples from the early Christian martyrs for his defense of Christianity against attack by non-Christians and unorthodox Christians. The martyrs were witnesses of Christ in blood who through their sufferings and death[68] had set excellent examples to the faithful to make manifest the true religion and expose the false.[69] The bodies of martyrs were often buried in churches, and it was hoped that their remains would perform miraculous healing to the sick.[70] St. Augustine also praised persons who carried with them relics of martyrs.[71] Many of the martyrs were regarded as saints, and again, it was believed that closeness and care of the bodies of saints would render beneficial miracles to the faithful.[72] Thus, a cult of martyrs, saints, miracles, and relics crept into medieval historiography, and since St. Augustine had approved

23.

of it, it not only held firm through the Middle
Ages, but also flourished and occupied a respectable place in medieval chronicles. Gradually
even a specific branch of history writing devel-
oped--hagiography--stories and legends about
saints, their lives and the miracles which they
performed.

In the City of God St. Augustine repeatedly
indicated that his goal was to write a history of
the heavenly--not earthly--city; therefore his
story about the human past actually is a sacred
history.[73] However, ample reference is made
throughout the work, particularly in books 3 and
18, to the history of man in antiquity. Who were
Augustine's authorities, what were his sources for
the profane history, for the city of man in the
ancient world? For biblical or Jewish history his
sources are almost entirely the Scripture, in particular the Psalms and Genesis. But Augustine also made thorough use of other books of the Old
Testament, including some apocryphal works. For
refuting pagan religious dogmas and affirming the
correctness of the Christian point of view Augustine's basic source is the New Testament; of the
twenty-seven New Testament books only the three
shortest ones are not referred to: Paul's Epistle
to Philemon and John's Second and Third Epistles.
Of the ancient pagan historians St. Augustine most
widely used several lost works by Varro, then Virgil's Aeneid, and Cicero's On Republic and Tuscu-
lan Disputations; in a lesser degree, Augustine
also made use of Sallust's Conspiracy of Catiline,
Lucan's Pharsalia, and Trogus Pompeius' and Justin's Histories. Beyond doubt, Augustine used
Eusebius' and Jerome's Chronological Tables extensively, particularly for the Near Eastern history and its correlation to biblical, Greek, and
Roman history,[74] though, following the tradition
of all ancient historians, he seldom indicated
his source directly. Thus, by the standards of
his own day Augustine probably used the best
sources available to him in Latin. And yet, St.
Augustine did not write a history of the earthly

city, a factual history of antiquity; that was not his intention. He used facts from secular history mostly for two purposes: to compare and to contrast with his story of sacred history, thus of the city of God; and secondly, to defend and refute accusations against Christianity and the heavenly city. Therefore St. Augustine's City of God is of little value as a source book, even as a text book for ancient history. St. Augustine's real importance in historiography lay in the field of philosophy of history, for he formulated more clearly and effectively than anyone else before him Christian attitude toward sacred history and history in general. St. Augustine has divided the whole mankind into those who follow the teachings of the Book, and consequently will be saved on the Day of Reckoning, and those who have rejected the messianic prophecies of the Old Testament and the message of Jesus Christ and His apostles in the New Testament. In the eyes of Augustine only the former group of people, the city of God on earth, are worthy of being described in history. Such a division of history, into Christian and non-Christian, then, was rigorously followed, at least ideologically, throughout the Middle Ages,[75] for European annalists, chroniclers, and historians wrote their works only about Christians and Christianity, completely ignoring history of non-Christian peoples. Many of the medieval historians called their works ecclesiastical or church histories; however, it would be wrong to assume that they wrote either sacred histories of the heavenly city, or even true religious histories. Their works all lack the dynamic, prophetic message of St. Augustine; therefore the best that the Westerners achieved during the Middle Ages in historiography was a secular history of Christian society, that is, according to St. Augustine's definition, a history of the earthly city in which are wayfaring, among others, the true Christians, "who live after the spirit," the citizens of the heavenly city on earch.

St. Augustine did not have a high esteem for secular or profane history. In his treatise <u>On Christian Doctrine</u> (<u>De doctrina Christiana</u>) Augustine noted the two-fold use of history. First, secular chronology, arranged according to Olympiads and consular lists, helps in understanding scriptural events and biblical history. Secondly, historical narratives describe former institutions of men. Augustine also believed that "history narrates what has been done, faithfully and with advantage," because "things that are past and gone and cannot be undone are to be reckoned as belonging to the course of time, of which God is the author and governor."[76] In making such a statement about the infallibility of history, Augustine most probably was thinking of biblical history, which in his mind was absolute truth, written by God Himself, or at least by divine inspiration. Secular or profane history is written by learned humans--thus men, not God--and men are preoccupied with trifles and lies.[77] In any case, Augustine's knowledge for writing a secular history of ancient peoples was too scanty, and his conception of divine and historical relationship too artificial. Neither was history of the earthly city his goal, nor did he have the scholarly approach to history of Thucydides or Tacitus or the eloquent tongue of Polybius or Caesar. Augustine was well aware of his shortcomings, and therefore, seeing the need for a secular history of ancient peoples for Christian readers, he asked his friend and fellow-wayfarer Orosius to write a profane history of the ancient world from the viewpoint of a Christian. "I have set forth," wrote Orosius in conclusion of his work, "with Christ's help, according to your bidding, most blessed father Augustine, the desires and punishments of sinful men, the struggles of the world, and the judgments of God, from the beginning of the world down to the present day, that is, during five thousand six hundred and eighteen years, as briefly and as simply as I could."[78]

PAULUS OROSIUS (ca. 380-after 418) was born
between 380 and 390 in the Iberian peninsula,
where he had become a priest. In 414 he left for
North Africa, and at Hippo he met St. Augustine.
The two men became friends. Upon Augustine's
suggestion, Orosius in 415 departed to Palestine,
taking with him Augustine's letter to St. Jerome
in Bethlehem. In the East Orosius became in-
volved in the Pelagian controversy by defending
the views of St. Augustine against Pelagianism.
In the following year Orosius returned to Hippo,
where upon Augustine's insistence he began to
compose his apologetic work Seven Books of History against the Pagans (Historiarum adversus
paganos libri septem); it was completed in 418.
After that year there is no trace of Orosius'
life.

Orosius' work can be regarded as the first
attempt to write a universal history of the
earthly city in accordance with the philosophy of
history of St. Augustine. As his model work for
writing universal history Orosius used an earlier
work, Justin's (Justinus, died ca. 226 A.D.)
History of the World (Historiarum ex Trogo Pompeio
excerptarum libri XLIV) which, in turn, was merely
an abridgment of the Augustan historian Trogus
Pompeius' Philippic Histories (Historiae Philip-
picae). Justin was a pagan, and Orosius' task was
to inject Augustinian dogmas, philosophy, and
apology of the new religion into his version of
world history. To achieve this end, Orosius used
as his main sources, first, the Bible, then Eusebius' "Chronological Tables" as translated and
extended by St. Jerome. Further, Orosius made
extensive use of the work of Trogus Pompeius,
through its abridger Justin, then Eutropius'
(died ca. 364) Short History of Rome (Breviarium
ab urbe condita), Tacitus' Histories, Suetonius'
Lives of the Twelve Caesars, Sallust's Jugurthine
War and Conspiracy of Catiline, and an abridgment
of Livy by Florus (fl. 1st half of 2nd cent.)
For the legendary and early history of Greece and
Rome Orosius consulted Virgil's Aeneid; informa-

tion about events of his own time Orosius drew
from personal knowledge. It is doubtful whether
Augustine made any use of Orosius' work; Augustine's main sources were Cicero, Livy, Pliny,
Sallust, Vergil, and Varro, the latter not even
referred to by Orosius.

Orosius began his world history with the rise
of the Assyrian Empire (which he frequently called
Babylonian Empire) contemporary to Abraham (whose
birth he, like Eusebius, fixed to 2015 B.C.), and
then in seven books brought it down to 417 A.D.
Thus, it had become a tradition to begin the history of secular states--or as St. Augustine would
have said, of the earthly city--with Abraham, the
Hebrew patriarch. Orosius briefly sketched biblical, Assyrian, Chaldean, Egyptian, Greek and
Macedonian history in the first three books of his
work. The founding of Rome is discussed already
in book two, early Roman history is described in
book three, and from book four on (or in two-
thirds of his work) Orosius pays attention only to
Roman history. In his sketch of the history of
mankind Orosius recognized four great ancient empires: the Babylonian (i.e. Assyrian) in the
east, the Roman in the west, the Macedonian in the
north, and the Carthaginian in the south. However, the greatest of the four were the Babylonian, which was the oldest, and the Roman, its
successor, unto which was passed over the power
from the east through the intermediary kingdoms
of Macedon and Carthage.[79] Already Augustine had
recognized four world empires in antiquity, though
his list differed slightly from Orosius': Augustine saw as the four greatest secular states Assyria, Egypt, Greece, and Rome, whereas Orosius,
retaining Assyria as the oldest, and Rome, of
which both of them were residents, as the strong-
est, replaced Greece with Macedon and Egypt with
Carthage. Most probably the idea of four world
empires was derived from the prophet Daniel's
dream about the four great beasts which came out
of the sea and according to verse 17: "These
four great beasts are four kingdoms which shall

28.

arise out of the earth." The concept of four
world monarchies for centuries appeared in Christian histories, and according to the time of interpretation, were differently identified. Paulus Orosius, however, explained that his purpose
for writing the history of the past was "to compare the periods of world history with one another, not to revile any part of it for its
troubles."[80]

For Roman history Orosius followed the chronological scheme of the preceding Roman historians by dating events from the legendary founding
of Rome in 753 B.C. Christ's birth Orosius has
fixed "in the seven hundred and fifty-second year
after the founding of the City."[81] However, the
birth of Christ did not yet become a milestone
for dating later events.

Orosius' History is not overladen with facts
or scholarly writing, nor could it be used today
as a source of information for Roman history: it
is a popular account of the past for an ordinary
reader. However, for its own times, for the poorly educated early Christians, it most probably was
a good and acceptable history of the ancient
world, correlated to biblical history, viewed
through the eyes of a fervent Christian, and rich-
ly adorned with messianic quotations from the
Scripture. Seemingly, such was the kind of history his contemporary Christians could understand
and needed. Christians of later centuries held
it indispensable and highly esteemed: almost two
hundred manuscript copies of Orosius' work have
survived to our day. The Church's approval of
its usefulness was sanctioned in 494 by a bull of
Pope Gelasius (492-496).[82]

Orosius' own philosophy of history is best
described with his words: "Among Romans, as I
have said, I am a Roman; among Christians, a
Christian; among men, a man; I implore the state
through its laws, the conscience through religion, nature through its universality. I enjoy

29.

every land temporarily as my fatherland, because
what is truly my fatherland and that which I love
is not completely on this earth. I have lost
nothing, when I have loved nothing, and I have
everything when He whom I love is with me, especially because He is the same among all, who
makes me known to all and very near to all."[83]
A truly Augustinian approach to human society, to
sojourners in this world! Although by the crite-
ria of modern historians Orosius' work is not
considered first rate, it was highly esteemed and
very popular throughout the Middle Ages because
its Christian orientation suited the minds of
medieval people.

Notes

[1] Samaria — a district in Palestine.

[2] Gentile — a non-Jew, a pagan.

[3] Sextus Julius Africanus has miscalculated
Elagabalus' reign for about three years.

[4] Nicomedia — a town in the northwestern
corner of Asia Minor.

[5] Caesarea — Roman capital for the province
of Palestine.

[6] The traditional year for the first Olympic
games is 776 B.C.

[7] Olympiad — the four-year period between
two Olympic games.

[8] Orthodoxy — conformity with the established
doctrine in religion.

[9] Hippo Regius - present day Bone in Algeria.

[10] Manichaeism - a dualistic religion, founded by the Persian prophet Mani, who began preaching in about 242 in the Valley of Tigris and Euphrates. Manichaeism is a mixture of Zorastrianism, Buddhism and Christianity, emphasizing the power and struggle of the dual forces, light and dark, spirit and flesh, the good God, as represented in Jesus, and the evil god, as represented in Satan. Manichaeism was regarded by Christians as a heresy and was practically eradicated in the West by the sixth century. Its revival from the East in twelfth-century Western Europe is usually known as the Albigensian heresy.

[11] Neo-Platonism - a philosophical religion, developed in the third century A.D. by an Egyptian Plotinus (d. 270), who did most of his writing in Rome. According to Plotinus there is one God, the supreme Light, the supreme Intelligence, the absolute One. The absolute One was the first being (Nous), though not a human being, not an active creator. From the absolute One, the God comes or emanates the Divine Mind which contains the individual or human intelligences, and the World Soul, from which individual people receive their individual souls. The World's Soul is eternal, it never comes down to earth. Plotinus, like Plato, believed that each man has a body and a soul; the latter is received from the World's Soul. A man's soul is the intelligence of man. If the soul can take over the flesh, which is less good than the soul, then the soul escapes the influence of the temptations of the body. After a person's death the soul through many migrations returns to the World Soul. Neo-Platonism, like Manichaeism, was attacked by contemporary Christians.

[12] Holy Saturday - Saturday before Easter Sunday.

31.

[13] Ostia – ancient harbor of Rome.

[14] To take the holy orders – ordination to priesthood.

[15] Arianism – A Near Eastern Christian controversy, advanced by a priest of Alexandria, Arius (ca. 256-336), who taught that Christ, though God, is a created being by the Father, and therefore, as the first creature, is subordinated to the Father and not eternal. Arianism was condemned as heresy by the Council of Nicaea in 325.

Donatism – a North African Christian controversy which arose after the persecutions of Diocletian about the validity of ordination of priests by bishops who have conformed with the emperor's order to hand over sacred Christian books during the persecutions, and the validity of sacraments administered by priests who were ordained by conformist bishops. One of the leaders of the nonconformist group of the African clergy was Donatus, bishop of Carthage (313-347), thus the name of the movement, Donatism.

Pelagianism – A Western Christian controversy advanced by the British monk Pelagius (ca. 355-ca. 425), who denied the seriousness of original sin, stressed the importance of free will and challenged St. Augustine's view that God's grace alone can save man from eternal perdition. Pelagianism was declared a heresy by the Council of Ephesus in 431.

[16] St. Augustine, "Expositions on the Book of Psalms," Psalm 93, para. 1, in Nicene and Post-Nicene Fathers, 1st series, vol. 8 (1888); cf. Vernon J. Bourke (ed.), The Essential Augustine (Indianapolis: Hackett Publishing Co., 1964; 2nd printing 1974), p. 224.

[17] St. Augustine, The City of God, book 14, ch. 1. All quotations from The City of God are given from Marcus Dods' transl., in Nicene and

<u>Post-Nicene Fathers</u>, 1st series, vol. 2 (1887).

[18] St. Augustine, "Literal Commentary on Genesis," transl. Vernon J. Bourke, <u>The Essential Augustine</u>, p. 201.

[19] St. Augustine, "Expositions on the Book of Psalms," Psalm 87, para. 5, as above, note 16. The phrase "City of God" Augustine borrowed from the Psalms 45:5-6, 47:1-2, 83:3, and in his works it is used interchangeably with the "eternal city," the "heavenly city," and "Jerusalem." Its opposite, or adversary, the "earthly city," is used interchangeably with "Babylon," the "city of devil," the "city of man," and the "city of the world."

[20] St. Augustine, "Expositions on the Book of Psalms," Psalm 99, para. 4, as above, note 16; cf. Bourke, p. 208.

[21] <u>City of God</u>, book 1, Preface.

[22] <u>City of God</u>, book 11, chs. 9 and 28.

[23] <u>City of God</u>, book 15, ch. 1.

[24] <u>City of God</u>, book 14, ch. 28; cf. ch. 13, and Bourke, p. 205.

[25] <u>City of God</u>, book 15, ch. 1; cf. ch. 5: "Thus the founder of the earthly city was fratricide. Overcome with envy, he /Cain/ slew his own brother, a citizen of the eternal city, and a sojourner on earth," cf. ch. 17.

[26] <u>City of God</u>, book 15, ch. 17; cf. chs. 1, 5 and 21.

[27] <u>City of God</u>, book 15, chs. 5 and 21; book 18, ch. 1; book 19, ch. 19.

[28] <u>City of God</u>, book 15, ch. 4; cf. ch. 17.

[29] City of God, book 1, ch. 35; book 15, ch. 2; Bourke, p. 201.

[30] City of God, book 17, ch. 3; cf. ch. 16 and book 15, ch. 20.

[31] City of God, book 18, ch. 2 and book 19, ch. 17; cf. book 5, ch. 16; book 14, ch. 13 and book 16, ch. 41.

[32] City of God, book 17, chs. 3, 14 and 16.

[33] City of God, book 15, chs. 17, 20 and 21; book 19, ch. 17; book 1, ch. 35; cf. book 14, ch. 13; book 16, ch. 41 and book 18, ch. 1.

[34] City of God, book 17, ch. 3 and book 19, ch. 18.

[35] St. Augustine, "Expositions on the Book of Psalms," Psalm 99, para. 4, as above, note 16; cf. City of God, book 13, ch. 16; and "On the Catechizing of the Uninstructed," ch. 21, para. 37, in Nicene and Post-Nicene Fathers, 1st series, vol. 3 (1887): "The Church of Christ in all His saints . . . are citizens of the heavenly Jerusalem."

[36] St. Augustine, "Of True Religion," ch. 8, para. 15 in John H. S. Burleigh, ed. and transl., Augustine: Earlier Writings ("The Library of Christian Classics," vol. 6) (Philadelphia: The Westminster Press, 1953), p. 233.

[37] St. Augustine, Confesssions, transl. R. S. Pine-Coffin (Baltimore: Penguin Books, 1961), book 11, ch. 15.

[38] St. Augustine, "Literal Commentary on Genesis," book 11, ch. 15 in Bourke, Essential Augustine, p. 201; cf. City of God, book 19, ch. 17; book 20, chs. 6 and 7; book 21, ch. 1; book 1, ch. 35.

39 St. Augustine, "Enchiridion," ch. 111, in *Nicene and Post-Nicene Fathers*, 1st series, vol. 3 (1887).

40 *City of God*, book 5, ch. 16; book 15, ch. 17.

41 *City of God*, book 22, ch. 1.

42 *City of God*, book 19, ch. 11; cf. ch. 4. For the word "eternal," which means everlasting, see book 22, ch. 1, and the *Vulgate* (Douey transl,), Luke 1:33: "of his kingdom there shall be no end."

43 *City of God*, book 19, ch. 13

44 *City of God*, book 15, ch. 20; book 17, ch. 1.

45 *City of God*, book 1, ch. 35; book 19, chs. 11 and 28.

46 *City of God*, book 13, ch. 14; cf. book 1, ch. 35 and book 5, ch. 21.

47 *City of God*, book 13, chs. 13 and 14.

48 *City of God*, book 2, ch. 21; cf. book 5, ch. 16. For "justice," see book 19, ch. 21; according to Cicero and St. Augustine "justice is that virtue which gives every one his due"; cf. book 19, ch. 14.

49 *City of God*, book 15, ch. 4; cf. book 14, ch. 28 and book 18, ch. 2.

50 *City of God*, book 15, ch. 8; cf. St. Augustine, "On Christian Doctrine," book 2, ch. 25, para. 38-40; ch. 26; ch. 39, para. 58, in *Nicene and Post-Nicene Fathers*, 1st series, vol. 2 (1887).

51 City of God, book 5, ch. 21: "We do not
attribute the powers of giving kingdoms and empires to any save to the true God, who gives
happiness in the kingdom of heaven to the pious
alone, but gives kingly power on earth both to
the pious and the impious, as it may please Him";
cf. ch. 1.

52 City of God, book 19, ch. 17 and book 5,
ch. 27.

53 City of God, book 19, ch. 21. Here St.
Augustine follows the description and definition
of state by Cicero in The Republic. His own
definition of state Augustine offers in ch. 24:
"A people is an assemblage of reasonable beings
bound together by a common agreement as to the
objects of their love."

54 City of God, book 4, ch. 3; cf. St. Augustine, "On the Catechizing of the Uninstructed,"
ch. 21, para. 37, in Nicene and Post-Nicene
Fathers, 1st series, vol. 3 (1887).

55 City of God, book 18, ch. 2: "Among the
very many kingdoms of the earth into which, by
earthly interest or lust, society is divided
(which we call by the general name of the city
of this world). . ."

56 City of God, book 18, ch. 22; book 5,
ch. 21; book 15, ch. 4.

57 City of God, book 16, ch. 17; cf. chs.
15 and 16 and book 18, ch. 2. Augustine's
chronology and historical facts seem completely
confused. During the day of Abraham the Near
East witnessed the fall and disappearance of
Sumerian political power with the conquest of
Ur III, the invasion of Amorites from the West
and the beginning of Old Babylonian kingdom
which reached its height with Hammurabi (fl. ca.
1792-1750 B.C.). In book 18, ch. 2 Augustine
mentions that Ninus was followed on the Assyrian
throne by his wife Semiramis. Semiramis is

identified by historians as the Assyrian queen
Samonuramat (810-805 B.C.) who was the wife of
Shamshi-Adad V (823-810 B.C.). Shamshi-Adad V
was preceded by his father Shalmaneser III (859-
823 B.C.), who was the contemporary of Jehu in
Israel and Athaliah in Judah. Ninus is identified as the old Assyrian king Tukulti-Ninurta I
(ca. 1244-1208 B.C.), and Belus--according to
Augustine the first king of the Assyrian king-
dom--as the Canaanite god Baal, the symbol of
idolatry in the Old Testament. Probably the
Grecian forms of "Balus," "Ninus" and "Semiramis"
have invaded Latin historical literature through
the Universal History (Bibliotheca universalis)
of Diodorus of Sicily (Diodorus Siculus), a
Graeco-Roman historian of Augustan age.

58 "Sacred history" to Augustine means history with a messianic or prophetic message, which
is divinely inspired, thus biblical history (book
16, ch. 2); cf. Robert Austin Markus, Saeculum:
History and Society in the Theology of St. Augustine. Cambridge, Eng.: University Press, 1970,
ch. 1 and passim. The opposite to "sacred history" is "profane history," as used by Augustine
in his treatise On Christian Doctrine (De doctrina Christiana), book 2, ch. 28, para. 43, to
indicate secular or temporal history.

59 City of God, book 18, chs. 2 and 22; cf.
book 16, ch. 17 and book 15, ch. 5.

60 City of God, book 18, ch. 22; book 19,
chs. 7 and 17; book 15, ch. 4 and book 20, ch.
30; and above, pp. 21-22.

61 City of God, book 12, ch. 13; cf. chs.
17 and 20; book 19, ch. 28; book 21, ch. 1.

62 Confessions, book 5, ch. 2.

63 St. Augustine, "On the Holy Trinity,"
book 3, ch. 2, para. 7, in Nicene and Post-
Nicene Fathers, 1st series, vol. 3 (1887).

[64] St. Augustine, "Reply to Faustus the Manichaean," book 26, para. 4 and 5, in <u>Nicene and Post-Nicene Fathers</u>, 1st series, vol. 4 (1887).

[65] St. Augustine, "Our Lord's Sermon of the Mount," book 2, ch. 5, para. 18, in <u>Nicene and Post-Nicene Fathers</u>, 1st series, vol. 6 (1888).

[66] St. Augustine, "Sermons on Selected Lessons of the New Testament," Sermon 19, para. 4, in <u>Nicene and Post-Nicene Fathers</u>, 1st series, vol. 6 (1888).

[67] <u>City of God</u>, book 5, ch. 11; cf. ch. 10.

[68] St. Augustine, "Reply to Faustus the Manichaean," book 22, para. 76, as above, note 64; cf. St. Augustine, "The Letters of Petilian the Donatist," book 2, ch. 23, para. 52, in <u>Nicene and Post-Nicene Fathers</u>, 1st series, vol. 4 (1887).

[69] <u>City of God</u>, book 8, ch. 27

[70] <u>Confessions</u>, book 8, ch. 6, para. 16; cf. St. Augustine, "On Care to be Had for the Dead," para. 6 and 7, in <u>Nicene and Post-Nicene Fathers</u>, 1st series, vol. 3 (1887).

[71] St. Augustine, "Letters," letter 212, in <u>Nicene and Post-Nicene Fathers</u>, vol. 1 (1892).

[72] St. Augustine, "On the Care to be Had for the Dead," para. 1, 6 and 7, as above, note 70; cf. <u>City of God</u>, book 19, ch. 10; St. Augustine, "Letters," letter 78, para. 3, in <u>Nicene and Post-Nicene Fathers</u>, 1st series, vol. 1 (1892).

[73] <u>City of God</u>, book 1, ch. 1; book 15, ch. 20; book 16, chs. 41 and 43; book 17, ch. 1; book 18, ch. 1.

[74] For the use of the Scripture as source, see the <u>City of God</u>, <u>passim</u>, and the "Index of

Scripture Citations" in <u>The City of God against
the Pagans</u>, by M. Green. <u>7</u> vols. ("Loeb Classical Library" Latin authors) (London: William
Heineman; Cambridge, Massachusetts: Harvard
University Press, 1957-1972), 7:389-405. For
classical Greek and Roman authors as Augustine's
source, see Ibidem, pp. 407-416.

Marcus Terentius Varro (116-ca. 27 B.C.),
Roman encyclopedic writer, regarded by Cicero and
St. Augustine as the most learned man of his day
(<u>City of God</u>, book 6, chs. 2 and 6), has written
works on practically every topic, which, unfor-
tunately, with the exception of two, are all lost
to us. Augustine makes reference to such works
by Varro: <u>On the Origin of the Roman People</u>,
<u>On the Race of the Roman Republic</u>, <u>On the Latin
Language</u> (in part extant), <u>On Divine Things</u>, <u>On
Philosophy</u>, and <u>Antiquities</u>.

Marcus Annaeus Lucan (39-65 A.D.), Roman
poet from Spain, wrote an epic poem on the civil
war between Pompey and Caesar, called <u>Pharsalia</u>.

About Trogus Pompeius and Justin, see
below, under Orosius. Augustine refers to their
works several times (book 18, chs. 8 and 25).

75 About Augustine's influence on medieval
Europe, see William M. Green, "Augustine on the
Teaching of History," in University of California
<u>Publications in Classical Philology</u>, vol. 12,
No. 18 (1944), pp. 327-332; John Neville Figgis,
<u>The Political Aspects of St. Augustine's 'City of
God.'</u> (London: Longmans, Green and Co., 1921),
pp. 81-100; Henri Marrow, <u>St. Augustine and His
Influence through the Ages</u>, transl. Patrick
Hepburne-Scott and Edmund Hill. (New York:
Harper, /1957/, pp. 147-180.

76 St. Augustine, "On Christian Doctrine,"
book 2, ch. 28, para. 42-44, as above, note 50.

77 <u>City of God</u>, book 6, ch. 6.

[78] Paulus Orosius, The Seven Books of History against the Pagans, transl. Roy J. Deferrari. ("The Fathers of the Church," vol. 50.) (Washington: The Catholic University of America Press, 1964), book 7, ch. 43; cf. book 2, Prologue.

[79] Paulus Orosius, book 2, ch. 1; all quotations taken from Deferrari's transl.; see above, note 78. Ososius' chronolgy and factual history of the ancient Near East, like that of St. Augustine's, is confused and follows the general pattern of biblical tradition, which ignores the greatness of ancient Egypt, the Hittite power and the vastness and importance of the conquests of Alexander the Great. This fact clearly indicates that Orosius' main source for ancient Near East was the Old Testament.

[80] Paulus Orosius, book 2, ch. 12.

[81] Paulus Orosius, book 6, ch. 22.

[82] Papal bull — a solemn papal letter to which a leaden seal is attached, usually issued to deal with matters of doctrine and faith.

[83] Paulus Orosius, book 5, ch. 2.

A SELECT BIBLIOGRAPHY

General Reference Works

The Cambridge Medieval History, planned by
J. B. Bury, ed. by H. M. Gwatkin and J. P. Whit-
ney. 8 vols. in 9. Cambridge, Eng.: The University Press, 1966-1969 (first ed. 1911-1936).

    The standard scholarly general reference
work on medieval history with elaborate bibliographies and maps at the end of each volume.

The New Encyclopedia Britannica. 30 vols.
15th ed. Chicago: Encyclopedia Britannica, 1974.

    The most scholarly American general ency-
clopedia with emphasis on European affairs.

The New Catholic Encyclopedia. 15 vols.
San Francisco: McGraw-Hill Book Co., 1967.

    The most up-to-date general church ency-
clopedia with accent on the Middle Ages.

General Historiographical Works

    Barnes, Harry Elmer, A History of Histori-
cal Writing. 2nd rev. ed. New York: Dover
Publications, 1962.

    A general survey of historiography from the
earliest times to the Second World War.

    Smalley, Beryl, Historians in the Middle
Ages. New York: Charles Scribner's Sons, 1974.

    The most recent general account of medieval
historiography.

    Thompson, James Westfal, A History of His-
torical Writing. 2 vols. New York: Macmillan
Co., 1942; reprint ed., Glouster, Mass.: Peter
Smith, 1967.

Vol. 1 contains the most extensive survey of
medieval historiography in English.

General Medieval Bibliographical Guides

Chevalier, Ulysse, Répertoire des sources
historiques du moyen age: bio-bibliographie.
2 vols.; 2nd rev. ed. Paris: A. Picard et fils,
1905-1907; reprint ed., New York: Kraus Reprint
Corp., 1960.

A biographical and bibliographical guide of
medieval authors and their works.

Chevalier, Ulysse, Répertoire des sources
historiques du moyen age: topo-bibliographie.
2 vols. Paris: Montbéliard, 1894-1903; reprint
ed., New York: Kraus Reprint Corp., 1959.

A bibliographical guide of medieval places,
institutions and families.

International Bibliography of Historical
Sciences. Published by the International Commit-
tee of Historical Sciences, Lausanne. Paris:
Librairie Armand Colin, 1930-.

Published annually, listing publications
year by year, beginning with 1926 (years 1940-
1946 not published) of books and articles in all
fields of history. Arranged by topics, historical periods and geographical areas.

International Guide to Medieval Studies:
A Quarterly Index to Periodical Literature, vol.
1-. Darien, Connecticut: American Bibliographic
Service, 1961-in progress.

Mimeographed guide that lists articles in
periodicals published in Europe and North America
on political, military, social, economic and ecclesiastical history of Western Europe from approximately sixth to fourteenth century as well
as articles on medieval science, arts and crafts,

language and literature. Articles are listed alphabetically by author's name with extensive subject index added. Published, presumably, annually.

International Medieval Bibliography, eds. R. S. Hoyt and P. H. Sawyer. Minneapolis: University of Minnesota, Department of History, 1967-in progress.

Lists books and articles on medieval history and civilization from Diocletian to the end of the fifteenth century; it includes Byzantine history.

Paetow, Louis John, A Guide to the Study of Medieval History. Rev. ed. with errata by Gray C. Boyce and an addendum by Lynn Thorndike. Millwood, N.Y.: Kraus Reprint, 1980.

Still the standard bibliographical guide in English for medieval history. Lists editions of original sources and modern scholarly works to 1930. The 1980 ed. is based on the 1931 edition.

Potthast, August, Bibliotheca historica medii aevi. Wegweiser durch die Geschichtswerke des europäischen Mittelalters bis 1500. 2 vols. Berlin: W. Weber, 1896.

Lists all major editions of medieval sources.

Repertorium fontium historiae medii aevi, ed. Istituto Italiano per il medio evo /Italian Historical Institute for the Middle Ages/. Vols. 1-. Rome: Istituto storico Italiano per il medio evo, 1962-in progress.

A new, amended and augmented edition of Potthast's Bibliotheca. First volume contains source editions in series; from second volume on editions of works of individual authors. In progress.

Rouse, Richard H., Serial Bibliographies for Medieval Studies. (University of California, Center for Medieval and Renaissance Studies, "Publications," vol. 3). Berkeley and Los Angeles: University of California Press, 1969.

Lists major serial publications according to countries and fields of study.

Farrar, Clarissa P. and Evans, Austin P., _Bibliography of English Translations from Medieval Sources_. (Columbia University, Department of History, "Records of Civilization: Sources and Studies," vol. 39.) New York: Columbia University Press, 1946.

Lists translations to 1942.

Ferguson, Mary Anne Heyward, _Bibliography of English Translations from Medieval Sources, 1943-1967_. (University of Columbia, Department of History, "Records of Civilization: Sources and Studies," vol. 88.) New York: Columbia University Press, 1974.

A continuation of Farrar and Evans' _Bibliography_.

Parks, George B. and Temple, Ruth Z., _The Greek and Latin Literatures_. ("The Literatures of the World in English Translation: A Bibliography," vol. 1.) New York: Frederick Ungar Publishing Co., 1968.

Contains a select list of translations from Greek of early Christian and Byzantine literature, and from Latin of Christian literature under the Empire, as well as medieval authors; collections and individual authors and works are included.

The American Historical Review. American Historical Association, 1895-.

A scholarly general historical journal, published quarterly by the American Historical Association. The journal includes an ample section of book reviews as well as detailed bibliography of recently published books and articles in all fields, including the Middle Ages.

Speculum: A Journal of Medieval Studies. Cambridge, Mass.: The Mediaeval Academy of America, 1926-.

A scholarly journal of medieval studies, published quarterly by the Medieval Academy of America. The journal includes an ample section of book reviews on medieval history as well as detailed bibliography of recently published books and articles.

Early Christian Historical Works in Source Collections and Serial Editions

Patrologiae cursus completus: series Graeca, ed. Jacques Paul Migne. 161 vols. in 168. Paris: J. P. Migne, 1857-1868; reprint ed., Turnhout, Belgium: Brepols, 1959-.

In this collection, usually referred to as Migne, Patrologia Graeca (abbr. PG), are printed the works of almost all of the Greek church writers, from Pseudo-Barnabas (120 A.D.) to the Council of Florence (1438-1439). The authors are arranged chronologically, and their works are given in Greek, with Latin translation. Brepols reprints all volumes that are out of print.

Cavallera, Ferdinand, Indices /of/ Migne, Patrologia Graeca. Paris: Fratres Garnier, 1912.

Hopfner, Theodore, Index locupletissimus "Patrologiae Graecae." 2 vols. Paris: Librairie orientaliste Paul Geuthner, 1928-1936.

Patrologia cursus completus: series Latina, ed. Jacques Paul Migne. 221 vols., incl. indices (vols. 218-221) in 216. Paris: J. P. Migne, 1844-1855; reprint ed. Turnhout, Belgium: Brepols, 1959-.

In this collection, usually referred to as Migne, Patrologia Latina (abbr. PL) are printed the works of the Latin church writers from Tertullian (200 A.D.) to Innocent III (1216).

Hamman, Adalbert, ed., Supplementum "Patrologiae Latinae." Fasc. 1-18. Paris: Éditions Garnier Frères, 1958-1975.

Both Migne's multi-volume publications are the basic and most ample collections of Greek and Latin church writers. Hamman's supplement contains the omitted texts from PL, vols. 1-96.

Corpus Christianorum: series Latina, /collected by the monks of the Benedictine Abbey of St. Peter in Steenbrugge/. Vols. 1-. Turnhout, Belgium: Brepols, 1954-in progress.

This series contains works of Christian Latin literature of the first eight centuries and partially supersedes Migne's collection by providing philologically better edited texts.

Corpus scriptorum ecclesiasticorum Latinorum, ed. Academiae litterarum caesareae Vindobonensis /Academy of Vienna; title of the academy varies/. Vols. 1-. Vienna: C. Gerold's Sons Academic Library (publishers vary), 1866-in progress.

This multi-volume collection partially supersedes Migne's collection by providing philologically better edited texts.

Die griechischen christlichen Schriftsteller der ersten /drei/ Jahrhunderte, ed. Kommision für spätantike Religions-geschichte der deutschen Akademie der Wissenschaften zu Berlin /Committee for Religious History of Later Antiquity of German Academy of Arts and Letters in Berlin; title of the academy varies/. Vols. 1-. Leipzig and Berlin: J. C. Hinrichs'sche Buchhandlung (publishers vary) 1897-in progress.

This edition contains the works of several early Greek ecclesiastical writers.

Monumenta Germaniae historica, inde ab anno Christi quingentesimo usque ad annum millesimum et quingentesimum, ed. Societas aperiendis fontibus rerum Germanicarum Medii Aevi /Society for Publishing Medieval German Historical Sources; name of the society varies/. General editor, George Heinrich Pertz, et al. Vols. 1-. Hanover: Hahn (imprint varies), 1826-in progress.

The most prestigious collection of European medieval historical sources from ca. 500-1500, with special attention to German history, usually referred to as Monumenta Germaniae historica (abbr. MGH). It was originally planned in five series: "Chronicles" (Scriptores; abbr. MGH, SS); "Law Books" (Leges; abbr. MGH, LL); "Charters" (Diplomata; abbr. MGH, Dipl.); "Royal and Papal Letters" (Epistolae; abbr. MGH, Epist.); and "Antiquities" (Antiquitates). Already in 1839 a sixth series was added--"German Chronicles for Use in Schools" (Scriptores rerum Germanicarum in usum scholarum ex Monumentis Germaniae historicis; abbr. MGH, Script. in usum schol.). Originally designed as reprint editions, with shortened variorum of selected individual chronicles from the Scriptores for the use of students, it later became the vehicle for publishing amended texts of the Scriptores editions. After 1875 were added several new series to the Monumenta of which for the early period the most important is the "Oldest Chronicles" (Auctores antiquissimi; abbr. MGH, AA). There are several reprint editions of the Scriptores, vols. 1-30. For a more detailed description, see below, p.116,under "Historians of the Early Middle Ages."

Source Collections and Serial Editions
in English Translation

The Ante-Nicene Fathers: Translations of the Writings of the Fathers down to A.D. 325, eds. Alexander Roberts and James Donaldson.

Rev. ed. of the Edinburgh edition by A. Cleveland
Coxe. 10 vols. New York: The Christian Literature Co., 1884-1886; several reprint eds.

Usually referred to as Ante-Nicene Fathers,
an older translation of the important works of
the earliest church writers from Justin Martyr
(ca. 100-ca. 165) to the Council of Nicaea (325).

A Select Library of Nicene and Post-Nicene
Fathers of the Christian Church, eds. Philip
Schaff and Henry Wace. 1st series, 14 vols.;
2nd series, 14 vols. New York: The Christian
Literature Co., 1886-1900; several reprint eds.

Usually referred to as Nicene and Post-Nicene
Fathers, an older translation of many works of
the early church writers. 1st series: St. Augustine (354-430), vols. 1-8; John Chrysostom (347-
407), vols. 9-14. 2nd series: Eusebius of
Caesarea (ca. 260-ca. 340) to Gregory the Great
(pop 590-604), vols. 1-14.

Ancient Christian Writers: The Works of The
Fathers in Translation, eds. Johannes Quasten et
al. Vols. 1-. Westminster, Maryland (from 1970,
New York): The Newman Bookshop (from 1948, The
Newman Press), 1946-in progress.

The Fathers of the Church: A New Translation,
eds. Ludwig Schopp et al. Vols. 1-. New York:
Fathers of the Church, 1947-1961; from vol. 43,
Washington: The Catholic University of America,
1962-in progress.

These two multi-volume editions contain the
principal works of the late classical and early
medieval Christian writers.

The Greek Ecclesiastical Historians of the
First Six Centuries of the Christian Era. 6 vols.
London: Samuel Bagster and Sons, 1843-1846.

This edition contains the ecclesiastical

48.

histories of Eusebius, Socrates, Sozomen,
Theodoret and Evagrius, and Eusebius' <u>Life of
Constantine</u>.

<u>Bohn's Ecclesiastical Library</u>. 9 vols.
London: Henry G. Bohn (publishers vary),
1851-1877.

This series reprints the church histories of
Eusebius, Socrates, Sozomen and Theodoret as published in <u>The Greek Ecclesiastical Historians</u>.

<u>The Loeb Classical Library. Greek authors</u>.
London: William Heinemann; New York: Macmillan
Co. (publishers vary), 1912-in progress.

<u>The Loeb Classical Library. Latin authors</u>.
London: William Heinemann; New York: Macmillan
Co. (publishers vary), 1912-in progress.

These two series, now published by Harvard
University, contain the works of classical and
some early Christian authors. On verso the text
is given in the original language, on recto--in
English translation.

Gay, Peter and Cavanaugh, Gerald, eds.,
<u>Historians at Work</u>. 4 vols. New York: Harper
and Row, 1972-1975.

Selections from the works of historians from
Antiquity to the 20th century. Vol. 1 contains
short selections from Eusebius, St. Augustine,
Orosius, Gregory of Tours, William of Malmesbury,
Otto of Freising, Matthew Paris and John
Froissart.

Modern Studies on Early
<u>Christian Historiography</u>

Altaner, Berthold, <u>Patrology</u>; transl. Hilda
C. Graef. Frieburg, Germany: Herder; London and
Edinburgh: Nelson, 1960.

A chronologically and topographically arranged biographical and bibliographical survey of church writers from the end of the first to the eighth century.

Milburn, Robert L. P., <u>Early Christian Interpretations of History</u>. London: A. and C. Black; New York: Harper Brothers, 1954.

Essays on the essential early Christian historians.

Quasten, Johannes, <u>Patrology</u>. 3 vols. Westminster, Maryland: The Newman Press, 1950-1960.

A chronologically and topographically arranged biographical and bibliographical survey of Christian writers from Clement of Rome (bishop 92-101 A.D.) to the Council of Chalcedon (451).

Individual Historians

EUSEBIUS OF CAESAREA (ca. 260-ca. 340)

Text Editions

"Chronicle"

"Eusebii Pamphili Caesariensis episcopi <u>Chronicorum libri duo</u>," in Migne, <u>Patrologia Graeca</u>, 19:99-598.

Contains both parts of the <u>Chronicle</u>: pp. 99-350 the "Chronicle" proper; pp. 349-598 the "Chronological Tables" with St. Jerome's commentaries and continuation. For a similar, though not identical version of the "Tables" see Migne, <u>Patrologia Latina</u>, 27:33-676. The complete works of Eusebius are printed in <u>Patrologia Gracea</u>, vols. 19-24.

Fotheringham, John Knight, ed., <u>Eusebii Pamphili "Chronici canones" Latine vertit, adauxit, ad sua tempora produxit S. Eusebius</u>

<u>Hieronymus</u>. London: Oxford University Press, 1923.

A modern, scholarly edition of the "Chronological Tables;" see also below, p.62, under "St. Jerome."

Karst, Joseph, transl. and ed., <u>Eusebius Werke fünfter Band</u>: "Die Chronik." A German transl. from Armenian texts ("Die griechischen christlichen Schriftsteller der ersten drei Jahrhunderte", vol. 20). Leipzig: J. C. Hinrichs'sche Buchhandlung, 1911.

"Ecclesiastical History"

"Eusebii Pamphili <u>Historia ecclesiastica</u>," in Migne, <u>Patrologia Graeca</u>, 20:45-906.

Greek text with Latin translation.

Schwartz, Edward and Mommsen, Theodor, eds., <u>Eusebius Werke zweiter Band</u>: "<u>Die Kirchengeschichte</u>." 2 vols. ("Die griechischen christlichen Schriftsteller der ersten drei Jahrhunderte", vol. 9, pts. 1 and 2.). Leipzig: J. C. Hinrichs'sche Buchhandlung, 1903-1908.

The Greek text on verso edited by Edward Schwartz, Rufinus' Latin translation on recto edited by Theodor Mommsen.

Schwartz, Edward, ed., <u>Eusebius</u> "<u>Kirchengeschichte</u>". 5th ed. Berlin: Akademie-Verlag, 1952.

Greek text only.

"Life of Constantine"

"Eusebii Pamphili Caesareae Palaestinae episcopi <u>De vita imperatoris Constantini libri quatuor</u>", in Migne, <u>Patrologia Graeca</u>, 20:905-1252.

Heikel, Ivar August, ed., Eusebius Werke erster Band: "Über das Leben Constantins" ("Die griechischen christlichen Schriftsteller der ersten drei Jahrhunderte," 7:1-148). Leipzig: J. C. Hinrichs'sche Buchhandlung, 1902.

Greek text only.

English Translations

"Ecclesiastical History"

Cruse, C. F., trans., "An Ecclesiastical History to the Twentieth Year of the Reign of Constantine, being the 324th of the Christian Era," by Eusebius ("The Greek Ecclesiastical Historians of the First Six Centuries of the Christian Era," vol. 2). London: Samuel Bagster and Sons, 1847.

_____, "Ecclesiastical History" of Eusebius Pamphilus, Bishop of Caesarea ("Bohn's Ecclesiastical Library"). London: Henry G. Bohn, 1851.

Deferrari, Roy Joseph, transl., Eusebius Pamphili "Ecclesiastical History." 2 vols. ("Fathers of the Church," vols. 19 and 29). New York: Fathers of the Church, 1953-1955.

Lake, Kirsopp and Oulton, J. E. L., transl., Eusebius "The Ecclesiastical History." 2 vols. ("The Loeb Classical Library," Greek authors). New York: G. P. Putnam's Sons, 1926-1932.

Greek text verso, English translation recto.

McGiffert, Arthur Cushman, transl., "The Church History" of Eusebius in Nicene and Post-Nicene Fathers, 2nd series, 1:73-403 (1890).

Williamson, G. A., transl., Eusebius "The History of the Church from Christ to Constantine." ("The Penguin Classics") Baltimore, Maryland: Penguin Books, 1965.

"Life of Constantine"

Richardson, Ernest Cushing, transl., "The Life of Constantine by Eusebius," in Nicene and Post-Nicene Fathers, 2nd series, 1:473-559 (1890).

/Translator unknown/ "The Life of the Blessed Emperor Constantine in Four Books, from 306 to 333 A.D." by Eusebius Pamphilus ("The Greek Ecclesiastical Historians of the First Six Centuries of the Christian Era," 1:1-234). London: Samuel Bagster and Sons, 1845.

Modern Studies

Mosshammer, Alden A., The Chronicle of Eusebius and Greek Chronographic Tradition. Cranbury, N.J.: Bucknell University Press, 1979.

Stevenson, James, Studies in Eusebius. Cambridge: The University Press, 1929.

Wallace-Hadrill, D.S., Eusebius of Caesarea. Westminster, Maryland: The Canterbury Press, 1961.

A good biography and analysis of his works.

ST. AUGUSTINE OF HIPPO (354-430)

Text editions

"Confessions"

"S. Aurelii Augustini Hipponensis episcopi Confessionum libri tredecim," in Migne, Patrologia Latina, 32:659-868.

The complete works of St. Augustine are printed in vols. 32-47.

Knoll, Pius, ed., Sancti Aurelii Augustini "Confessionum libri tredecim" ("Corpus scriptorum ecclesiasticorum Latinorum," vol. 33). Vienna: F. Tempsky, 1896.

"City of God"

"S. Aurelii Augustini Hipponensis episcopi ad Marcellinum De civitate dei contra paganos libri viginti duo," in Migne, Patrologia Latina, 41:13-804.

Hoffmann, Emanuel, ed., Sancti Aurelii Augustini episcopi "De Civitate Dei libri XXII." 2 vols. ("Corpus scriptorum ecclesiasticorum Latinorum," vol. 40, pts. 1 and 2). Vienna: F. Tempsky, 1899-1900.

"On Christian Doctrine"

"S. Aurelii Augustini Hipponensis episcopi De doctrina Christiana libri quatuor," in Migne, Patrologia Latina, 34:15-122.

Green, G. M., ed., Sancti Aurelii Augustini "De doctrina Christiana libri IV" ("Corpus scriptorum ecclesiasticorum Latinorum," vol. 80). Vienna: Hoelder-Pichler-Tempsky, 1963.

English Translations

"Confessions"

Pilkington, J. G., transl., The "Confessions" of St. Augustine ("The Works of Aurelius Augustine, Bishop of Hippo," ed. Marcus Dods., vol. 14). Edinburgh: T. and T. Clark Co., 1874. Several reprint eds.; see also in Nicene and Post-Nicene Fathers, 1st series, 1:27-297 (1886).

Pine-Coffin, R. S., transl., Saint Augustine "Confessions." ("The Penguin Classics"). Baltimore, Maryland: Penguin Books, 1961.

Watts, William, transl., St. Augustine's "Confessions." 2 vols. ("The Loeb Classical Library," Latin authors). New York: The McMillan Co., 1912; several reprint eds.

Latin text verso, English translation recto.

"City of God"

Dods, Marcus, transl., The City of God. 2 vols. ("The Works of Aurelius Augustine," ed. Marcus Dods, vols. 1-2). Edinburgh: T. and T. Clark Co., 1871. Several reprint eds.; see also in Nicene and Post-Nicene Fathers, 1st series, 2:1-511 (1886).

McCracken, G. E., et al, transl., Saint Augustine "The City of God against the Pagans." 7 vols. ("The Loeb Classical Library," Latin authors). Cambridge, Mass.: Harvard University Press, 1957-1972.

Latin text verso, English translation recto.

Zema, Demetrius B., et al., transl., Saint Augustine "The City of God." 3 vols. ("The Fathers of the Church," vols. 8, 14, 24). New York: Fathers of the Church, 1950-1954.

"On Christian Doctrine"

Gavigan, John J., transl., "Christian Instruction" in Writings of Saint Augustine, 4:11-235. ("The Fathers of the Church," vol. 4). New York: Cima Publishing Co., 1947.

Shaw, J. F., transl., "On Christian Doctrine" in The Works of Aurelius Augustine, ed. W. Marcus Dods, 9:1-171. Edinburgh: T. and T. Clarke Co., 1873. Several reprint eds.; see also in Nicene and Post-Nicene Fathers, 1st series, 2:512-597 (1886).

Modern Studies

Brown, Peter, Augustine of Hippo: A Biography. London: Faber and Faber, 1967.

The most scholarly biography of St. Augustine.

Deane, Herbert A., *The Political and Social Ideas of St. Augustine.* New York: Columbia University Press, 1963.

Figgis, John Neville, *The Political Aspects of S. Augustine's "City of God."* London: Longman's, Green and Co., 1921.

Green, William M., *Augustine on the Teaching of History.* (University of California, "Publications in Classical Philology," vol. 12, pt. 18: 315-322). Berkeley: University of California Press, 1944.

Hagendahl, Harold, *Augustine and the Latin Classics.* 2 vols. ("Studia Graeca et Latina Gothoburgensia," vol. 20, part 1; also "Acta universitatis Gothoburgensis"). Goteborg: /The University Press/, 1967.

The first vol. contains extensive quotations from Latin authors; the second vol., an analysis of their influences on St. Augustine's writings.

Keyes, Gordon L., *Christian Faith and the Interpretation of History: A Study of St. Augustine's Philosophy of History.* Lincoln: University of Nebraska Press, 1966.

McCabe, Joseph, *Saint Augustine.* London: Duckworth and Co., 1902.

A good but somewhat outdated study of St. Augustine.

Markus, Robert Austin, *Saeculum: History and Society in the Theology of St. Augustine.* Cambridge: University Press, 1970.

Marrou, Henri, *Men of Wisdom: St. Augustine and His Influence through the Ages*, transl. Patrick Hepburne-Scott and Edmund Hill. New York: Harper Torchbooks, 1957.

Possidius, "Life of St. Augustine," transl. Mary Magdeleine Müller and Roy J. Deferrari, in Roy J. Deferrari, ed., Early Christian Biographies, pp. 67-124 ("The Fathers of the Church," vol. 15). New York: Fathers of the Church, 1952.

A life-story of St. Augustine by his contemporary, Possidius, bishop of Calama in Numidia.

Van der Meer, F., Augustine the Bishop: The Life and Work of a Father of the Church, transl. Brian Battershaw and G. R. Lamb. London and New York: Sheer and Ward, 1961.

PAULUS OROSIUS (ca. 380-after 418)

Text editions

"Pauli Orosii Hispani presbyteri Historiarum libri septem," in Migne, Patrologia Latina, 31:663-1174.

Zangemeister, C., ed., Pauli Orosii "Historiarum adversum paganos libri VII" ("Corpus scriptorum ecclesiasticorum Latinorum," vol. 5). Vienna: C. Gerold's Sons, 1882.

English Translations

Deferrari, Roy J., transl., Paulus Orosius "The Seven Books of History Against the Pagans" ("The Fathers of the Church," vol. 50). Washington: The Catholic University Press, 1964.

Raymond, Irving Woodworth, transl., Seven Books of History Against the Pagans: The Apology of Paulus Orosius (University of Columbia, Department of History, "Records of Civilization: Sources and Studies," vol. 26). New York: Columbia University Press, 1936.

Minor Historians

Text editions, English Translations, Modern Studies

JUSTIN MARTYR (ca. 100–ca. 165)

"Sancti Justini philosophi et martyris Apologia prima pro Christianis," in Migne, Patrologia Graeca, 6:377–440.

Dods, Marcus, transl., "The First Apology of Justin," in Ante-Nicene Fathers 1:163–187 (1884).

Falls, Thomas B., transl., "The First Apology" in Saint Justin Martyr, pp. 29–111 ("The Fathers of the Church," vol. 6). Washington: Catholic University Press, 1948.

"Sancti Justini philosophi et martyris Apologia secunda pro Christianis," in Migne, Patrologia Graeca, 6:441–470.

Dods, Marcus, transl., "The Second Apology of Justin for the Christians," in Ante-Nicene Fathers, 1:188–193 (1884).

Falls, Thomas B., transl., "The Second Apology" in Saint Justin Martyr, pp. 117–135 ("The Fathers of the Church, vol. 6). Washington: Catholic University Press, 1948.

"Sancti Justini philosophi et martyris Dialogus cum Tryphone Judaeo," in Migne, Patrologia Graeca, 6:471–800.

Falls, Thomas B., transl., "Dialogue with Trypho" in Saint Justin Martyr, pp. 141–366 ("The Fathers of the Church," vol. 6). Washington: Catholic University Press, 1948.

Reith, G., transl., "Dialogue of Justin, Philosopher and Martyr, with Trypho, a Jew," in Ante-Nicene Fathers, 1:194–270 (1884).

Barnard, L. W., Justin Martyr: His Life and Thought. Cambridge: The University Press, 1967.

TERTULLIAN (ca. 155-ca. 230)

"Quinti Septimi Florentis Tertulliani Apologeticus adversus gentes pro Christianis," in Migne, Patrologia Latina 1:257-536.

Dekkers, E., ed., "Quinti Septimi Florentis Tertulliani Apologeticum" in Opera, 1:77-171 ("Corpus Christianorum," series Latina, vol. 1). Turnhoult: Brepols, 1954.

Hoppe, Heinrich, ed., Quinti Septimi Florentis Tertulliani "Apologeticum." 2nd ed. ("Corpus scriptorum ecclesiasticorum Latinorum," vol. 69). Vienna: Hoelder-Pichler-Tempsky, 1939.

Arbesmann, Rudolph, Daly, Emily Joseph and Quain, Edwin A., transl., "Apology" in Tertullian "Apologetical Works," and Minucius Felix "Octavius," pp. 7-126 ("Fathers of the Church," vol. 10). New York: Fathers of the Church, 1950.

Glover, T. R., transl., "Apology" in Tertullian /and/ Minucius Felix, transl. T. R. Glover and W. C. A. Kerr, pp. 1-227, ("Loeb Classical Library," Latin authors). New York: G. P. Putnam's Sons, 1931.

Thelwall, S., transl., /Tertullian/ "Apology," in Ante-Nicene Fathers, 3:17-55 (1885).

"Quinti Septimi Florentis Tertulliani Ad nationes," in Migne, Patrologia Latina, 1:559-608.

Borleffs, J. G. Ph., ed., "Quinti Septimi Florentis Tertulliani Ad nationes" in Opera, 1:9-75 ("Corpus Christianorum," series Latina, vol. 1). Turnhoult: Brepols, 1954.

Reifferscheid, August and Wissowa, Georg, eds., "Quinti Septimi Florentis Tertulliani Ad nationes libri duo" in Opera, 1:59-133 ("Corpus scriptorum ecclesiasticorum Latinorum," vol. 20). Vienna: F. Tempsky, 1890.

Holmes, Peter, transl., /Tertullian/ "Ad
Nationes," in <u>Ante-Nicene Fathers</u>, 3:109-147
(1885).

Barnes, Timothy David, <u>Tertullian: A Historical and Literary Study</u>.   Oxford: Clarendon Press,
1971.

Excellent study of Tertullian's life and
works.

SEXTUS JULIUS AFRICANUS (ca. 160-ca. 240)

"Julii Africani quae supersunt ex quinque
libri <u>Chronographiae</u>," in Migne, <u>Patrologia
Graeca</u>, 10:63-94.

Routh, Martin Joseph, ed., "Julius Africanus
chronologus" in <u>Reliquae sacrae sive auctorum
fere jam perditorum secundi tertiique saeculi post
Christum natum quae supersunt</u>, 2:238-309 (1846).
5 vols.; 2nd ed.   Oxford: University Press,
1846-1848.

Contains the extant fragments of his
<u>Chronography</u> in Greek, with Latin translation.

Salmond, S. D. F., transl., "The Extant
Fragments of the <u>Five Books of the Chronography</u>
of Julius Africanus," in <u>Ante-Nicene Fathers</u>,
6:130-138 (1886).

A translation from Migne, 10:63-94.

CYPRIAN (ca. 210-258)

"Divi Thascii Calcilii Cypriani episcopi
Carthaginensis et martyris <u>Epistolae</u>," in Migne,
<u>Patrologia Latina</u>, 4:191-438.

Hartel, Wilhelm, ed., "Thasci Caecili
Cypriani <u>Epistolae</u>" in <u>Opera omnia</u>, vol. 2
("Corpus scriptorum ecclesiasticorum Latinorum,"
vol. 3, part 2).   Vienna: C. Gerold's Sons, 1871.

Donna, Rose Bernard, transl., Saint Cyprian "Letters 1-81" ("The Fathers of the Church," vol. 51). Washington: Catholic University of America Press, 1966.

Wallis, R. E., transl., "The Epistles of Cyprian," in Ante-Nicene Fathers, 5:275-409 (1886).

"Divi Thascii Calcilii Cypriani episcopi Carthaginensis et martyris Liber de lapsis," in Migne, Patrologia Latina, 4:465-494.

Hartel, Wilhelm, ed., "Thasci Calcili Cypriani De lapsis" in Opera omnia, 1:235-264 ("Corpus scriptorum ecclesiasticorum Latinorum," vol. 3, part 1). Vienna: C. Gerold's sons, 1868.

Bevenot, Maurice, transl., "The Lapsed" in Cyprian "The Lapsed; The Unity of the Catholic Church," pp. 13-42 ("Ancient Christian Writers," vol. 25). Westminster, Maryland: Newman Press, 1957.

Wallis, R. E., transl., "The Treatises of Cyprian: On the Lapsed," in Ante-Nicene Fathers, 5:437-447 (1886).

Hinchliff, Peter, Cyprian of Carthage and The Unity of the Christian Church. London: Geoffrey Chapman, 1974.

Pontius, "Life of St. Cyprian," transl. Mary Magdeleine Müller and Roy J. Deferrari, in Roy J. Deferrari, ed., Early Christian Biographies, pp. 1-24 ("The Fathers of the Church," vol. 15). New York: Fathers of the Church, 1952.

A life-story of Cyprian by his contemporary, Pontius.

Sage, Michael M. Cyprian ("Patristic Monograph Series," vol. 1). Philadelphia: The Philadelphia Patristic Foundation, 1975.

LACTANTIUS (ca. 260-ca. 340)

"Lucii Caecilii Finmiani Lactantii Liber ad Donatum confessorem de mortibus persecutorum," in Migne, Patrologia Latina, 7:189-276.

Brandt, Samuel and Laubmann, Georg, eds., "Lucii Caeli Finmiani Lactanti De mortibus persecutorum liber" in Opera omnia, vol. 2, part 2: 169-238 ("Corpus scriptorum ecclesiasticorum Latinorum," vol. 27, part 2). Vienna: F. Tempsky, 1893.

Fletcher, William, transl. "Lactantius, Of the Manner in which the Persecutors Died," in Ante-Nicene Fathers, 7:301-322 (1886).

McDonald, Mary Francis, transl., "The Death of the Persecutors" in Lactantius "Minor Works," pp. 137-203 ("The Fathers of the Church," vol. 54). Washington: Catholic University of America Press, 1965.

Hartwell, Kathleen Ellen, Lactantius and Milton. Cambridge, Mass.: Harvard University Press, 1929.

This study deals with Lactantius' influence on Milton.

ST. JEROME (ca. 347-ca. 420)

"S. Eusebii Hieronymi Stridonensis presbyteri Interpretatio chronicae Eusebii Pamphili cui subjecta sunt continentur fragmenta quae extant operis Graeci," in Migne, Patrologia Latina, 27:33-676.

The "Chronological Tables" of Eusebius of Caesarea from Abraham to A.D. 339 as augmented and commented upon by St. Jerome. This is a similar, though not identical, version with the "Tables" as printed in Migne, Patrologia Graeca, 19:349-598. See above, p.50.

"S. Hieronymi Chronicon," in Migne,
Patrologia Latina, 27:675-702.

St. Jerome's continuation of Eusebius'
"Chronological Tables" from 330 to 381 A.D.

Helm, Rudolf, ed., Eusebius Werke siebenter
Band: "Die Chronik" des Hieronymus. Hieronymi
"Chronicon." ("Die griechischen christlichen
Schriftsteller der ersten Jahrhunderte," vol. 47).
Berlin: Akademie-Verlag, 1956.

A modern edition of Jerome's version of
Eusebius' "Chronological Tables;" see also above,
p.50, under Eusebius of Caesarea Chronicle.

Hagendahl, Harold, Latin Fathers and the
Classics: A Study of the Apologists, Jerome and
Other Christian Writers ("Acta universitatis
Gothoburgensis. Goteborgs Universitets Årsskrift,"
vol. 64 (1958); also published as "Studia Graeca
et Latina Gothoburgensia," vol. 6). Goteborg:
⟨The University Press⟩, 1958.

The main emphasis in this study is put on
St. Jerome.

Kelly, John Norman Davidson, Jerome: His
Life, Writings and Controversies. London:
Duckworth and Co., 1975.

PROSPER OF AQUITAINE (ca. 400-460)

"Prosperi Aquitanici Chronicon," in Migne,
Patrologia Latina, 27:703-724.

Prosper's continuation of St. Jerome's
"Chronological Tables" from 382-419 A.D.

"S. Prosperi Aquitani Chronicum integrum in
duas partes distributum," in Migne, Patrologia
Latina, 51:535-606.

Prosper's world chronicle from Adam to
A.D. 455.

Mommsen, Theodor, ed., "Prosperi Tironis
Epitoma chronicon ed. primam a. CCCCXXXIII,
continuata ad a. CCCCLV" in Chronica minora saec.
IV, V, VI, VII, 1:341–485; 3 vols. (MGH, AA,
Vol. 9) Berlin: Weidmann, 1892.

ISIDORE OF SEVILLE (ca. 560–636)

"Sancti Isidori Hispalensis episcopi
Etymologiarium libri XX," in Migne, Patrologia
Latina, 82:73–1054.

Lindsay, W. M., ed., Isidori Hispalensis
episcopi "Etymologiarum sive originum libri XX."
2 vols. Oxford: The University Press, 1911;
reprint eds. 1957, 1962.

Isidor's "Chronicle" from the Creation to
A.D. 627 is included in book 5, chs. 38–39 of the
Etymologies.

Brehaut, Ernest, transl., An Encyclopedist
of the Dark Ages: Isidore of Seville. New York:
Columbia University Press, 1912; reprint ed.,
("Burt Franklin Research and Source Work Series,"
vol. 107) New York: Burt Franklin, 1965.

Partial translation of the Etymologies.

RUFINUS OF AQUILEIA, or RUFINUS TYRANNIUS (ca.
345–410)

"Rufinus Aquileiensis presbyteri Historiae
ecclesiasticae libri duo," in Migne, Patrologia
Latina, 21:465–540.

Schwartz, Eduard and Mommsen, Theodor, eds.,
Eusebius Werke zweiter Band: "Die Kirchenge-
schichte." See above, p.51, under Eusebius,
Ecclesiastical History.

The Greek text of Eusebius on verso edited
by Eduard Schwartz; Rufinus' Latin translation on
recto ed. by Theodor Mommsen.

Murphy, Francis X., _Rufinus of Aquileia_
(345-411): His Life and Works. (The Catholic
University of America, "Studies in Medieval
History." N.S., vol. 6; Ph.D. Diss.). Washington:
The Catholic University of America Press, 1945.

SOCRATES (ca. 380-ca. 450)

"Socrates scholastici _Historia ecclesias-_
tica," in Migne, _Patrologia Graeca_, 67:29-842.

Chronologically Socrates' work is a continuation of Eusebius' _Ecclesiastical History_, covering
the years from 305-439.

For a more recent edition of the text in
Latin see below, p.67 under Cassiodorus'
Historia ecclesiastica tripartita.

Zenos, A. C., transl., "_The Ecclesiastical_
History by Socrates Scholasticus," in _Nicene and_
Post-Nicene Fathers, 2nd series, 2:1-178 (1890).

"_Ecclesiastical History: A History of the_
Church in Seven Books, from the Accession of
Constantine, A.D. 305, to the 38th year of
Theodosius II, Including a Period of 140 Years,"
by Socrates. Transl. from the Greek ("The Greek
Ecclesiastical Historians of the First Six Cen-
turies of the Christian Era," vol. 3). London:
Samuel Bagster and Sons, 1844: reprint ed. in
"Bohn's Ecclesiastical Library," London: Henry G.
Bohn, 1851.

SOZOMEN (ca. 400-ca. 450)

"Hermiae Sozomeni _Ecclesiastica historia_,"
in Migne, _Patrologia Graeca_, 67:843-1630.

Bidez, Joseph and Hansen, Günther C., eds.,
Sozomenus "Kirchengeschichte" ("Die griechischen
christlichen Schriftsteller der ersten Jahrhunderte," vol. 50). Berlin: Akademi-Verlag,
1960.

Like Socrates, Sozomen continues Eusebius'
Ecclesiastical History from 323 to 423. For
another edition of the text in Latin see below,
under Cassiodorus' _Historia ecclesiastica tri-_
partita.

Hartranft, Chester D., transl., "The Ecclesiastical History of Sozomen, Comprising a History of the Church from A.D. 323 to A.D. 425," in
Nicene and Post-Nicene Fathers, 2nd series,
2:181-427 (1890).

"_Ecclesiastical History: A History of the_
Church in Nine Books, from A.D. 324 to A.D. 440"
by Sozomen. Transl. from the Greek. ("The Greek
Ecclesiastical Historians of the First Six Cen-
turies of the Christian Era," vol. 4). London:
Samuel Bagster and Sons, 1846; reprint ed. in
"Bohn's Ecclesiastical Library," London:
Henry G. Bohn, 1851.

THEODORET OF CYRUS (ca. 393-before 466)

"Beati Theodoreti episcopi Cyrensis
Ecclesiasticae historiae libri quinque," in
Migne, _Patrologia Graeca_, 82:882-1280.

Parmentier, Leon and Scheidweiler, Felix,
eds., Theodoret "_Kirchengeschichte._" 2nd ed.
("Die griechischen christlichen Schriftsteller
der ersten Jahrhunderte," vol. 44). Berlin:
Akademie-Verlag, 1954.

Theodoret's _History_ covers the years from
324 to 429. For another edition of the text in
Latin, see below under Cassiodorus' _Historia_
ecclesiastica tripartita.

Jackson, Blomfield, transl., "The Ecclesiastical History of Theodoret," in _Nicene and Post-_
Nicene Fathers, 2nd series, 3:34-159 (1892).

"_Ecclesiastical History: A History of the_
Church in Five Books, from A.D. 322 to the Death

of Theodore the Mopsuestia A.D. 427" by Theodoretus, Bishop of Cyrus. A new transl. from the
original. ("The Greek Ecclesiastical Historians
of the First Six Centuries of the Christian Era,"
vol. 5). London: Samuel Bagster and Sons, 1843;
reprint ed. in "Bohn's Ecclesiastical Library,"
London: Henry G. Bohn, 1851.

CASSIODORUS (ca. 487-ca. 583)

   "M. Aurelii Cassiodori Historia ecclesiastica vocata tripartita," in Migne, Patrologia
Latina, 69:879-1214.

   Jacob, Walther and Hanslik, Rudolph, eds.,
Cassiodorus-Epiphanius "Historia ecclesiastica
tripartita: Historiae ecclesiasticae ex Socrate
Sozomeno et Theodorito in unum collectae et nuper
de Graeco in Latinum translatae libri numero
duodecim." ("Corpus scriptorum ecclesiasticorum
Latinorum," vol. 71). Vienna: Haelder-Pichler-
Tempsky, 1952.

   Cassiodorus' Historia ecclesiastica tripartita is Epiphanius' condensed Latin translation
of Socrates', Sozomen's and Theodoret's church
histories (see above).

   The Vienna edition of Cassiodorus distin-
guishes the information taken from the three
individual authors, though it prints their works
intermittingly, preserving the chronological
sequence of events.

   "M Aurelii Cassiodori Chronicon ad Theodorum
regem," in Migne, Patrologia Latina, 69:1213-1248.

   Mommsen Theodor, ed., "Cassiodori Senatoris
Chronica ad a. DXIX" in Chronica minora saec.
IV, V, VI, VII, 2:109-161. 3 vols. (MGH, AA,
vol. 11). Berlin: Weidmann, 1894.

   Cassidorus' own continuation of the three
Greek ecclesiastical historians in the form of

chronological tables to the year A.D. 519.

For other English translations of all listed
works see Bibliography of English Translations
from Medieval Sources (listed above, p. 44).

HISTORIANS OF THE EARLY MIDDLE AGES
(to Mid-eleventh Century)

Both St. Augustine and Orosius witnessed the imperial legislation of late fourth and early fifth centuries which established Christianity as the only legal religion in the classical Roman Empire. Both men also lived at the beginning of the great Germanic invasions of Europe, which event coincided with the suppression of worshipping pagan gods. The defense of Christianity after the sack of Rome by the Arian Visigoths in 410 was St. Augustine's main reason for writing the <u>City of God</u>. However, the Visigoths only began the long series of barbarian migrations in the Empire; their invasions continued throughout the fifth and sixth centuries and came to a close with the appearance of the Lombards in Italy in 568. During these two hundred years the Visigoths and the Ostrogoths, the Vandals, the Burgundians, the Suevi, the Juts, the Angles, the Saxons, the Alemanni, the Ripurian and Salian Franks and finally the Lombards had left their original homelands and settled down in the western part of the Empire. Hand in hand with barbarian invasions progressed the spread of Christianity, for the Germanic peoples were converted to Christianity before their migrations. The chieftains of the conquering German tribes established their rule as kings over a mixed native, Roman and German population. Gradually new monarchies emerged in Western Europe: the most powerful became the Merovingian and Carolingian kingdoms in Gaul, the Lombard kingdom in northern Italy, the Anglo-Saxon Heptarchy[1] in England and the Ottonian and Salian Empires in Germany. The new kings and emperors now became the defenders of the Faith in their realms.

Naturally, none of these major events escaped the attention of contemporary historians. However, the task of the new generation of

history writers was quite different from that of
their predecessors. No longer did they have to
defend Christianity, or formulate Christian attitude toward the great changes they noticed, recorded and described: that had already been
achieved or made a fait accompli by the pens of
Eusebius of Caesarea and St. Augustine of Hippo.
The early medieval historians, therefore, either
paid little attention to dogmatic problems and
concentrated mostly on military and political history, though from a Christian point of view, or
wholeheartedly described the renewed expansion of
the Christian faith to the periphery of Europe.
Nevertheless, in historiography two important in-
novations were accomplished during the early Middle Ages: first, the introduction of Christian
chronology, or the dating of events in the past
according to the birth of Christ, and secondly,
the beginnings of medieval annals. Gradually the
annals were expanded into chronicles.

      After St. Augustine had written the City of
God in 426 a century passed till a new generation
of Christian historians came to prominence.
Their task now was to record the great changes
that had taken place in the Roman Empire during
and after the migrations. The Germanic peoples
who set the invasions in motion were the Goths,
and the earliest of the migration historians,
CASSIODORUS[2] (ca. 487-ca. 575), the chief minister to the Ostrogothic King Theodoric (471-526)
and co-compiler of the Tripartite History, composed between 526 and 533 a History of the Goths
in twelve books. Another important work by
Cassiodorus is his Letters (Epistulae Theodericianae variae), a collection of official state
papers and correspondence of the Ostrogothic
Kingdom; the latter work is still extant, but his
Gothic history is lost. However, in an abridged
form it is preserved in Jordanes' Gothic History
(De origine actibusque Getarum, also known as
Historia Getarum and Getica).

      JORDANES was probably a Romanized Goth who

70.

lived in the sixth century and was employed as
secretary by a noble Gothic family in Ravenna.
It is assumed that he was a Catholic, probably a
priest, and presumably he had accompanied Pope
Vigilius (537-555) to Constantinople in 551. At
about the same time Jordanes compiled the history
of the Goths, mainly Ostrogoths, by epitomizing
Cassiodorus' work. However, it is evident that
he also used other writings as well as oral traditions of the Goths. His aim in compiling the
History was twofold: to turn the Arian Ostrogoths to orthodox Catholicism. and secondly, to
explain Gothic domination over the Roman people.
For the latter purpose Jordanes narrated the preserved legends of Gothic migration from their
original homeland in Scandinavia to the great
plains north of the Black Sea, and then their advance and conquest of Italy under their great
King Theodoric. To aggrandize Theodoric's ancestry Jordanes introduced into his work a fictitious
lineage of Theodoric; to emphasize Roman and
Ostrogothic long ties Jordanes created a myth of
the close relations of the two nations in ancient
past. Notwithstanding the legendary element,
Jordanes is our best narrative source about the
Ostrogoth's wanderings from Pannonia to Italy,
their rule in the Apennine peninsula and their
relations with the Eastern Empire. Jordanes also
sketched Ostrogothic wars and ties with other
Germanic tribes during Theodoric's dominance of
Italy, thus giving a rather vivid picture of
Western Europe in turmoil during the great migrations. In describing Ostrogothic contributions to western civilization Jordanes always
emphasized Gothic merits in preserving classical
culture and Roman traditions. Though a Christian,
Jordanes cannot be regarded a church historian;
his work falls in the category of military and
political history; thus Jordanes continued the
line of profane or secular historians, begun by
Orosius.

About the other Gothic people, the Visigoths,
an unpretentious and sketchy history was written by ISIDORE OF SEVILLE[3] (ca. 560-636),

71.

the bishop of Spain's southern province. Isidore
was of noble birth, but he chose to join the
clergy, and as bishop of Seville after 600 he had
played an important role in Spain's seventh century church life: he added his hand to the conversion of the Arian Visigoths to Catholicism,
and presided at several Spanish church councils.
Besides his purely church work Isidore also was
interested in the past of his native country and
wrote a History of the Goths, Vandals and Suevi
(Historia Gothorum, Vandalorum et Sueborum), a
concise and rather inaccurate account of Visigothic rule in Spain. Isidore's main work, however, is the Etymologies (Etymologiae), an encyclopedic compilation in twenty books, which contain a comprehensive summary of all ancient and
contemporary knowledge of things, places, art
and science, including some information on history. Both Isidore of Seville and Jordanes wrote
in Latin.

The Ostrogoths in 493 established their rule
in Italy, the Visigoths in 426 in Spain, and the
Vandals in 439 in western North Africa. In 533
Justinian's excellent general Belisarius (ca.
505-565) invaded the Vandal Kingdom and destroyed
it; a year later Belisarius invaded Ostrogothic
Italy and for twenty years the Byzantine Empire
waged wars against the Ostrogoths until their
kingdom succumbed in 554. Visigothic Spain alone
held out until 711; then it came under Moslem
rule. The Byzantine wars under Justinian (527-
565) against the Ostrogoths and Vandals are described by Justinian's contemporary PROCOPIUS OF
CAESAREA (Procopius Caesariensis, ca. 505-565).
Biographical data about Procopius is very scanty;
however, it is known that in 527, thus in the
year Justinian assumed sole emperorship, he was
already in Constantinople and became the secretary to general Belisarius. Procopius remained
in Belisarius' employ and accompanied him in
wars until 540 or 542, when Procopius returned to
Constantinople and, it seems, served the emperor
then in several administrative capacities. It is
believed that Procopius had received a good educa-

tion in Constantinople; he was well versed in classical Greek historiography and was particularly familiar with the works of Herodotus, Thucydides and Polybius. Being closely associated with Belisarius and later with the imperial court, Procopius had excellent first-hand knowledge of Justinian's wars, the administration and court intrigues. Procopius wrote three works in which he has left a rather detailed history of the reign of his great contemporary, Justinian I.

Procopius' main work is the History in Eight Books (De bellis) composed in about 550 and published in 551. The History describes Justinian's or Belisarius' wars[4] against the Persians in the first two books (covering the years 530-531), the Vandal war in the next two books (years 533-534) and the Gothic war in the last four books (years 534-552). The last book of the Gothic wars is a partial summary of Justinian's wars against the Persians and Ostrogoths and, it seems, was published only in 553. Since the main subject of description in Procopius' History is wars, the work frequently is called the History of the Wars, or simply the Wars.

In the History Procopius attests himself as a good narrator and trustworthy contemporary historian. And that is understandable: he accompanied Belisarius to the battlefields, thus was an actual eyewitness of the action, and as personal friend and secretary to the general, Procopius had access to important documents and military archives; therefore, he was the most qualified man to write a history of Justinian's wars. One has to assume that Procopius made some notes during the campaigns and used them as well as other eyewitness evidence, and perhaps also official state papers when he sat down to compose the History. Procopius is regarded as reporting events and dates correctly, and since there are practically no other sources to check Procopius, one has to take his narrative at face value. However, modern historians often indicate that he was biased in favor of the Byzantines; certainly

he was an admirer and adherent of Belisarius, particularly during the early years of their compan-
ionship. Interesting is Procopius' grouping of
Justinian's wars: he did not follow the more traditional annalistic form but divided the subject-
matter according to the opponents of the Byzantines. Thus, he described separately the campaigns
against the Persians, then against the Vandals and
finally against the Ostrogoths, though some of the
military actions took place concurrently. However,
within each group of wars Procopius pursued a
strict chronological pattern, as devised by the
great ancient military historians Thucydides and
Polybius.

The History of the Wars covers the military
events during Justinian's reign. It is generally
assumed that concurrently with the History Procopius wrote another work, called in Greek the
Anecdota, meaning an unpublished work. The given
Latin title is the Historia Arcana, meaning the
hidden or private history, and the traditional
English title of this work is the Secret History.
This work was not meant for publication during
Justinian's reign, for its narrative is too scan-
dalous to be tolerated by any person, and certainly by an autocratic emperor. Whether this work
was published after Justinian's and Procopius'
deaths, cannot be established, but its existence
was known to the Byzantines. It was rediscovered
in 1623 in the Vatican library and published in
the same year in Lyons. The Secret History sheds
light on the private lives of Emperor Justinian
and General Belisarius. The History of the Wars
may be regarded as a semiofficial and in any case
an honest and respectable account of the publicly
known events during the wars; the Secret History
describes the many behind-the-scene facts of the
imperial court and the deceitful trickery of the
royal couple, with particular emphasis on lewed-
ness and treacheries of the empress Theodora
(died 548) and the coquetry and ambitions of the
general's wife Antonina. Both of these women are
depicted as whores and intrigantes, holding immense power over their husbands. The Secret

History, therefore, may be looked upon--and probably it was done so by Procopius himself--as a component to the History of the Wars, the former narrating the social and moral history of the court, the highest nobility and the members of the imperial administration. Allowing that Procopius has treated his master, Belisarius, with a certain degree of respect, for Belisarius' wife, the emperor, and the empress in particular Procopius reserved the very slanderous passages of the work. After reading the Secret History it becomes rather obvious that Procopius was spewing pure venom, giving vent to his personal feelings, distaste and even hate against the imperial couple and the general's wife.

The third work of Procopius is called On Buildings (De aedificiis); it was written either in 554 or in 560. The Buildings is a work distinctly opposite to the Secret History: it is an acclaim of Justinian, a song of praise of the many buildings he had constructed throughout the empire. Some modern historians have branded the Buildings even as a panegyric to Justinian, expressing the views that it was composed at the request of the emperor. Nevertheless, this work, after the exaggerated rhetoric is overlooked, offers a good account of Justinian's building activities; it includes a description of Hagia Sophia[5] as well as a valuable, though concise geographical and economic survey of the Byzantine Empire.

Historians alwys have questioned why Procopius had written two diametrically contrasting evaluations about the same man--Justinian; even doubts have been expressed whether Procopius was the author of the Secret History. However, after careful analysis of its style and phraseology all doubts about the authorship have been dismissed. The probable answer to the question of two different attitudes may lie in the fact that the Secret History was not intended for immediate publication; therefore, in it Procopius has expressed his deepest personal feeings and displeasure about the imperial government. A possibility that the <u>Secret History</u> was Procopius' retaliation against the emperor for not receiving some expected honor or hoped-for office cannot be ruled out. In the <u>Buildings</u>, an officially commissioned work, Procopius was compelled to glorify the emperor and his achievements. Consequently, one has to read both the <u>Secret History</u> and the <u>Buildings</u> with some reservations and not take literally every slanderous or laudatory remark.

As a historian, Procopius deserves a high, though somewhat unique place in early medieval historiography. He seems to be quite unaware of Eusebius' and St. Augustine's new philosophies of history; their schemes of universal Christian history and theorization of the two cities remained foreign to Procopius. Though a Christian, he wrote a secular contemporary history, a history of wars which were fought not so much to spread the orthodox faith as to regain lost territory, to conquer Western Europe in order to restore the classical Roman Empire under the rule of Justinian. For his models Procopius looked back to classical antiquity: his teachers were the ancient military historians Herodotus and Thucydides. In regard to imperial biography the <u>Secret History</u> is closer by far to Suetonius' <u>Lives of the Twelve Caesars</u> than to Eusebius' <u>Life of Constantine</u>. In sum, Procopius stands out as the best historian after Polybius who write in Greek. Even his language and style is praiseworthy: he avoided the use of the colloquial Greek of his day, but retained much of classical forms and phraseology of ancient historians. The classical school of Greek historians came to an end with Procopius, just as the use of Latin as the official language of the Byzantine Empire disappeared with the reign of Justinian.

Neither the Goths nor the Vandals established long-lasting states: Procopius is our best witness to that. More lucky than the Goths were the Salian Franks, who began their conquests under King Clovis (481-511) from their homeland on the banks of lower Rhine at about the same time that the Ostrogoths under Theodoric entered Italy. On Christmas Day, 800 the Frankish state became the revived Roman Empire in the West under Charlemagne. Likewise, the Franks were more lucky than the Goths in finding a greater talent than Jordanes and Isidore to record their deeds and achievements. The Frankish historian par excellence was the celebrated bishop of Tours, St. Gregory, the most prominent ecclesiastic of Merovingian Gaul.

GREGORY OF TOURS (Georgius Florentius Gregorius, 538-594), born in a noble Gallo-Roman family in Auvergne,[6] entered the service of the Church in early youth; after ordination to the priesthood in 563 he became bishop of the city of Tours[7] in 573 and held this office for twenty-one years, till his death in 594. Apparently Gregory had received a good contemporary education, though it was short of a good classical Roman one. Gregory certainly had studied Martianus Capella's (d. 429) Marriage of Mercury and Philology; thus he mastered the trivium, and undoubtedly had also some understanding of the quadrivium.[8] However, his knowledge of the Scripture was by far more profound than his secular learning, although it is questionable whether Gregory was familiar with the dogmatic works of the early church fathers. It seems that Gregory was more concerned about practical church problems than religious philosophy; even his Latin was colloquial rather than striving after purity and eloquence.

Gregory wrote several works, mainly in the field of hagiography. This segment of his literary production usually is grouped together under a common title The Miracles (Libri octo miraculorum), which includes the legendary lives of several saints, such as St. Martin of Tours, St. Julian the Martyr, the blessed apostle Andrew and several others. In these works, as the title indicates, the miracles performed by saints are moved to the foreground, leaving the true biographical element obscure and wrapped up with legends. Gregory wrote also a work on The Course

77.

of the Stars (De cursu stellorum ratio) and
A Commentary on the Psalms (In psalterii tractatum
commentarius).

The most significant of all of his works,
however, and the one for which Gregory has won
universal acclaim is the History of the Kings of
the Franks (Historia Francorum), composed between
574 and 593 in ten books. Though Gregory is a
truly Frankish historian and particularly a historian who described events of his own day in his
own country, his following of the established
Christian approach to historiography cannot be
denied: in the first book of his work Gregory
briefly sketched events of universal history from
the Creation to 397 A.D., to the death of St.
Martin of Tours (ca. 316-397), the great predecessor in his see. As sources for the introductory
book of the History Gregory used Jerome's translation of Eusebius' "Chronological Tables," Orosius'
History against the Pagans, Rufinus' translation
of Eusebius' Ecclesiastical History and local
Frankish annals. With the second book Gregory began the true history of the Franks, and the hero
in this book is Clovis, the founder of the Frankish
kingdom. With Clovis' death in 511 ends the second book of the History. Books three and four
describe Gaul under Frankish rule down to 575.
The remaining six books narrate the events to 591,
with an epilog written in his last year of life.
Thus, the last six books cover the events during
his episcopate when Gregory was not only the most
influential Frankish ecclesiastic, but on several
occasions also an eyewitness of many contemporaneous occurrences. For the earlier period of
Frankish history Gregory gathered information from
the works of several Frankish annalists, such as
the Chronicle (Chronica) of Sulpicius Severus (ca.
365-425) and other chronicles, now lost, as well
as from his seniors who had firsthand knowledge
of some particular event. For his own times Gregory made ample use of knowledge and observations
of events he witnessed, and where his personal
reach for news fell short, he listened to narra-
tions from other eyewitnesses and incorporated

these stories into his work.

Gregory's approach to history follows the
Christian pattern worked out by Eusebius: he
uses the year-by-year or annalistic form of
narration, includes a catalogue of the bishops of
Tours, and concludes the last book with an epilogue which lists his works and provides a summary
of events from the Creation to the year he wrote
the epilogue, i.e. till the fifth year of the pontificate of Gregory the Great, which was, according to Gregory, 5792 years since Adam, or 609
after the Resurrection. Ignoring Gregory's
faulty chronology, the fact remains that the resurrection of Christ was regarded by the bishop of
Tours important enough for reference, whereas the
birth of Christ was not used as a milestone for
dating events.

However, more significant than Gregory's
following of Eusebius' chronological pattern is
his attitude toward Christianity and his concept
of a historian's mission. Already in the introductory paragraph of the History Gregory solemnly
declares: "I am Catholic," and then recites,
with brief commentaries, the Nicene Creed, thus
emphasizing his orthodoxy. From this premise
evolves Gregory's concept of a historian's mission: "to describe the wars waged by kings
against hostile people, by martyrs against the
heathen, and by the pagans, of Churches against
the heretics."[9] Thus again, Gregory of Tours is
following St. Augustine's division of mankind into
two societies or two cities: into true Christians
and non-Christians or bad Christians. The historian's duty, according to Gregory, is to describe how the true or Catholic Christians, led by
kings under the guidance of the Church and aided
by martyrs, wage wars against pagans and heretics
in order to expand Christianity and enhance the
strength of the true religion. As a Catholic
bishop, Gregory had unreserved faith in God's own
omnipotence and righteousness. Moreover, Gregory
strongly believed in God's active role in shaping
the human past and in punishing all his foes and

79.

and adversaries. The classical example of God's direct interference on behalf of Christians is Gregory's story about Clovis' conversion to Catholicism after the Frankish king had promised to turn away from paganism if the Christian God would grant him victory over the Alemanni: "Even as he said this, the Alemanni turned their backs and began to run away."[10]

Closely connected with Gregory's confidence in divine intervention in shaping human history is his unshaken belief in miracles: Gregory not only narrated numerous miraculous deeds from the lives of saints who had lived long before him and about whom too few historical facts were available, but also ascribed many wondrous and incredible achievements to fully historical persons, such as to the founder of the Frankish kingdom, Clovis. Again, a good example is Gregory's story about the Christian king's victory over the city of Agoulême: "The Lord showed him /Clovis/ such favor that the city walls collapsed of their own weight as he looked at them."[11] Such a statement would sound completely unacceptable in our days, but to Gregory of Tours and to many of his contemporaries the idea of God's active participation in guiding human affairs and performing miracles for the benefit of the faithful was nothing extraordinary. Apparently the Bible served Gregory well as a model for relating miraculous events. Likewise, Gregory had unshakeable belief in the power of relics and the merit of adoring saints; therefore, his History is literally overburdened with miraculous stories, descriptions of marvels and legends of saints and martyrs. However, the inclusion of the irrational in his work does not mean that the purely historical material is either false or absent: besides describing Frankish expansion in Gaul and their military and political history, Gregory conveyed to posterity the best description of Franco-Gallic institutions, administration, society, morals and the church. Gregory also narrated the lives and deeds of the Frankish kings and queens. In short, Gregory is our best source for Frankish history up to his own day.

Gregory's language is colloquial and his Latin vulgar: he was neither a great stylist nor a truly scholarly historian in the sense of the great classical historians, but Gregory, like Herodotus, is a vivid and lively narrator who without set purpose and in good faith has related Franco-Gallic history as he observed and understood it. If one can trace prejudice in Gregory's work, then it is demonstrated against non-Christians and Arian Christians: he regarded every crime by a Catholic a lesser evil than heresy or paganism.

The period of Frankish history between Gregory of Tours and Charlemagne is, perhaps, best treated by the so called FREDEGAR (Fredegarius, fl. mid-seventh cent.), a sixteenth century name given to an anonymous Frankish chronicler. The original part of the chronicle, called the Fourth Book of Fredegar (Fredegarii chronica), covers events from 584 to 642, but later additions brings it down to 768, to the death of Pepin the Short (king 751-768) and accession of Charlemagne. The chronicle's first three books are an epitome of the first six books of Gregory of Tours' History of the Franks.

The northern neighbors of the Franks were the Saxons, whose early association with the Angles and their joint migration across the English Channel began well before Clovis' conquest of Gaul. To stop the massive barbarian invasions of the Empire, Emperor Honorius (395-423) in 407 withdrew Roman legions from Britain in order to bolster the garrisons on the Rhine-Danube frontier. The removal of the Roman army from Britain left the island defenseless against German incursions, and seemingly by about 450 the Jutes, the Angles and the Saxons, living in modern Denmark and round the estuary of the Elbe river, had begun their raids on Britain. The Jutes were the first who crossed the Channel, followed by Angles and Saxons. The earliest English historian who has left a description of Anglo-Saxon migration to Britain is GILDAS (ca. 516-ca. 570). Gildas

probably was a Welsh monk who fled England during
the invasions, settled down in Brittany and there
wrote a narrative On the Destruction and Conquest
of Britain (De exidio et conquestu Britanniae),
probably before 550. Gildas began his work with
a description of Britain and its early inhabitants,
then outlined Roman occupation and rule in England,
later turned to the introduction of Christianity
in Roman Britain, to Pictish and Scottish attacks
on the Britons,[12] and in the final chapters described the Roman withdrawal from England and the
Anglo-Saxon invasions. However, it seems that
Gildas was writing the Destruction not only to
narrate historical events but also to prove divine providence at work in England. Consequently,
his history is heavily overshadowed with religious
motifs and attempts to apply biblical parallels to
his native country. Besides, Gildas wrote in a
style of an emotional poetic story-teller rather
than a substantiated chronicler. Therefore, fact
and fancy are frequently interwoven in his narrative. Nevertheless, Gildas is our only contemporary source of Anglo-Saxon migrations across the
Channel and the subsequent destruction of Romano-
Briton civilization in England. All successive
historians writing about this period had to rely
on Gildas' Destruction. About Gildas' sources
one can only surmise.

A later work, from the early ninth century,
commonly known as Nennius' History of the Britons
(Historia Brittonum), is still less reliable as a
historical source than Gildas' Destruction, for
imagination and fantasy dominate this compilation
of Briton history. Many modern scholars believe
that NENNIUS (fl. ca. 800) was a Welsh clerk who
had either compiled the many oral traditions or
revised an earlier work or works, no longer extant, about Roman Britain and the Anglo-Saxon
invasions. Occasionally Nennius took over information also from Gildas. The real significance
of Nennius' History of the Britons lay in the fact
that it became the original basic source for legendary Briton history, particularly for the
celebrated Arthurian cycle[13] and partly also for

St. Patrick (ca. 385-461).

For the first truly scholarly historian on early Britain, the Anglo-Saxon invasions, the revival of Christianity in England and the Heptarchy, one has to look to the VENERABLE BEDE (Baeda, also Beda Venerabilis, ca. 673-735) who in 731 completed his major work the Ecclesiastical History of the English People. The main source about Bede's life is Bede himself. Apparently he was born in about 673 in Northumbria,14 near Wearmouth. At the age of seven he was placed by his parents, of whom we know nothing, in the Benedictine abbey at Wearmouth, and it seems that two years later, in 682, he was transferred to the newly built nearby twin monastery at Jarrow, where he spent the remaining years of his sixty-two-year-long life as a monk. At the age of nineteen Bede was made deacon, at thirty he was ordained a priest. Bede travelled around but little; he spent his life quietly at Jarrow, studying, teaching other monks and writing many works—about forty in number. At Bede's time the monastery of Jarrow was one of the great centers of learning in northern England, with an excellent library, and Bede had wasted no time in reading all the books available in patristic literature, descriptions of the lives of saints and martyrs; he certainly knew the Scripture well, was familiar with the Etymologies of Isidore of Seville, and had read many works on history and chronology. Modern scholarship has acclaimed Bede as the most learned man in the West of his day and the most scholarly historian of the early Middle Ages.

Bede's own works may be grouped into religious, educational and historical writings. By far the greatest part falls in the first group, viz., several commentaries on the books of the Bible, homilies, lives of the saints and a book of hymns. His educational works, such as On Time, On the Nature of Things, On Orthography, On the Art of Poetry were meant as textbooks for the monastery's school. However, Bede's real

contribution to medieval scholarship lays in his
historical works.

Bede became interested in the chronology of
history, in dating events according to some well-
established and extremely important and popular
fact.   Late antiquity used many different dating
schemes.   During the first centuries of Christianity, as in the case with Sextus Julius Africanus
and Eusebius of Caesarea, the most prevalent had
become the practice of dating events according
either to the first man Adam, or the Greek Olympiads.   The former, however, was actually a Jewish
system of recording time, though recognized and
adopted by Christians.   Besides, there was no real
agreement about the exact year of the creation of
the world.   The Olympic games were truly pagan
festivities in honor of the Greek god Zeus.   As a
pagan festival, the Olympic games had been for-
bidden already in 394; therefore this handy way of
dating events, so consistently used by Eusebius
and St. Jerome, had become obsolete.   Another common practice--dating events after the Roman consuls and regnal years of the emperors--also had
lost its value, for the office of the consuls had
fallen into disuse, and after 476 there were no
emperors in the West.   On the other hand, with the
spread and triumph of Christianity the fixing of the
correct date of religious festivals, related to Jesus'
life, had grown to great importance.   Particularly
intricate had become the finding of the accurate date
in the year of the most solemn of all Christian
feasts--Jesus' resurrection and the celebration of
Easter.   According to Luke, 24:1-7, the resurrection had fallen on the first day of the week
(Sunday) after the Hebrew feast of the unleavened
bread (cf. Matt. 26:17).   The latter was celebrated by the Jews on the fourteenth day in the
month of Nisan (March-April) which was identical
with the vernal equinox.[15]   However, the Jewish
feast of the unleavened bread or the Passover was
calculated according to a lunar year consisting
of 354 days.   To the early Christians, who followed the calendar of a solar year of $365\frac{1}{4}$ days,
a problem arose: how to reconcile the lunar

with the solar year, and how to determine the
Christian Easter according to a lunar calendar.

The Council of Nicaea in 325 had established
the date of Easter on the Sunday following the
full moon after the vernal equinox. However, in
a solar year the appearance of the full moon after
the spring equinox fluctuates from March 21 till
April 18; therefore Easter became one of the move-
able Christian feasts. In order to determine what
Sunday following March 21 is Easter Sunday in every particular year, special Easter Tables were
prepared for the use of the clergy. The best
known Easter Tables were compiled by the patriarch of Alexandria CYRIL (Cyrillus, ca. 370-444).
Computing the tables, Cyril had made use of the
old astronomical knowledge that after every
twenty-eight solar years the days of the week
again fall on the same dates of the month. This
twenty-eight year period in astronomy is known as
the solar cycle. Further, Cyril relied on the
calculation of Meton (fl. ca. 432 B.C. in Athens)
that after every 235 lunar or synodic months the
phases of the full moon appear on the same dates
of the month as in the previous period, and that
235 lunar months are equal to 223 solar months,
or nineteen years. This period of nineteen years
after which the lunar and solar years again are
in concordance, is called either the Metonic or
more frequently the Lunar cycle; in astronomical
tables it is referred to as the golden number.
To calculate an Easter cycle or prepare the Easter
Tables a period of time was to be found after
which the sun and the moon again were in the same
positions and the day of the week fell on the
same date of the month. Such a period, called the
Greek cycle, is obtained by multiplying the number
of years in the Lunar cycle with the number of
years in the Solar cycle (19 x 28 = 532). Thus
after every 532 years Easter Sunday occurs on the
same date of the month. Cyril of Alexandria had
prepared his Easter Tables for a period of five
Lunar cycles or ninety-five years, from 436 to
531, and had correlated the year 436 to the 153rd
and 531 to the 247th year after Diocletian's

reign. Cyril had used the accession to the throne of Diocletian on August 29, 284 as the beginning of an era, in historiography known as Diocletian's or Martyr's era,[16] for under the Emperor Diocletian the great persecutions of Christians took place in 305. Thus the first year of Diocletian's reign, or A.D. 284 in Cyril's mind became year one in Diocletian's era, and it was accepted by Cyril as the chronological basis for his Easter Tables. Although Cyril of Alexandria used Diocletian's era only for compiling Easter Tables, nevertheless, in time this era was used also for dating historical events; thus it acquired a wider usage than Cyril had intended.

Since Cyril's tables terminated with the year 247 of Diocletian's era (equivalent to A.D. 531), a learned monk DIONYSIUS EXIGUUS (Denis the Little, died after 525) at Rome in 525 prepared a continuation of Cyril's tables by computing the date of Easter for five additional lunar cycles or ninety-five years. However, Dionysius Exiguus made one remarkable advancement: he abandoned counting years according to Diocletian's era, for he found it unacceptable to tie the most solemn Christian feast to the memory of an ungodly persecutor of Christians. Instead, Dionysius began reckoning years according to the "incarnation of our Lord Jesus Christ."[17] Dionysius calculated that until the accession of Diocletian 284 years had lapsed since the birth of Christ (an error of about four years), and consequently the year 248 in Diocletian's era became 532 in Dionysius', or the Christian era, meaning that Dionysius Exiguus computed his ninety-five year Easter Tables beginning with the 532nd year after the birth of Christ.[18] Dionysius Exiguus, thus, became the first who used Christ's birth as the point of departure for counting years in Easter Tables. However, there is no evidence that Dionysius' method of chronology was followed until the Synod of Whitby in 664, nor did it become a practice to date historic events according to the Nativity until the day of the Venerable Bede.

86.

Bede, like Cyril of Alexandria and Dionysius
Exiguus, was concerned with the correct date for
celebrating Easter. However, seventh century
Britain was religiously torn between the Irish or
Celtic[19] and the Roman form of Christianity, each
fixing the celebration of Easter according to different practices. In order to establish unifor-
mity the king of Northumbria, Osway (641-670), in
663 or 664 convoked a synod at Whitby, where the
eloquent St. Wilfried (634-ca. 709), bishop of
Ripon, persuaded the synod and the king to adopt
the Roman rites and Roman way of fixing Easter
Sunday. The Church of Rome followed the tradition
established by Cyril of Alexandria and Dionysius
Exiguus. Bede, who was brought up in rigid Roman
orthodoxy, gave his full support to Dionysius'
method of computing Easter, and in a lengthy treatise On the Reckoning of Time (De temporum ratione),
composed in 725, he carefully explained how various
aspects of time were calculated in antiquity, including the date of Easter. Two chapters of this
work are of particular importance to historians.
In one, "On the Years of the Lord's Incarnation,"
quoting verbatim Dionysius Exiguus, Bede approved
the method of counting years according to Christ's
birth. The other chapter, "The Chronicle, or the
Six Ages,"[20] is a world chronicle faithfully compiled after the patterns of Eusebius and Jerome
and describes events from Adam to A.D. 725. This
"Chronicle" may be regarded as a continuation of
Isidore of Seville's chronicle. Noteworthy is
Bede's recognition and strict following of St.
Augustine's division of the world's history into
six ages according to the six days of Creation.
However, Bede has ignored Orosius' approach to
history according to four secular monarchies. In
the concluding chapters of the treatise On the
Reckoning of Time Bede, like St. Augustine, offers
a vision on the day of the Last Judgment, and ends
his story with the last age of mankind, with the
blissful life in the heavenly city of God for the
saved, and eternal perdition for the damned.
Though Bede in an earlier chapter of this treatise
had advocated the acceptance of Christ's incarnation as the year of departure for dating events,

he does not follow this method in On the Reckoning of Time. The work, however, in which Bede does pursue rigorously such a chronological scheme is his other major historical composition, the Ecclesiastical History of the English People. Nevertheless, it is Bede who set the pattern which was followed and gradually adopted by the whole of Western Christendom—dating historic events in relation to the Nativity. Contributing to this end were English missionaries who worked on the continent, particularly among the Franks, and carried with them and popularized Bede's works On the Reckoning of Time and the Ecclesiastical History. Although the latter became England's major literary export item to continental Europe, in the Frankish Empire dating events after the Incarnation is not noticed until 839; in the papal chancery not until 963. Thus, it took more than two centuries after Bede, and more than four hundred years after Dionysius Exiguus to make the Christian era the general pattern for dating events in European historiography. It also means that the factor that effectively lead to Christian chronology was the desire to fix correctly the date of Easter, which fact in turn resulted in the computation of Easter Tables using the birth of Christ as the point of departure for listing years in chronological sequence.

Bede's other great contribution to medieval historiography is the Ecclesiastical History of the English People, also translated as the History of the English Church and People (Historia ecclesiastica gentis Anglorum), completed in 731. It consists of five books, each book further divided into many chapters. In the first book, after the introductory chapter on Britain's geography and early inhabitants, Bede narrates (in twenty-one chapters) English history from Caesar's first landing in 55 B.C. to the arrival of Augustine of Canterbury (archbishop of Centerbury, 601-ca. 605) in Kent in 597. In the following twelve chapters he describes Augustine's mission in England during the pontificate of Gregory the Great (590-604). The next two books bring English history down to the arrival of Theodore of Tarsus (archbishop of Canterbury, 669-690) in England in 669, thus approximately to the time of Bede's birth. The last two books, comprising one-third of the entire work, deal with English history during Bede's lifetime, till 731. The concluding chapter contains a chronological summary of many important dates in English history as well as a sketch of Bede's life and a list of his works.

Bede certainly intended to write, as the title of the work indicates, a history of Christianity and the Catholic church in England, and beyond doubt, he accomplished his task very successfully. Already in the fourth chapter—in the year 156—Bede mentions the first Christians among the Britons; he continues his story about the struggle of Christianity in England till the arrival of Augustine in 597, then vividly depicts the conversion of the Anglo-Saxons to Orthodoxy, and lastly, describes the spread of Catholicism and Catholic institutions in the British Isles. His narrative is detailed, accurate and convincing. Bede calls English bishops and abbots by name; he describes their appointments, lives and successors and gives accounts of the building of churches and the founding of new monasteries. In Bede's story of the christianization of England historical facts are not infrequently interwoven with legend and miracles, but that was the tradition of the day for writing ecclesiastical history, and for certain Bede had taken over this manner from Eusebius and Gregory of Tours. Besides that, several descriptions of the lives of saints were in circulation, and undoubtedly Bede had read them and relied upon their information in compiling his history.

Though Bede wrote a history of the advancement of Christianity, he could not avoid mentioning and describing temporal rulers and secular events. He portrayed the Anglo-Saxon kings and their deeds, he sketched many political and military events in England, and occasionally he inserted a piece of information about Anglo-Saxon customs and idolatry. Therefore, Bede's <u>Eccle-siastical History</u> is not only a sacred history but also the best extant narrative of secular events in England for the period of the great migrations and the Anglo-Saxon kingdoms. For this reason, then, it is justifiable to translate Bede's Latin title as the <u>History of the English Church and People</u>.

Moreover, Bede is also our best source of information about cultural and itellectual life in England. During the early Middle Ages all writing and learning rested in the hands of the clergy, as the only literate people of the day. By describing life and work in English monasteries, Bede sheds light on the cultural and intellectual achievements of English and Irish monks, on their literary activities, on monastic libraries, on his own search for books and documents, and on the flourishing copying trade.

This fact leads to an inquiry into Bede's sources and authorities. The "Preface" of the <u>Ecclesiastical History</u> offers a good account of the method by which Bede obtained information. It has been noted already that Bede had travelled but little; therefore, he had not done research in archives of the great churches and abbeys of England, nor could he question participants in battles and witnesses of miracles who lived in other districts than his own. Bede had to rely almost entirely upon written accounts and oral narratives brought to him and the "Preface" reveals how diligently he had inquired for information. Most of the information was transmitted to him in the form of narratives from the archives at Canterbury and to a lesser degree also from several other dioceses and abbeys. Thus, Anglo-Saxon England had rich ecclesiastical records which could be used for compiling narratives about the introduction and dissemination of Christianity as well as secular events in Britain. Accounts of the progress of Christianity in Northumbria Bede had partly copied himself upon his visit to the nearby monastery of Lindisfarne. Moreover, Bede reveals that he had taken into consideration "old traditions" and evidence conveyed to him "by word of mouth" by "countless faithful witnesses who either know or remember the facts apart from what I know myself."[21] Through a priest in London who had visited Italy, Bede had obtained copies of documents from the papal archives in Rome, particularly those relating to the pontificate of Gregory the Great. Consequently, several papal letters are copied verbatim in the Ecclesiastical History. For using word by word quotes from documents Bede had a good example to follow--Eusebius' Ecclesiastical History.

But Bede took Eusebius' history as his model for more than just inserting edicts and letters. Both men selected carefully the best literary and oral information available; both searched for accounts of events from witnesses; both included in their histories lives of saints and martyrs; both adorned their narratives with legends and miracles; both frequently and openly indicated their source of information; even Bede's very idea of writing a church history is Eusebius'. Furthermore, both were study historians who compiled their works from information that was brought to them. Neither had travelled much, nor visited historic sites. Therefore, in this respect they would not meet the requirements of the best ancient historians. Neither of them, being priests, had a thorough understanding or any experience in diplomacy and military affairs; nor had they firsthand knowledge of the geography or the material resources of their respective regions. Bede differs from Eusebius mostly in that the latter wrote a universal history of the Church, the former an account of the triumph of Christianity in his native country.

For the Roman period and the age of the migrations Bede's sources were Tacitus' Agricola, Orosius' History, Jerome's translation of Eusebius' Chronicle, several saints' lives, and Gildas' Destruction, or as Bede puts it, "earlier writers." All of these works he could find in

91.

the libraries of Wearmouth and Jarrow. The most
influential of these authors upon Bede seems to
have been Gildas, particularly for his information
on Scottish and Pictish attacks on Roman Britain,
the Roman withdrawal from England and the Anglo-
Saxon invasions; some of Bede's descriptions are
very close to Gildas'.

Bede's language is a much better Latin than
Gregory of Tours'; his style is scholarly rather
than vulgar. Bede used longer and shorter quotations from direct speeches, though he never included elaborate oratory. In the "Preface" Bede
also reveals his philosophy and zeal of history:
he wanted to put into record "the doings and say-
ings of_great men of the past, and of our /i.e.
English/ nation in particular. For if history
records good things and good men, the thoughtful
hearer is encouraged to imitate what is good."
Thus, Bede had a vision of the usefulness of history similar to that of Polibius (ca. 201-120
B.C.)--"to transmit whatever I could ascertain
from common report for the instruction of posterity."22

To conclude the survey of the historians of
the great migrations a look need be taken at the
last of the important Germanic peoples who de-
scended into southern Europe--the Lombards, who
in 568 arrived in northern Italy and settled down
in the Po Valley, in present day Lombardy, and
from there established two Lombard duchies in
southern Italy--Spoleto and Benevento. The Lombard historian was Paul, usually called PAUL THE
DEACON or PAUL THE LOMBARD (Paulus Diaconus, ca.
720-ca. 800). Paul was a member of the Lombard
nobility, and before retiring to the monastery
of Monte Cassino in 774 he had lived in the Lombard capital, Pavia, where he probably was a
teacher at the royal court. It appears that Paul
has had a rather good education: he knew some
Greek, had travelled widely in northern Italy, and
in 783 visited the court of Charlemagne in Gaul,
where he remained for a few years before returning
to Monte Cassino. He died in the monastery around

800. Paul wrote several poems and many letters, of which some are extant, a life story of Gregory the Great and the History of the Bishops of Metz (Liber de episcopis Metensibus).

However, Paul's real contribution to historiography is his last work, the History of the Lombards (Historia Langobardorum) in six books, begun in the later years of his life at Monte Cassino and never completed. Paul's History first recites the legendary period of the Lombards' origins in Scandinavia and their descent into central Europe; it then turns to the Lombard conquest of northern Italy, and brings the narrative down to 744, to the death of their king Luitprand (712-744). For the early period of Lombard history Paul relied on oral tradition and several older authors, among others on Isidore of Seville, Gregory of Tours, Bede, episcopal biographies, and a brief anonymous treatise Origin of the Lombard People (Origo gentis Langobardorum). None of these authorities had any competence in the Lombards' past, nor had Paul the erudition to separate historical facts from legend; therefore, his story is rather confused and often imaginary. For the later period his narrative is more credible, and it seems that he was rather well informed about Lombard history during the seventh and eighth centuries. Not only the Lombard past is described by Paul; quite often he has news also about the Byzantines in Constantinople and their wars in Italy, and now and then he reports events from the Frankish Kingdom and the wars with the Avars; likewise, he mentions attacks by the Saracens[23] in the Mediterranean and the rising power of the papacy. Probably much of the information Paul had picked up at the Lombard royal court, though his direct sources or informers remain a puzzle. Paul's weakest point throughout the work is chronology; one may also question his ability to move to the foreground important events and de-emphasize the role of minor happenings. Nevertheless, Paul's History of the Lombards was a popular work during the Middle Ages (over one hundred manuscript copies are extant), for it is written in good

Latin, his narrative in general is smooth and flowing, and frequently a degree of drama is achieved, especially when events of war are related. However, when Paul attempts to go into minute description of the many petty skirmishes and strifes for power, his talent often breaks down and he turns into a rather dull and monotonous narrator. Paul's literary style is neither as barbarous as Gregory of Tours', nor as scholarly as Bede's: he wrote in the manner of his day, at the beginning of the Carolingian Renaissance (ca. 770-ca. 900) when continental learning began to gain prominence and refinement. For his literary achievement the History of the Lombards is regarded as part of the Carolingian Renaissance.

The zenith of the Carolingian Renaissance in historiography, however, was achieved by Paul's later contemporary, the biographer of Charlemagne EINHARD (Einhardus), also called EGINHARD (Eginhardus, ca. 770-840). Einhard was born in the Main river valley, probably of noble parents, and was given for education to the monastery of Fulda,[24] which was a great center of education during the Carolingian Renaissance. It seems that Einhard had been a very talented student, for the abbot of Fulda recommended him to Charlemagne, and in ca. 791 Einhard joined the scholarly circle of the royal court and became one of Charles' confidants. In the palace school Einhard received further training under Alcuin (ca. 735-804), the headmaster of the school, and apparently again had excelled himself as a Latin scholar. Einhard had read many of the Roman classical historians, such as Cicero, Caesar, Livy, Tacitus, Suetonius, as well as some of the early Frankish annalists. Since education in the early Middle Ages was aimed toward preparation of monks and priests, it is natural that Einhard also was well versed in the Scripture and patristic literature.

After Charlemagne's death in 814 Einhard served the emperor's son Louis the Pious (814-840) as a secretary and as a tutor to Louis' son Lothair (emperor 840-855). In 830 Einhard left the court

of Louis and retired to the monastery of Seligenstadt,[25] which he had founded; there he died ten
years later, in 840.

Einhard had written a history of the transfer
of the relics of two Frankish saints to his monastery, a poem in honor of these saints, letters
of which several are extant, and The Life of
Charlemagne (Vita Caroli Magni). This biography
is regarded not only as Einhard's greatest contribution to historiography but also as one of the
finest biographies written during the early Middle
Ages. Most probably Einhard composed it between
817 and 830, thus after the emperor's death. The
relationship between Charles and his confidant
was, to say the least, friendly; therefore, Einhard's Life of the great emperor is a laudatory
narrative of Charles' wars, public works, court,
palace school and religious policies. It also
describes briefly Charles' ancestry and youth,
his private life and his last hours. Thus, Einhard has left to posterity the only contemporary
narrative of the age of Charlemagne and the Carolingian Renaissance.

As sources Einhard used first of all his personal observations and impressions about the emperor. Secondly, being an assistant to Charles
and later on a secretary to the emperor's successor Louis the Pious, Einhard had access to official court documents, and no doubt he made use of
some information gathered from the imperial archives, as well as from the contemporary Royal
Frankish Annals. However, for writing the biography Einhard took as his model Suetonius'
Lives of the Twelve Caesars. From Suetonius Einhard not only adopted the structural scheme and
many parallel descriptions of Charlemagne and the
Roman emperors but also copied almost verbatim
several phrases from the Lives of the Twelve
Caesars into his own work. Probably the most frequently mentioned citation as evidence of Einhard's borrowing is the description of Charles'
physical appearance in chapter 22 and the appear-

ance of Augustus in Suetonius' biography, paragraph 79: both emperors are described as being almost six feet tall. Many modern historians have criticized Einhard for plagiarism, for none believed that Charlemagne was so tall a man. However, Charlemagne's tomb in Aachen has been opened several times, and the measurements taken in 1861 suggest that Charles really was about six feet tall. Thus, one may believe that Einhard, though copying Suetonius' style and method of description, has applied to Charles only those expressions by Suetonius which were relevant to Charlemagne.

From the early Middle Ages other biographies of famous emperors are extant, the most popular being that of Constantine by Eusebius and Justinian by Procopius. In comparing Einhard's Life of Charlemagne with the two former life stories, it could be said that Eusebius' work falls into the category of pure panegyric; Procopius' Secret History emphasizes court intrigues and the depravity and the wickedness of the Byzantine imperial couple. Einhard's biography, though underlining the good side of Charles' life and the emperor's great deeds, never sinks to mere eulogy of the dead ruler, nor brings to the foreground the vices and injustice of Charlemagne's reign. For this reason--relative objectivity--Einhard's work is superior to the other two Lives, and it has enjoyed a great popularity throughout the Middle Ages and even today. The other reason, of course, is the fame and importance of Charlemagne himself. The greater credibility of Einhard's work does not mean that he had striven to achieve an absolutely true picture of Charles, nor that Einhard's Life meets modern standards of a biography: Einhard's description of the emperor leaves much to be desired, particularly in regard to Charles' early life, the first years of his reign, his coronation and his administration of the realm. Nor can one excuse Einhard's superficiality in exploring the rich material in the imperial archives, nor his passing over in silence of the unpleasant acts and manners of his patron. Einhard wrote a commending, if not a glorifying life story of his friend and a

great emperor in gratitude for "the benefits con-
ferred upon" him, and in such light, then Einhard's Life of Charlemagne should be read.

Einhard wrote the biography in a simple,
somewhat official, but flowing style, using epi-
thets sparingly. He fashioned his language as
closely to classical Latin as he could imitate it,
for he took the ancient historians and biographers
as his teachers not only for composition, but also
for phraseology. Partly for these reasons Einhard's Life is regarded as one of the best original compositions of the Carolingian Renaissance.

Around the year Einhard died, another biographer of Charlemagne was born, the MONK OF ST.
GALL (Monachus Sangallensis), who is usually identified with NOTKER THE STAMMERER (Notkerus Balbu-
lus, ca. 840-912), a monk at St. Gall monastery.
He was a German, born in the vicinity of Lake Constance, who evidently spent his life at the nearby
monastery of St. Gall. Between 883 and 887, thus
some seventy years after the death of Charles the
Great, he composed a work The Deeds of Charlemagne
(Gesta Karoli Magni imperatoris) in two books for
the entertainment of the emperor's great-grandson
Charles the Fat (emperor 876-887). As his chief
authorities Notker mentions a veteran of Charlemagne's wars and an abbot of St. Gall who in his
youth had been a pupil of Alcuin. Their reminis-
cences, together with Einhard's biography and the
Royal Frankish Annals provided the historical
background for Notker's compilation. However, it
appears that the greater part of the monk's narrative contains funny stories or anecdotes which
he most probably had heard at various times in
the monastery of St. Gall and later inserted in
his work and attributed either to Charlemagne or
to Charles' son Louis the Pious or his grandson
Louis the German (king 843-876). These anecdotes
may be regarded as international monkish pastime
stories whose origin no one knows, and they
therefore have little biographical and historic
value for reconstructing the life story of
Charles. The real significance of Notker's work

97.

is twofold. First, it sheds light on how gossip
and tales gradually began to envelop the great
emperor until the legend developed into cycles of
romances about the alleged deeds of Charlemagne,
and finally produced the oldest French epic, the
Song of Roland (Chanson de Roland). Secondly,
Notker's work provides a closer insight into the
social and intellectual history of the Carolingian
Renaissance as reflected and preserved in monastic
literature; bishop and monks, clerics and jews,
soldiers and courtiers parade through the pages of
Notkers' tales.

Another biography, compiled slightly later
than Notker's, commonly known as Asser's "Life of
King Alfred" (De rebus gestis Aelfredi) deserves
mention. Though the authorship of this work is
still questioned, it is generally believed, since
W. H. Stevenson published in 1904 a critical edition of the Life accompanied with textual criticism, that it belongs to the pen of the bishop of
Sherborne,[26] ASSER (Asserius, bishop 892-910).
Asser, a Welshman and for many years a monk at St.
David's monastery in Wales, in about 884 joined
the household of King Alfred (871-899) and became
his teacher and helper in literary works, and in
about 893, thus six years before the king's death,
composed his life story. It is a unique work:
Asser took as the base for his compilation a now
lost version of the Anglo-Saxon Chronicle, translated the annals from the years 849 to 887 into
Latin and interpolated them with his personal observations about the king's life, without organ-
ically fusing the chronicle's information with
Alfred's biography. Moreover, Asser was negli-
gent in chronology, in dating correctly many
events in the king's life. Nevertheless, he was
an admirer, adherent and protégé of Alfred, and
his narrative is lively and rather laudatory, not
infrequently even attributing magic powers to
Alfred.

As his model for writing Alfred's biography
Asser took Einhard's Life of Charlemagne. Therefore, many similar patters are noticeable in both

works: birth, ancestry, youth, piety of the king, his wars, building activities, devotion to learning and interest in the native language. The real value of Asser's _Life_ lies in the fact that it was written by a close associate and contemporary of the Anglo-Saxon king.

Reference has been made to the Royal Frankish Annals (as Einhard's source) and the Anglo-Saxon Chronicle (as Asser's source). Annals and particularly chronicles became an integral and very prominent part of medieval historiography. By annal usually is understood a brief entry or record of an event during a single year in some kind of a register or a yearbook. An aggregation of such entries, arranged in strictly yearly or annual sequence is known as annals. Their origin dates back to republican Rome where each pontifex maximus entered on tablets the most significant occurrences during his year of office. It is fairly well established that medieval annals developed from Easter Tables, first in England, and from there, through the work of English missionaries in Gaul, spread to continental Europe. It is demonstrated that frequently clerics and monks in particular began to record in the Easter Tables in the margin or between the lines the most important local events during the current year. Gradually a tradition evolved whereby these brief notes were recorded independently from the Easter Tables in some sort of a notebook or roll (though in some monasteries events in the Easter Tables were recorded as late as the twelfth century). These were extremely short notes, usually a few words or a very abrupt sentence for the entire year. Recorded were some natural phenomena, such as eclipses, great flood or excessively harsh winters, or happenings connected with the monastery: death of the local abbot or bishop, rebuilding or adding a new structure to the monastery complex, or erecting a new church. Sometimes even political or military events were written down: accession or death of a king, or some other political or military occurrence of great importance. However, generally these were entries of

99.

local significance; records of wider or even national consequence were rather occasional.

Since the Easter Tables frequently were lent
to a neighboring monastery or parish for copying,
they were copied together with the brief annals.
In time it became traditional to add to the local
annals entries from the borrowed Easter Tables;
often events from past years were also copied down.
Such borrowed information usually was recorded in
the same roll or notebook where the local events
were entered. Thus, man's natural curiousity about
events in the neighborhood as well as interest in
the past was aroused and kept alive, and monks,
and to a lesser degree also priests, became the
local historians of the early Middle Ages. Such a
tradition had become rather common already during
the period of the early Carolingians in the eighth
century. However, the ninth century is regarded
as the golden period of annals.

It is further conjectured by historians that
the local annals frequently were circulated from
monastery to monastery, where new information was
added, often facts from one collection copied into
another, and now and then descriptions of earlier
events included, sometimes even at a length of a
paragraph or two. Thus, a new form of medieval
historiography gradually took shape--the chronicle.
The medieval chronicle is a narrative in which the
description of events still was arranged in chronological sequence, but the information was more
comprehensive, occasionally running into some detail and not infrequently covering a longer period
of time or events from a wider area than the local
monastery or bishopric. Such a chronicle might be
prefaced by a compendium of world history, usually
in the form of an epitome of Eusebius' "Chronological Tables," as translated and expanded by St.
Jerome, and further augmented from Isidore of
Seville, Bede and some other source no longer
extant.

Though it is traditional today to speak of
medieval annals and chronicles, there is, however,

in fact no definite limit that would separate annals from chronicles. Ordinarily a chronicle
would be more extensive in scope and content than
annals, though some chronicles were still called
annals, such as the Royal Frankish Annals, and
some literary narratives known as chronicles, such
as the Anglo-Saxon Chronicle in its earlier part
(roughly to mid-ninth century), are made up of
short annals. For certain, medieval annals differ
from classical Roman annals, especially as phrased
by Tacitus, who applied this term to highly pol-
ished narratives of past events, whereas the word
"history" he used to describe and evaluate in detail contemporary events. Likewise, early medieval chronicle is different from Eusebius' and his
epigones' chronicles, for the latter wrote universal chronicles, beginning either with the Creation
or Abraham, while typical chronicles of the early
Middle Ages (as an outgrowth of annals) were restricted to the time period and surroundings of
the residence of the author. However, the structural model after which to pattern the local
chronicle already was at hand: Eusebius and Bede.
Only gradually, during the Middle Ages the medieval chronicle evolved into a contemporary-world
or a universal chronicle. Early medieval chronicles also are distinguished from classical and
modern histories in that a historian presents his
narrative "in an ample and elegant style, whereas
the Chronicler writes simply and with brevity.
The historian aims at relating facts as they really happened, but he does this in a literary form;
he pleases his readers by a gracefulness with
which he describes men and manners. The chronicler, on the other hand, sets down the year of
Grace, calculates the months and days, notes
shortly the doings of kings and princes, and records events, portents or miracles. But. . .
there are some chroniclers who travel beyond
their limits, who make broad their phylacteries
and enlarge their borders."27 To this it may be
added that historians frequently feel free to in-
terrupt a chronological sequence in order to dem-
onstrate their point and, above all, to include
analysis and interpretation in their narrative in

in order to explain events and actions, whereas a
chronicler just records facts without elaborating
on causes and results.

The authorship of medieval annals and chronicles is still a puzzle to modern scholars, because for the most part such works are either whol-
ly anonymous or the name of the author must be
established from the content of the narrative or
from the dedication of the work to a patron. This
problem is further complicated by the fact that
annals and chronicles frequently were continued
by several authors through several generations,
and usually none of the scribes revealed his iden-
tity. However, with practically no exception, all
chronicles were the works of a monk or monks or,
in fewer cases, a priest. Medieval annals and
chronicles almost as a rule were written in Latin.

The authorship partially determined also the
character and scope of the chronicle: the early
chronicles, in general, described either the history of a monastery, a diocese, a town, or at most,
a geographical region. Only seldom did a chronicle reach the extent of a national or universal
history.

Another peculiarity requires mentioning.
Though by far the majority of medieval chronicles
were private compositions (i.e., were composed
of a person's own accord), there are, however,
some works which were compiled by official commission from a royal court for keeping a favorable record, one may assume, of the ruling dynasty, its ancestry and deeds for posterity.
Such annals and chronicles usually are classified
as "royal" annals and chronicles. The most popular work in this group is the ANGLO-SAXON CHRON-
ICLE (Annales Saxonici), a product, as the title
indicates, of England. It is a typical medieval
chronicle because it originated from brief annals
and gradually developed into extended narratives.
The Anglo-Saxon Chronicle, however, is atypical in
that it is not written in the traditional Latin
language of medieval historical works, but in

vernacular--in Anglo-Saxon, or Old English. There are several theories which attempt to explain the origin of the Chronicle. There is, however, a general agreement among scholars that the oldest extant version, known as manuscript "A" and pre-served at Corpus Christi College in the University of Cambridge, is a copy of a code which was com-piled from several sources in the late ninth or very early tenth century. Probably that was done at the court of Alfred the Great, presumably by his commission or at least under his inspiration, and possible using entries from Easter Tables, written originally perhaps in Latin. However, these latter hypotheses are mere conjectures. It is, however, established that the compiler used as his source Bede's Ecclesiastical History and some earlier West Saxon annals along with some regional lists and genealogies of Anglo-Saxon kings. Who the compiler was, is not known, but it is assumed that he was closely associated with King Alfred's court, for the dominant part of the factual infor-mation refers to Wessex, Alfred's kingdom, and Alfred's dynasty is presented in a favorable light. The historical material of the Alfredian chronicle covers the period from Caesar's landing in England in 54 B.C. to 891, the year which by several schol-ars is presumed as the year of the compilation of the Chronicle. However, independent information in the Chronicle starts only with the cessation of Bede's History and the appearance of Danish Vikings in England in late eighth century. The material is scanty and extremely laconic, arranged in strict annalistic form and chronological sequence. How-ever, the information conveyed is the only con-temporary narrative for the post-Bede period.
Once the Alfredian chronicle was compiled, several copies were prepared from the original manuscript (no longer extant), and these copies were kept and continued at various English monasteries, notably at Canterbury, Winchester, Abingdon, Worcester and Peterborough. It is again believed that the monas-teries where the Alfredian copies were continued received supplemental information till 1018 from some center unknown to us; after that year each continuator obtained his information locally.

103.

Consequently, several versions of the Anglo-Saxon Chronicle came into existence, for even the continuators between 892 and 1018 felt free to interpolate local or other information into their continuations. It also means that each of the extant manuscripts ends at a different date: the manuscript coded "B," assumed to have originated at Canterbury, ends with 977; the version "E," known as the "Peterborough Chronicle," with the year 1154. To our day seven manuscript copies are extant. It is noteworthy that the Chronicle is chiefly concerned with secular matters, with raids, wars and politics; church affairs have only secondary ranking. After the year 891 the factual information becomes more detailed, the narrative smoother and story-like, and the language more modern; however, the strict chronological sequence was retained. The most authentic, thus the most valuable, information of the Chronicle is confined to the period from the beginning of the Norsemen's raids (mid-ninth cent.) to the Norman invasion of England by William the Conqueror in 1066. For this period of Anglo-Saxon history the Chronicle as the main contemporary original narrative source is indispensable.

Much discussion is concerned with the authorship of the Anglo-Saxon Chronicle. Since it was continued over a long period of time and compiled at many independent centers, it should be regarded as an anonymous work, as a product of many compilers and continuators.

A scholarly edition, entitled The Anglo-Saxon Chronicle and prepared by B. Thorpe in 1861, gives all the various versions of the chronicle in the original language. The best translation into modern English, giving again all seven versions, was prepared by Dorothy Whitelock in 1961 and published as The Anglo-Saxon Chronicle.

The other important chronicle which today is regarded as an official composition, is the so-called ROYAL FRANKISH ANNALS (Annales regni Francorum). They cover the period between 741, the death of major domus[28] Charles Martel (689-741) and 829, the fifteenth year of the reign of Emperor Louis the Pious. The <u>Royal Frankish Annals</u>, it is believed, were put together at the Carolingian court in three installments. The first part was written down by a single author between 787 and 795, using as sources older annals, now lost, for the early period, but from 787 onward, contemporary information. The second portion was written concurrently with the described events by another scribe between 795 and 807, and the last segment was probably the work of several authors, again writing contemporaneously with the events. Who the authors were cannot be established; however, it is generally agreed that they were, like the original compiler of the <u>Anglo-Saxon Chronicle</u>, closely associated with the court, were well versed in political and military affairs of the day, and were favorable toward the reigning Carolingian dynasty. Whether the chronicle was begun by a commission of Charlemagne cannot be proven. Unlike the <u>Anglo-Saxon Chronicle</u>, the <u>Royal Frankish Annals</u> are written in simple, but comparatively good Latin, and they make up part of the achievement of the Carolingian Renaissance (as the <u>Anglo-Saxon Chronicle</u> is a product of the Alfredian Renaissance). Again, like the English counterpart, the <u>Royal Frankish Annals</u> is a secular history, placing events within the Church in the background. Einhard knew the <u>Frankish Annals</u> and used them as a source for the <u>Life of Charlemagne</u>; the unused information of the chronicle is a handy supplemental cross-reference for the reign of Charlemagne and his predecessor Pepin the Short (king 751-768) and a first-hand original source about Charles' successor Louis the Pious. The original version, down to the year 800 was revised and augmented in the early ninth century by an unknown author but, again, one closely associated with the Carolingian court. Though the official title of the work is "annals," in fact, because of the extent of the information and character of description, it should be regarded as a chronicle.

Chronologically, a direct continuation of the
Royal Frankish Annals is Nithard's Four Books of
Histories (Historiarum libri quatuor), a third
important work in the royal annal group. NITHARD
(Nithardus, ca. 795-845), a bastard grandson of
Charlemagne, was, like Einhard, a layman, a knight
and a strong supporter of Louis the Pious and his
younger son Charles the Bald, king of the Franks
(843-877). Upon the latter's request, Nithard in
841 began to write his chronicle, covering the
years 829 to 843, thus the later period of Emperor
Louis the Pious and the early years of the reign
of his rebellious sons. In Frankish history these
years are known for the bitter struggle among
Charlemagne's successors for power and the crown.
The civil wars finally resulted in the disintegration of the Carolingian Empire. Nithard's Histories contain the famous "Oath of Strassbourg of
842" between Charles the Bald and Louis the German
(843-876), giving the earliest example of the two
dialects spoken in the Carolingian Empire--Old
French and Old German. Nithard, one may assume,
had received a good education in Charlemagne's
palace school; he wrote the Histories in simple,
but good Latin, using as the main source his own
observations and knowledge of events. However, it
is proven that he also made use of many official
documents and probably of the Royal Frankish Annals.
For the introductory paragraphs he had looked even
into Einhard's Life of Charlemagne. Though
Nithard's work is termed Histories, it actually
falls in the category of royal chronicles; the
English translator of the Royal Frankish Annals
and Nithard's Histories, Professor Bernhard W.
Scholz has properly called them, Carolingian
Chronicles.

Of the numerous monastic or privately written chronicles mention need be made of Richer's
Four Books of History (Historiarum libri quatuor).
RICHER (Richerus, died ca. 1000) was a Frankish
monk of St. Remi of Reims, a student of the most
learned man of his day Gerbert of Aurillac, later
Pope Sylvester II (999-1003), to whom he dedicated
his chronicle. Richer's work covers the years

888 to 995; however, the most valuable part is books three and four, which describe contemporary events from 966 to 995. In Frankish history, these years are a transition period from the Carolingian dynasty to the early Capétians (987-1328). Richer was well read in Latin classics and is a fluent narrator who occasionally tried to imitate the Roman historian Sallust (86-ca. 34 B.C.). Richer wrote the later part of the History as a contemporary, and his work contains much factual material about political and military maneuvering as well as descriptions of intellectual life in late tenth century France. However, he was biased in favor of the rising Capetian house; therefore, his work should be read with some critical alertness.

Richer's contemporary in Germany was WIDUKIND (Widukindus, ca. 925-ca. 1004), a Saxon monk from the monastery of Corvey at the River Weser, where he wrote the Deeds of the Saxons (Rerum gestarum Saxonicarum) in three books from the earliest times to the late years of Emperor Otto I (936-973). Following the pattern of Jordanes and Paul the Deacon, Widukind relied heavily upon Saxon legends and unwritten tradition, but for the later period, particularly for the reigns of the Saxon kings Henry I the Fowler (919-936) and his son Otto I the Great, he is reliable and rich in a rather detailed narrative of events. Widukind was of noble stock; consequently his interest centered on wars and the emperors' deeds. His pictures of Henry and Otto are rather glorified, and it seems that in this regard he was influenced by Einhard's Life of Charlemagne. A bishop of Merseburg,29 THIETMAR (Thietmarus Merseburgensis, died 1018) wrote a Chronicle (Chronicon) in eight books, covering Saxon history down to the reign of Emperor Henry II (1002-1024), and a monk at the Abbey of Reichenau30 HERMAN THE CRIPPLE (Hermannus Contractus, 1013-1054)--a universal Chronicle (Chronicon) describing historical events from the beginning of the Christian era to his own death. The most important part of Herman's work deals with the reigns of Emperor Conrad II (1024-1039) and Henry III (1039-1056). For these years the

Chronicle is actually a universal history of his own day. All these German chroniclers were interested predominantly in secular affairs.

For German eastward expansion during the eleventh century the best narrative source is ADAM OF BREMEN (Adamus Bremensis, died ca. 1085), a canon at the cathedral chapter, who wrote a History of the Archbishops of Hamburg - Bremen (Gesta Hammaburgensis ecclesiae pontificum) in four books, beginning with the year 788. The last three books, however, are the most valuable: the second book contains a well documented narrative from 936 to 1043; the third, contemporary events to 1072; the last book actually is a geographical and ethnographical treatise offering a good description of all north European lands and peoples known to the westerners at that time. Adam's sources for the early period were Frankish and German annals, Einhard, Gregory of Tours, lives of saints and missionaries, and imperial and papal letters. For the later period he made extensive use of his own knowledge as well as that of his contemporaries. The geographical and ethnical outline in the fourth book was based on information obtained from classical Roman authors, early Christian historians and people who were familiar with the remote northern regions of Europe, among others the King of Denmark Swein Estridsson (988-1014), and some Swedish bishops.

Notes

1 Heptarchy — the seven kingdoms established in England after the Anglo-Saxon invasion.

2 For Cassiodorus, see above, p. 12, under "Early Christian Historians."

3 For Isidore of Seville, see above, p. 8, under "Early Christian Historians."

[4] Justinian was not a warrior emperor; he did
not lead his troops in any war; the high command
was entrusted to Justinian's generals, among whom
the most famous was Belisarius.

[5] Hagia Sophia - Holy Wisdom, the main and
the most beautiful church in Constantinople.

[6] Auvergne - region in southern France.

[7] Tours - city in west central France on the
banks of River Loire.

[8] Trivium - Latin grammar, rhetoric and logic,
forming the lower division of the medieval cur-
riculum of the Seven liberal arts, which were
taught in monastic and cathedral schools during the
Middle Ages. The basic textbook for acquiring the
trivium was Martianus Capella's work.

Quadrivium - arithmetic, geometry, astronomy and music, forming the upper division of the
Seven liberal arts.

[9] Both quotations are from the preliminary
to book 1, taken from Lewis Thorpe's translation,
The History of the Franks (Harmondsworth, England:
Penguin Books, 1974).

[10] Book 2, ch. 30.

[11] Book 2, ch. 37.

[12] Picts and Scots - ancient inhabitants of
Scotland. Britons - Celtic inhabitants of England
before the Anglo-Saxon invasion.

[13] Arthurian cycle - a mass of legends cen-
tering around the legendary Briton king Arthur
(ca. 600) and his knights.

[14] Northumbria - uppermost northern kingdom
of the Anglo-Saxon Heptarchy.

[15] Vernal equinox – time in spring when day and night are the same length.

[16] Era – a period in history begun by a memorable date from which a series of years is reckoned.

[17] Quoted from Dionysius Exiguus "Liber de Paschate" in Migne, Patrologia Latina, 67:487.

[18] Dionysius Exiguus "Easter Tables" are printed in Migne, Patrologia Latina, 67:493-498.

[19] Irish or Celtic Christianity – Christianity under strong influence from Eastern or Byzantine ecclesiastical tradition.

[20] "On the Years of the Lord's Incarnation" and "The Chronicle, or the Six Ages" from the chapters 47 and 66, respectively, of the treatise On the Reckoning of Time.

[21] Quoted from the "Preface" to the History of the English Church and People, transl. Leo Shirley-Price (Baltimore: Penguin Books, 1955).

[22] Both quotations from Shirley-Price's translation, mentioned above.

[23] Avars – Asiatic people who in the seventh century settled down in the Hungarian plain and marauded central western Europe; they were destroyed by Charlemagne.

Saracens – medieval term for Arabs and Moslems in general.

[24] Fulda is located in medieval Franconia, in central Germany. The abbey at Fulda was founded in 744 by St. Boniface (ca. 675-ca. 754), the Apostle of Germany.

[25] Seligenstadt – on lower Main river, near Frankfurt.

[26] Sherborne is located in south central England.

[27] Gervase of Canterbury, "The Chronicle of the Reigns of Stephen, Henry II, and Richard I" in William Stubbs, ed., The Historical Works of Gervase of Canterbury, 1:87, as quoted in Reginald L. Poole, Chronicles and Annals (Oxford: The University Press, 1926), pp. 1-2.

[28] Major domus – "stewart of the palace"; head of the royal household in Merovingian Gaul.

[29] Merseburg – in east central Germany on the River Saale.

[30] Reichenau – in southwestern Germany, near Lake Constance.

A SELECT BIBLIOGRAPHY

Historiographical Works

Balzani, Ugo, <u>Early Chronicles of Europe:
Italy</u>. London: Society for Promoting Christian
Knowledge, 1883.

A somewhat outdated survey of Italian medieval historical writings from Cassiodorus to the
fourteenth century.

Gransden, Antonia, <u>Historical Writing in
England c. 550 to c. 1307</u>. Ithaca, New York:
Cornell University Press, 1974.

An excellent up-to-date survey of historical
writings in England for early and high Middle Ages.

Masson, Gustave, <u>Early Chronicles of Europe:
France</u>. London: Society for Promoting Christian
Knowledge, 1879; reprint ed. ("Burt Franklin:
Research and Source Works Services," vol. 738)
New York: Burt Franklin, 1971.

A somewhat outdated survey of French medieval historical writings from Prosper of Aquitaine to ca. 1500.

Wattenbach, Wilhelm, <u>Deutschlands
Geschichtsquellen im Mittelalter bis zur Mitte
des dreizehnten Jahrhunderts</u>. 2 vols. 7th edition
ed. by Ernst Dummler. Stuttgart and Berlin:
Cotta'sche Buchhandlung Nachfolger, 1904.

The standard survey of German historical
writings to mid-thirteenth century.

Wattenbach-Levinson, <u>Deutschlands
Geschichtsquellen im Mittelalter: Vorzeit und
Karolinger</u>, ed. Wilhelm Levinson and Heinz Loewe.
5 parts. Weimar: Hermann Bohlaus Nachfolger,
1952-1973.

Wattenbach-Levinson, Deutschlands
Geschichtsquellen im Mittelalter: Vorzeit und
Karolinger. Beiheft: Die Rechtsquellen, ed.
Rudolf Buchner. Weimar: Hermann Bohlaus
Nachfolger, 1953.

A revised ed. of the early part (to ca. 900)
of Wattenbach's Deutschlands Geschichtsquellen.

Wattenbach, Wilhelm, Deutschlands
Geschichtsquellen im Mittelalter: Deutsche
Kaiserzeit, ed. Robert Holtzmann. Vol. 1 in 4
parts. 2nd ed. (part 1 - 3rd ed.) Tübingen:
Dr. M. Matthiesen and Co., 1948.

A revised ed. of the period 900-1125 of
Wattenbach's Deutschlands Geschichtsquellen.

Bibliographical Guides

Bonser, Wilfrid, Romano-British Bibliography
(55 C.C.-A.D. 449). 2 vols. Oxford: Basil
Blackwell, 1964.

Bonser, Wilfrid, An Anglo-Saxon and Celtic
Bibliography (450-1087). 2 vols. Oxford: Basil
Blackwell, 1957.

These two publications list sources and
modern works, incl. articles, arranged by topics
and geographical areas.

Cognasso, Francesco, Avviamento agli studi
di storia medievale ("Guide Bibliografiche
Gheroni"). Turin: Silvio Gheroni, 1951.

Mimeographed bibliography in Italian of
Italian medieval history incl. modern works and
source editions, arranged according to topics
and historical periods.

Dahlmann-Waitz, Quellenkunde der deutschen
Geschichte. 2 vols. 9th edition ed. by Hermann
Haering. Leipzig: Koehler, 1931-1932.

The standard bibliography for German history, listing original sources and modern works, arranged by topics and historical periods.

Dahlmann-Waitz, Quellenkunde der deutschen Geschichte. 10th ed. by Hermann Heimpel and Herbert Geuss. Stuttgart: Anton Hiersemann, 1969- in progress.

Graves, Edgar, ed., A Bibliography of English History to 1485. Based on "The Sources and Literature of English History from the Earliest Times to about 1485" by Charles Gross. New York: Oxford University Press, 1975.

The standard up-to-date bibliography of medieval England, listing original sources and modern works, alphabetically arranged by topics and historical periods, frequently with good annotations and brief bibliographical introductions to chapters.

Molinier, Auguste, et al, Les Sources d'histoire de France depuis les origenes jusqu'en 1789. Part I: Molinier, Auguste, Des origines aux guerres d'Italie (1494). 6 vols. ("Manuels de bibliographie historique," III) Paris: Alphonse Picard et fils, 1901-1906.

The six vols. covering the years till 1494, still constitute the standard bibliography on medieval French history, listing original sources and modern works.

Source Collections and Serial Editions

Patrologiae cursus completus: series Graeca, ed. Jacques Paul Migne: see above, p. 45, under "Early Christian Historians."

Patrologiae cursus completus: series Latina, ed. Jacques Paul Migne: see above, p. 45, under "Early Christian Historians."

Monumenta Germaniae historica; see above, p. 47, under "Early Christian Historians."

Of the several series of this gigantic collection of medieval sources, for early medieval historiography the most useful are the following: "Chronicles" (Scriptores; abbr. MGH, SS) "Oldest Chronicles" (Auctores antiquissimi; abbr. MGH, AA); "Chronicles of the Merovingian Period" (Scriptores rerum Merovingicarum, abbr. MGH, Script. rer. Mer.); "Lombard and Italian Chronicles of the 6th-9th centuries" (Scriptores rerum Langobardicarum et Italicarum saec. vi-ix; abbr. MGH, Script. rer. Lang.); "German Chronicles, New Series" (Scriptores rerum Germanicarum, Nova series; abbr. MGH, Script. N.S.) and the "German Chronicles for Use in Schools" (Scriptores rerum Germanicarum in usum scholarum; abbr. MGH, Script. in usum schol.). See also above, p. 47, under "Early Christian Historians."

Monumenta Germaniae Historica: Indices eorum quae Monumentorum Germaniae historicorum tomis hucusque editis continentur, eds. Oswald Holder-Egger and Karl Zeumer. Hanover and Berlin: Hahn and Weidmann, 1890.

Detailed "Table of Contents" of all volumes published till 1890.

Monumenta Germaniae historica: Gesamtverzeichnis der Veroffentlichungen nach dem Stande vom Juli 1958. Publ. by the "Deutsches Institut für Erforschung des Mittelalters." /no place; no date/

A summary "Table of Contents" of all volumes published till 1958.

Ausgewählte Quellen zur deutschen Geschichte des Mittelalters: Freiherr vom Stein-Gedächtnisausgabe, gen. ed. Rudolf Buchner. Vols. 1-Darmstadt: Wissenschaftliche Buchgesellschaft (imprint varies), 1955; reprint ed. of early volumes, Berlin: Deutsche Verlag der Wissenschaften, 1966-.

A new edition of revised texts, based on <u>MGH</u>, of the most important German chronicles, letters and charters. Original language on verso, modern German translation on recto.

Muratori, Ludovico Antonio, ed., <u>Rerum Italicarum scriptores ab anno aerae christianae quingentesimo ad millesimum quingestesimum</u>. 25 vols. in 28. Milan: Typographia Societatis palatinae, 1723-1751.

The earliest of the respectable collections of national medieval sources, in which Italian chronicles from 500-1500 are printed.

Muratori, Ludovico Antonio, ed., <u>Rerum Italicarum scriptores: Raccolta degli storici Italiani dal cinquecento al mille cinquecento ordinata da L. A. Muratori</u>. A new augmented and revised ed., gen. ed. Giosue Carducci et al., under the auspices of "Instituto storico Italiano per il medio evo." Vol. 1-. Citta di Castello (from 1917: Balogna): Lapi (Publishers vary), 1900- in progress.

An amended edition of Muratori.

<u>Rerum Britannicarum Medii Aevi scriptores, or Chronicles and Memorials of Great Britan and Ireland during the Middle Ages</u>. Published by the Authority of the Majesty's Treasury, under the Direction of the Master of the Rolls. 99 vols. in 253. London: Longman, Brown, Green, Longmans, and Roberts (publishers vary), 1858-1911; reprint ed., New York: Kraus Reprint Corporation, 1964-.

This collection, usually referred to as "Rolls Series" (abbr. <u>R.S.</u>) is an edition similar to the <u>M.G.H.</u>, though not of the same magnitude. It contains several important medieval English chronicles in original language, some with modern English translation.

117.

Rolls Series; see above, under Rerum
Brittannicarum Medii Aevi scriptores.

Les Classiques de l'histoire de France au
moyen age, gen. ed. Louis Halphen et al. Paris:
Librairie Honor Champion (publishers vary),
1923- in progress.

This publication prints several important
medieval French historical sources in original
language on verso, with modern French translation
on recto.

Source Collections and Serial
Editions in English Translation

Bohn's Antiquarian Library. 31 vols.
London: Henry G. Bohn (publishers vary), 1847-
1872; several reprint eds.

Still the most popular series of translations
of the important English medieval chronicles, incl.
the works of Gildas, Nennius, Bede, Asser, William
of Malmesbury, Geoffrey of Monmouth, Orderic
Vitalis, Henry of Huntingdon, Roger of Howden,
Roger of Wendower, Matthew Paris and others, as
well as the Anglo-Saxon Chronicle. There are
several reprint eds., the most recent by AMS
Press in New York.

The Church Historians of England, ed.
Joseph Stevenson. 5 vols. in 8. London:
Seeleys, 1853-1858.

This edition includes the Anglo-Saxon
Chronicle, the Acts of Stephen, and the works of
Venerable Bede, Florence of Worcester, Asser,
William of Malmesbury, Simeon of Durham, William
of Newburgh, Giraldus Cambrensis, Richard of
Devizes, Gervase of Canterbury, and others.

Columbia University, Department of History,
Records of Civilization: Sources and Studies,
gen. ed. James T. Shotwell, et al., vol. 1-.
New York: Columbia University Press, 1915- in

progress.

In this series are published in English translation original sources from all fields of history, incl. works of several medieval chroniclers: Paulus Orosius, Gregory of Tours, Helmold of Bosau, Adam of Bremen, Otto of Freising, William of Tyre, Robert of Clari, Philip of Novare, and others.

English Historical Documents, gen. ed. David C. Douglas. Vol. 1-. New York: Oxford University Press (imprint varies), 1955- in progress. Vol. 1: English Historical Documents c. 500-1042, ed. Dorothy Whitelock (1955).

The most elaborate selection of all kinds of English historical sources, including excerpts from chronicles, in English translation, with scholarly commentaries, extensive introductions and updated bibliographies. In vol. 1, which covers the early medieval or Anglo-Saxon period, the material is grouped according to subjects, with further chronological arrangement.

Gay, Peter and Cavanaugh, Gerald, eds., Historians at Work; see above, p. 49, under "Early Christian Historians."

A Select Library of the Nicene and Post-Nicene Fathers of the Christian Church; see above, p. 48, under "Early Christian Historians."

Vryonis, Speros, Jr., ed., Readings in Medieval Historiography. Boston: Houghton Mifflin Co., 1968.

This reader includes selections from St. Augustine, Einhard, Liuprand of Cremona, Procopius, Michael Psellus, Anna Comnena and some Arabic historians.

119.

Modern Studies on Early
Medieval Historiography

Brandt, William J., The Shape of Medieval History: Studies in Modes of Perception. New York and London: Yale University Press, 1966.

A philosophical approach to selected problems of medieval historiography.

Hanning, Robert W., The Vision of History in Early Britain from Gildas to Geoffrey of Monmouth. New York and London: Columbia University Press, 1966.

Essays on Gildas, Bede, Nennius and Geoffrey of Monmouth.

Jones, Charles W., "Development of the Latin Ecclesiastical Calendar," in Bedae "Opera de temporibus," ed. Charles W. Jones, pp. 1-122 (The Mediaeval Academy of America, "Publications," vol. 41). Cambridge, Mass.: The Mediaeval Academy of America, 1943.

The best treatise in English on the development of Easter Tables and Christian reckoning of time.

Knowles, David, "The Monumenta Germaniae Historica," in Great Historical Enterprises. Problems in Monastic History, pp. 63-97. London: Thomas Nelson and Sons, 1963.

Knowles, David, "The Rolls Series," in Great Historical Enterprises. Problems in Monastic History, pp. 99-134. London: Thomas Nelson and Sons.

Laistner, M. L. W., Thought and Letters in Western Europe A.D. 500-900. Ithaca, New York: Cornell University Press, 1957, paperback ed. 1966.

An excellent study of the literary activities of western scholars during the early Middle Ages.

Poole, Reginald, *Chronicles and Annals: A Brief Outline of Their Origin and Growth*. Oxford: The Clarendon Press, 1926.

The best study in English of the development of medieval annals and chronicles.

Ware, R. Dean, "Medieval Chronology: Theory and Practice," in James M. Powell, ed., *Medieval Studies: An Introduction*, pp. 213-237. Syracuse: Syracuse University Press, 1976.

Individual Historians

JORDANES (6th century)

Text Editions

"Gothic History"

"Jordanis seu Jordani episcopi Ravennatis *De Getarum sive Gothorum origine et rebus gestis*," in Migne, *Patrologia Latina*, 69:1251-1296.

Garetius, Johann and Antonius Joseph, eds., "Jordanis *Historia de Getarum, sive Gothorum origine, et rebus gestis*," in Ludovico A. Muratori, ed., *Rerum Italicarum scriptores*, vol. 1, part 1:187-221. Milan: Typographia societatis palatinae, 1723.

Giordano, Oronzo, ed., *Jordanes "De origine actibusque Getarum."* Bari: Adriatica, 1972.

Latin text verso, Italian translation recto.

Mommsen, Theodor, ed., "De origine actibusque Getarum" in *Jordanis Romana et Getica*, pp. 53-138 (*MGH,AA*, vol. 5, part 1). Berlin: Weidmann, 1882.

The standard edition of Jordanes *Gothic History*.

English Translation

"Gothic History"

Mierow, Charles Christopher, transl., The "Gothic History" of Jordanes, 2nd ed. Princeton: Princeton University Press, 1915; reprint ed. New York: Barnes and Noble, 1960.

Translation based on Mommsen's edition.

Modern Studies

Korkkanan, Irma, The Peoples of Hermanaric Jordanes, "Getica 116" ("Annales Academiae scientiarum Fennicae," ser. B, vol. 187). Helsinki: Suomalainen Tiedeaktamia, 1975.

PROCOPIUS OF CAESAREA (ca. 505-565)

Text editions

"History of the Wars"

Haury, Jakob, ed., "Procopii Caesariensis De bellis" in Opera omnia, vols. 1-2; 3 vols. in 4. ("Bibliotheca scriptorum Graecorum et Romanorum Teubneriana"). Leipzig: Teubner, 1905-1913; reprint ed. 1962-1964.

"Secret History"

Haury, Jakob, ed., "Procopii Caesariensis Historia quae dicitur arcana" in Opera omnia, vol. 3, part 1, as above.

"On Buildings"

Haury, Jakob, ed., "De aedificiis," as above, vol. 3, part 2.

The standard edition of Procopius' works in Greek.

English Translations

"History of the Wars"

Dewing, H. B., transl., "History of the Wars" in Procopius /complete works/ vols. 1-5 (1914-1928); 7 vols. ("Loeb Classical Library," Greek authors). London: William Heinemann, 1914-1940; several reprint eds.

"Secret History"

Atwater, Richard T., transl., Procopius "Secret History." Ann Arbor: University of Michigan Press, 1961.

Dewing, H. B., transl., "The Anecdota or Secret History" in Procopius, vol. 6 (1935), as above.

Williamson, G. A., transl., Procopius "The Secret History." ("Penguin Classics"). Baltimore: Penguin Books, 1966.

"On Buildings"

Dewing, H. B. and Downey, Glanville, transl., "Buildings" in Procopius, vol. 7 (1940), as above.

Cameron, Averil, transl., Procopius ("The Great Histories"). New York: Washington Square Press, 1967.

Abridged translations of the History of the Wars, the Secret History and the Buildings.

Modern Studies

Evans, James A. S., Procopius ("Twayne's World Authors Series: A Survey of the World's Literature," vol. 170). New York: Twayne Publishers, 1972.

The most comprehensive analysis in English of Procopius and his works.

GREGORY OF TOURS (538-594)

Text Editions

"History of the Franks"

"Sancti Georgii Florentii Gregorii episcopi
Turonensis Historiae ecclesiasticae Francorum
libri decem," in Migne, Patrologia Latina,
71:161-571.

Arndt, Wilhelm, ed., "Gregorii episcopi
Turonensis Historia Francorum," in MGH, Script.
rer. Mer., 1:1-450. Hanover: Hahnsche Buchhandlung, 1885; reprint ed., 1951.

Buchner, Rudolf, ed., Gregorii episcopi
Turonensis "Historiarum libri decem." Gregor von
Tours "Zehn Bücher Geschichten." 2nd ed. of
Bruno Krusch's radaction. 2 vols. ("Ausgewählte
Quellen zur deutschen Geschichte des Mittelalters,"
vols. 2-3). Darmstadt: Wissenschaftliche
Buchgesellschaft, 1955-1956: reprint ed., Berlin:
Deutscher Verlag der Wissenschaften, 1967.

Latin text verso, German translation recto.

Latouche, Robert, ed., Grégoire de Tours
"Histoire des Francs." 2 vols. ("Les Classiques
de l'histoire de France au moyen age," vols. 27-
28). Paris: Société d'édition "Les Belles
Lettres," 1963-1965.

Latin text verso, French translation recto.

"The Miracles"

"Sancti Georgii Florentinii Gregorii
episcopi Turonensis Libri miraculorum," in Migne,
Patrologia Latina, 71:704-827.

Krusch, Bruno, ed., "Gregorii episcopi
Turonensis Libri octo miraculorum, in MGM, Script.
rer. Mer., 1:451-820. Hanover: Hahnsche Buchhandlung, 1885.

English Translations

"History of the Franks"

Brehaut, Ernest, transl., "History of the Franks," by Gregory Bishop of Tours. Abridged transl. (Columbia University, Department of History, "Records of Civilization: Sources and Studies," vol. 2). New York: Columbia University Press, 1916; reprint ed. in paperback, New York: W. W. Norton and Co., 1969.

Dalton, O. M., transl., The "History of the Franks" by Gregory of Tours. 2 vols. Oxford: Clarendon Press, 1927.

The first vol. contains an extensive study of Gregory, his times and work; the second vol. contains the translation.

Thorpe, Lewis, transl., Gregory of Tours "The History of the Franks." ("The Penguin Classics"). Harmondsworth, Eng.: Penguin Books, 1974.

The most recent complete translation of The History of the Franks (in paperback).

"The Miracles"

McDermot, William C., transl., Gregory of Tours: Selections from the Minor Works. (University of Pennsylvania, Department of History, "Translations and Reprints from the Original Sources of History," 3rd series, vol. 4). Philadelphia: University of Pennsylvania Press, 1949.

Selected miracles.

Modern Studies

The most extensive study of Gregory of Tours in English is the "Introduction" by O. M. Dalton in the 1st vol. of his translation of The History of the Franks.

VENERABLE BEDE (ca. 673-735)

Text Editions

"Ecclesiastical History"

"Bedae Venerabilis presbyteri Anglo-Saxonis Historia ecclesiastica," in Migne, Patrologia Latina, 95:23-290.

The complete works of Bede are printed in vols. 90-95.

Giles, J. A., ed. and transl., "Historia ecclesiastica gentis Anglorum. Ecclesiastical History of the English Nation" in Venerabilis Bedae opera quae supersunt omnia. The Complete Works of Venerable Bede in the Original Latin... accompanied by a New English translation of the Historical Works, vols. 2-3 (1843). 12 vols. London: Whittaker and Co., 1843-1844.

Only those works which are printed in the first five vols., are translated into English.

Plummer, Charles, ed., "Historia ecclesiastica gentis Anglorum" in Venerabilis Baedae opera historica, 1:1-363. 2 vols. Oxford: Clarendon Press, 1896; reprint ed. 1961.

The standard edition of Bede's Ecclesiastical History in Latin. Vol. 1 contains Plummer's Introduction and Latin texts; vol. 2, Commentaries and Indices.

"On Time"

"Bedae Venerabilis Anglo-Saxonis presbyteri De temporibus liber," in Migne, Patrologia Latina, 90:277-294.

Giles, J. A., ed., "De temporibus liber" in Venerabilis Bedae opera quae supersunt omnia. The

Complete Works of Venerable Bede, 6:123-138.
London: Whittaker and Sons, 1843; see also
above, p.126.

Jones, Charles W., ed., "Bedae De temporibus
liber" in Bedae "Opera de temporibus," pp. 293-
303 (The Mediaeval Academy of America, "Publications," vol. 41). Cambridge, Mass." The Mediaeval Academy of America, 1943.

"On the Reckoning of Time"

"Bedae Venerabilis Anglo-Saxonis presbyteri
De temporum ratione," in Migne, Patrologia Latina,
90:293-578.

Contains the treatise on reckoning time and
the "Chronicles of the Six Ages" (pp. 520-573).

Giles, J. A., ed., "De temporum ratione" in
Venerabilis Bedae opera quae supersunt omnia. The
Complete Works of Venerable Bede 6:139-342.
London: Whittaker and Sons, 1843; see also above,
p.126.

Contains the treatise on reckoning time and
the "Chronicle of the Six Ages."

Jones, Charles W., ed., "Bedae Liber de
temporibus major sive De temporarum ratione" in
Bedae "Opera de Temporibus, pp. 173-291 (The
Mediaeval Academy of America. "Publications,"
vol. 41). Cambridge, Mass.: The Mediaeval
Academy of America, 1943.

The best scholarly edition of the treatise
on reckoning time, without the "Chronicle."

Mommsen, Theodor, ed., "Bedae De temporum
ratione /chapt./ LXVI: De sex huius saeculi
aetatibus" in Chronica minora saec. IV, V, VI, VII,
3:247-327 (MGH,AA, vol. 13). Berlin: Weidmann,
1898; reprint ed. 1961.

The best scholarly edition of the "Chronicle of the Six Ages" only.

English Translations

"Ecclesiastical History"

Colgrave, Bertram and Mynors, R.A.B., eds. and transl., Bede's "Ecclesiastical History of the English People" ("Oxford Medieval Texts"). Oxford: Clarendon Press, 1969.

Latin text verso, English translation recto.

Giles, J. A., ed. and transl., Historia ecclesiastica; see above p.126.

Latin text verso, English translation recto.

Giles, J. A., transl., "The Ecclesiastical History of the English Nation by Venerable Bede" in The Venerable Bede's "Ecclesiastical History of England." Also the "Anglo-Saxon Chronicle," pp. 1-300. ("Bohn's Antiquarian Library"). London: Henry G. Bohn, 1847; several reprint eds.

King, J. E., ed. and transl., "Ecclesiastical History of the English Nation" in Baedae opera historica. Bede, Historical Works. 2 vols. ("Loeb Classical Library," Latin authors). Cambridge, Mass.: Harvard University Press, 1954.

Latin text verso, English translation recto.

Sherley-Price, Leo, transl., Bede "A History of the English Church and People" ("Penguin Classics"). Baltimore: Penguin Books, 1955, several reprint eds.

"On the Reckoning of Time"

Stevenson, Joseph, transl., "The Chronicle of the Venerable Presbyter Beda, the Anglo-Saxon; or, Concerning the Six Ages of the World" in The

Historical Works of the Venerable Beda, pp. 624–652 ("The Church Historians of England," vol. 1, part 2). London: Seeleys, 1853.

Only the "Sixth Age," or the period of Christianity of the "Chronicle" is translated in full; for the period from the Creation till the Nativity merely a brief synopsis is given in English. The exposition on reckoning time, or chs. 1–65 of the treatise "On the Reckoning of Time," is not translated.

Modern Studies

Duckett, Eleanor Shipley, "Bede of Jarrow," in *Anglo-Saxon Saints and Scholars*, pp. 217–336. New York: Macmillan Co., 1948.

Hunter Blair, Peter, *The World of Bede*. London: Secker and Warburg, 1970.

The most comprehensive survey of Bede and his works in English.

Thompson, Hamilton A., ed., *Bede: His Life, Times and Works*. Oxford: Clarendon Press, 1935; reprint ed., 1966.

Essays in commemoration of the twelfth century of Bede's death.

PAUL THE LOMBARD (ca. 720–ca. 800)

Text Editions

"History of the Lombards"

"Pauli Warnefridi diaconi Forojuliensis *De gestis Langobardorum*," in Migne, *Patrologia Latina*, 95:433–672.

Bethmann, L. and Waitz, G., eds., "Pauli *Historia Langobardorum*," in *MGH, Script. rer. Lang.*, pp. 12–187. Hanover: Hahnsche Buchhandlung, 1878.

The anonymous treatise Origo gentis Langobardorum printed pp. 1-6.

Bethmann, L. and Waitz, G., eds., Pauli
"Historia Langobardorum" (MGH, Script. in usum
schol.). Hanover: Hahnsche Buchhandlung, 1878;
reprint ed., 1930.

Lindenbrogius, Frederick and Blancus,
Horatius, eds., "Pauli Warnefridi Langobardi
diaconi Forojuliensis De gestis Langobardorum
libri VI," in Ludovico A. Muratori, ed., Rerum
Italicarum scriptores, vol. 1, part 1:395-511.
Milan: Typographia societatis palatinae, 1723.

"History of the Bishops of Metz"

"Pauli Warnefridi diaconi Forojuliensis
Libellus de ordine episcoporum Metensium," in
Migne, Patrologia Latina, 90:699-724.

Pertz, Georg Heinrich, ed., "Pauli Warnefridi
Liber de episcopis Mettensibus," in MGH,SS,
2:260-270. Hanover: Hahnsche Buchhandlung, 1829.

English Translations

"History of the Lombards"

Foulke, William Dudley, transl., "History
of the Langobards" by Paul the Deacon (University
of Pennsylvania, Department of History, "Translations and Reprints from the Original Sources of
History," 2nd series, vol. 3). Philadelphia:
University of Pennsylvania Press, 1907; reprint
edition ed. by Edward Peters, History of the
Lombards, Philadelphia: University of Pennsylvania
Press, 1974.

These editions also contain a translation of
the Origo gentis Langobardorum.

EINHARD (ca. 770-840)

Text Editions

"The Life of Charlemagne"

"B. Caroli Magni imperatoris vita, auctore
Einhardo," in Migne, Patrologia Latina, 97:25-62.

Halphen, Louis, ed., Eginhard "Vie de Charlemagne" ("Les Classiques de l'histoire de France au
moyen age," vol. 1). Paris: Librairie ancienne
Honoré Champion, 1923; several reprint eds.

Holder-Egger, O., ed., Einhardi "Vita Karoli
Magni" (MGH, Script in usum schol.) 6th ed.
Hanover and Leipzig: Hahnsche Buchhandlung, 1911;
several reprint eds.

This edition is based on Pertz's and Waitz's
ed. in MGH, SS; see below.

Pertz, Georg Heinrich, ed., "Einhardi Vita
Karoli imperatoris," in MGH, SS, 2:426-463.
Hanover: Hahnsche Buchhandlung, 1829.

Rau, Reinhold, ed., "Einhardi Vita Karoli
Magni. Einhard, Das Leben Karls des Grossen" in
Quellen zur Karolingischen Reichsgeschichte,
1:163-211; 3 vols. ("Ausgewählte Quellen zur
deutschen Geschichte des Mittelalters," vol. 5).
Darmstadt: Wissenschaftliche Buchgesellschaft,
1955; reprint ed., Berlin: Deutsche Verlag der
Wissenschaften, 1966.

English Translations

"Life of Charlemagne"

Firchow, Evelyn S. and Zeydel, Edwin H.,
eds. and transl., Einhard "Vita Karoli Magni.
The Life of Charlemagne." Coral Gables, Florida:
University of Miami Press, 1972.

Latin text verso, English translation recto.

Grant, A. J., transl., "The Life of Charlemagne by Eginhard" in Early Lives of Charlemagne,
pp. 1-56 ("The Medieval Library"). New York:

Cooper Square Publishers, 1966.

Thorpe, Lewis, transl., "The Life of Charlemagne by Einhard" in Einhard and Notker the Stammerer: Two Lives of Charlemagne, pp. 47-90 ("The Penguin Classics"). Harmondsworth, England: Penguin Books, 1969; several reprint eds.

Turner, Samuel Epes, transl., The "Life of Charlemagne" by Einhard, ed. Sidney Painter. ("Ann Arbor Paperbacks"). Ann Arbor: The University of Michigan Press, 1960; several reprint eds.

NOTKER THE STAMMERER or THE MONK OF ST. GALL (ca. 840-912)

Text Editions

"Deeds of Charlemagne"

Haefele, Hans S., ed., Notkeri Balbuli "Gesta Karoli Magni imperatoris." Notker der Stammler "Taten Kaiser Karls des Grossen" (MGH, Script, N.S., vol. 12). Berlin: Weidmannsche Verlagsbuchhandlung, 1959.

Pertz, Georg Heinrich, ed., "Monachi Sangallensis De gestis Karoli imperatoris libri duo," in MGH, SS, 2:726-763. Hanover: Hahnsche Buchhandlung, 1826.

Rau, Reinhold, ed., "Notkeri Gesta Karoli. Notker Taten Karls" in Quellen zur Karolingischen Reichsgeschichte, 3:321-427. 3 vols. ("Ausgewählte Quellen zur deutschen Geschichte des Mittelalters," vol. 7). Darmstadt: Wissenschaftliche Buchgesellschaft, 1960; reprint ed., Berlin: Deutscher Verlag der Wissenschaften, 1966.

English Translations

"The Deeds of Charlemagne"

Grant, A. J., transl., "The Life of Charlemagne by the Monk of St. Gall" in Early Lives of

Charlemagne, pp. 57-158 ("The Medieval Library").
New York: Cooper Square Publishers, 1966.

Thorpe, Lewis, transl., "Charlemagne by
Notker the Stammerer, Monk of Saint Gall" in
Einhard and Notker the Stammerer: Two Lives of
Charlemagne, pp. 91-172 ("The Penguin Classics").
Harmondsworth, England: Penguin Books, 1969.

ASSER (bishop 892-910)

Text Editions

"Life of King Alfred"

Stevenson, William Henry, ed., "Asserius
De rebus gestis Aelfredi" in Asser's "Life of King
Alfred" together with the "Annals of Saint Neots"
erroneously ascribed to Asser, pp. 1-96. 2nd ed.
Oxford: Clarendon Press, 1959.

The 2nd ed. contains an article "Present work
on Asser's Life of Alfred" by Dorothy Whitelock.

English Translations

"Life of King Alfred"

Cook, Albert S., transl., Asser's "Life of
King Alfred." Boston and New York: Ginn and Co.,
1906.

Translation based on Stevenson's edition.

Giles, J. A., transl., "Annals of the Reign
of Alfred the Great from A.D. 849 to A.D. 887 by
Asser of Saint David's," in Six Old English Chronicles, pp. 41-86. London: Henry G. Bohn, 1848;
reprint ed., New York: AMS Press, 1968.

Jane, L. Cecil, transl., Asser's "Life of
King Alfred." ("The Medieval Library"). London:
Chatto and Windus, 1926.

Stevenson, Joseph, transl., "Annals of the Exploits of Alfred the Great by Asser of St. David's," in "The Church Historians of England," vol. 2, part 2:441-479. London: Seeleys, 1854.

ANGLO-SAXON CHRONICLE

Text Editions

Plummer, Charles, ed., Two of the Saxon Chronicles Parallel; rev.ed. based on an edition by John Earle. 2 vols. Oxford: The Clarendon Press, 1892-1899; reprint ed., 1952.

This publication is regarded as the best edition of the text; it prints versions "A" and "E".

Thorpe, Benjamin, ed. and transl., "The Anglo-Saxon Chronicle" according to the Several Original Authorities. 2 vols. (RS, vol. 23 in 2). London: Longman, Green, Longman, and Roberts, 1861; reprint ed., New York: Kraus Reprint Corp., 1964.

The only edition which contains the various versions of the Chronicle. Vol. 1 prints the texts in Anglo-Saxon; vol. 2, modern English translations.

English Translations

Garmonsway, George, N., transl., The Anglo-Saxon Chronicle; rev. ed. ("Everyman's Library"). London: Dent; New York: Dutton, 1960.

Giles, J. A., transl., "The Anglo-Saxon Chronicle," in The Venerable Bede's "Ecclesiastical History of England." Also the "Anglo-Saxon Chronicle," pp. 301-508 ("Bohn's Antiquarian Library"). London: J. A. Bohn, 1847; several reprint eds.

Stevenson, Joseph, transl., "The Anglo-Saxon Chronicle," in The Church Historians of England, vol. 2, part 1:1-168. London: Seeleys, 1853.

Thorpe, Benjamin, transl., The Anglo-Saxon Chronicle; see above.

Tucker, S. I., transl., "The Anglo-Saxon Chronicle (1042-1154)." in English Historical Documents, 2:107-203. London: Eyre and Spottiswoode, 1968.

Whitelock, Dorothy, transl., The Anglo-Saxon Chronicle. A rev. transl. with David C. Douglas and Susie J. Tucker. New Brunswick, N.J.: Rutgers University Press, 1961.

This edition contains the translations of the various extant versions.

Whitelock, Dorothy, transl., "The Anglo-Saxon Chronicle (60 B.C.-A.D. 1042)," in English Historical Documents, 1:135-235. New York: Oxford University Press, 1955.

A shorter version of the above-mentioned edition.

Modern Studies

The most extensive study of the Chronicle is prepared by C. Plummer in vol. 2 of his edition of the work; see above.

NITHARD (ca. 795-845)

Text Editions

"Histories"

"Nithardi De dissensionibus filiorum Ludovici pii liber quatuor," in Migne, Patrologia Latina, 116:45-76.

Lauer, Ph., ed., Nithard "Histoire des fils de Louis le Pieux" ("Les Classiques de l'histoire de France au moyen age," vol. 7.) Paris:

Librarie ancienne Honoré Champion, 1926.

Latin text verso, French translation recto.

Müller, Ernst, ed., Nithardi "Historiarum
libri IV," 3rd ed. (MGH, Script. in usum schol.)
Hanover: Hahnsche Buchhandlung, 1907; several
reprint eds.

Pertz, Georg Heinrich, ed., "Nithardi
Historiarum libri IV," in MGH, SS, 2:649-672.
Hanover: Hahnsche Buchhandlung, 1829.

Rau, Reinhold, ed., "Nithardi Historiarum
libri IV. Nithard Vier Bücher Geschichte," in
Quellen zur Karolingischen Reichsgeschichte,
1:385-461. 3 vols. ("Ausgewählte Quellen zur
deutschen Geschichte des Mittelalters," vol. 5).
Darmstadt: Wissenschaftliche Buchgesellschft,
1955: reprint ed., Berlin: Deutscher Verlag der
Wissenschaften, 1966.

Latin text verso, German translation recto.

English Translation

"Histories"

Scholz, Bernhard Walter, transl., "Nithard's
Histories," in Carolingian Chronicles, pp. 127-174
("Ann Arbor Paperback"), Ann Arbor: The Univer-
sity of Michigan Press, 1972.

RICHER (died ca. 1000)

Text Editions

"Histories"

"Richeri Historiarum libri quatuor," in
Migne, Patrologia Latina, 138-17-170.

Latouche, Robert, ed., Richer "Histoire de
France (888-995)." 2 vols. ("Les Classiques de
l'histoire de France au moyen age," vols. 12 and

17). Paris: Libraire ancienne Honoré Champion,
1930-1937.

Latin text verso, French translation recto.

Pertz, Georg Heinrich, ed., "Richeri Historiarum libri IV," in MGH, SS, 3:561-657. Hanover:
Hahnsche Buchhandlung, 1839.

Waitz, Georg, ed., Richeri "Historiarum
libri IV" (MGH, Script. in usum schol.); 2nd ed.
Hanover: Hahnsche Buchhandlung, 1877.

WIDUKIND (ca. 925-ca. 1004)

Text Editions

"Saxon History"

"Vidukindi Res gestae Saxonicae," in Migne,
Patrologia Latina, 137:115-212.

Bauer, Albert and Rau, Reinhold, eds.,
"Widukindi Res gestae Saxonicae. Die Sachsengeschichte des Widukind von Korvei," in Quellen zur
Geschichte der sächsischen Kaiserzeit, pp. 12-183
("Ausgewählte Quellen zur Deutschen Geschichte
des Mittelalters," vol. 8) Darmstadt: Wissenschaftliche Buchgesellschaft, 1971.

Latin text verso, German translation recto.

Hirsch, Paul and Lohmann, H. E., eds.,
Widukindi monachi Corbeiensis "Rerum gestarum
Saxonicarum libri tres." "Die Sachsengeschichte"
des Widukind von Korvei; 5th ed. (MGH, Script.
in usum schol.). Hanover: Hahnsche Buchhandlung,
1935.

Waitz, Georg, ed., "Widukindi Res gestae
Saxonicae," in MGH, SS, 3:408-467. Hanover:
Hahnsche Buchhandlung, 1839.

English Translation

"Saxon History"

Davis, Charles T., transl., "Widukind of Corvey: Battle of the Lechfeld (955)," in Charles T. Davis, ed., The Eagle, The Crescent, and the Cross, pp. 228-230. ("Sources of Medieval History," vol.1 c.250-c.1000). New York: Appleton-Century-Crofts, 1967.

THIETMAR OF MERSEBURG (died 1018)

Text Editions

"Chronicle"

"Thietmarus Merseburgensis episcopus Chronicon," in Migne, Patrologia Latina, 139:1183-1422.

Holtzmann, Robert, ed., Thietmari Merseburgensis episcopi "Chronicon." "Die Chronik" des Bishofs Thietmar von Merseburg und ihre Korveier Überarbeitung (MGH, Script. N.S., vol. 9). Berlin: Weidmannsche Buchhandlung, 1935.

Lappenberg, Johann, M., ed., "Thietmari Chronicon," in MGH, SS, 3:723-871. Hanover: Hahnsche Buchhandlung, 1839.

HERMAN OF REICHENAU, also HERMANNUS CONTRACTUS (1013-1054)

Text Editions

"Chronicle"

"Hermanni Contracti Chronicon," in Migne, Patrologia Latina, 143:55-264.

Buchner, Rudolf, ed., "Herimanni Augiensis Chronicon," in Quellen des 9. and 11. Jahrhunderts zur Geschichte der hamburgischen Kirche und des Reiches, pp. 628-707 ("Ausgewählte Quellen zur deutschen Geschichte des Mittelalters," vol. 11). Berlin: Rütten and Loening, 1961.

Pertz, Georg Heinrich, ed., "Herimanni Augiensis Chronicon," in MGH, SS, 5:67-133. Hanover: Hahnsche Buchhandlung, 1844.

ADAM OF BREMEN (died ca. 1085)

Text Editions

"History of the Archbishops of Hamburg-Bremen"

"Magister Adami Gesta Hammaburgensis ecclesiae pontificum," in Migne, Patrologia Latina, 146:451-668.

Lappenberg, Johann M., ed., "Magister Adami Gesta Hammaburgensis ecclesiae pontificum," in MGH, SS, 7:267-389. Hanover: Hahnsche Buchhandlung, 1846.

Trillmich, Werner, ed., "Adami Bremensis Gesta Hammaburgensis ecclesiae pontificum. Adam von Bremen Bischofsgeschichte der Hamburger Kirche," in Quellen des 9. und 11. Jahrhunderts zur Geschichte der hamburgischen Kirche und des Reiches, pp. 160-499 ("Ausgewählte Quellen zur deutschen Geschichte des Mittelalters," vol. 11). Berlin: Rütten and Loening, 1961.

Latin text verso, German translation recto.

English Translation

"History of the Archbishops of Hamburg-Bremen"

Tschan, Francis J., transl., Adam of Bremen "History of the Archbishops of Hamburg-Bremen" (Columbia University, Department of History, "Records of Civilization: Sources and Studies," vol. 53). New York: Columbia University Press, 1959.

Minor Historians

Text Editions, English Translations, Modern Studies

CASSIODORUS (ca. 487-ca. 575)

"M. Aurelii Cassiodori Variarum libri duodecim," in Migne, Patrologia Latina, 69:501-880.

Fridh, A. J., ed., "Magni Aurelii Cassiodori Variarum libri duodecini" in Opera, 1: (XLVI) + 1-499 ("Corpus Christianorum." series Latina, vol. 96). Turnhout: Brepols, 1973.

Mommsen, Theodor, ed., "Epistulae Theodericianae variae" in Cassiodori Senatoris "Variae," pp. 1-392 (MGH, AA, vol. 12). Berlin: Weidmann, 1894.

Hodgkin, Thomas, transl., The Letters of Cassiodorus. London: H. Frowde, 1886.

A condensed translation.

Zimmermann, Odo John, The Late Latin Vocabulary of the "Variae" of Cassiodorus with Special Advertence to the Technical Terminology of Administration (The Catholic University of America, "Studies in Medieval and Renaissance Latin Language and Literature," vol. 15; Ph. diss.). Washington: The Catholic University of America Press, 1944.

ISIDORE OF SEVILLE (ca. 560-636)

"Sancti Isidori Historia de regibus Gothorum, Wandalorum et Suevorum," in Migne, Patrologia Latina, 83:1057-1082.

Mommsen, Theodor, ed., "Isidori Junioris episcopi Hispalensis Historia Gothorum, Wandalorum, Sueborum ad a. DCXXIV," in Chronica minora saec, IV, V, VI, VII, 2:241-303; 3 vols. (MGH, AA, vol. 11). Berlin: Weidmann, 1894; reprint ed. 1961.

Donini, Guido and Ford, Gordon, B., transl., Isidore of Seville's "History of the Kings of the

Goths, Vandals and Suevi." Leiden: Brill, 1966.

SULPICIUS SEVERUS (ca. 365-425)

"Sulpicii Severi Chronicorum quae vulgo inscribuntur Historia sacra libri duo," in Migne, Patrologia Latina, 20:95-160.

Halm, Karl, ed., "Sulpicii Severi Chronica" in Opera, pp. 1-105 ("Corpus scriptorum ecclesiasticorum Latinorum" vol. 1). Vienna: C. Gerod's Sons, 1866.

"FREDEGAR" (fl. mid-seventh cent.)

"Sancti Georgii Florentinii Gregorii episcopi Turonensis Historia Francorum epitomata per Fredegarium Scholasticum," in Migne, Patrologia Latina, 71:573-604.

Krusch, Bruno, ed., "Chronicarum quae dicuntur Fredegarii Scholastici libri I-III" in Fredegarii et aliorum chronica. Vitae sanctorum, pp. 1-118. (MGH, Script. rer. Merov., vol. 2). Hanover: Hahnsche Buchhandlung, 1888.

"Fredegar's" epitome of the first six books of Gregory of Tours.

"Fredegarii Scholastici Chronicum," in Migne, Patrologia Latina, 71:605-664.

Krusch, Bruno, ed., "Chronicarum quae dicuntur Fredegarii Scholastici liber IV" in Fredegarii et aliorum chronica. Vitae sanctorum, pp. 118-168. (MGH, Script. rer. Merov, vol. 2).

Hanover: Hahnsche Buchhandlung, 1888.

The Fourth Book of Fredegar, covering the years 583 to 642.

"Fredegarii Scholastici Chronicum continuatum auctoribus anonymis," in Migne, Patrologia Latina, 71:665-704.

Krusch, Bruno, ed., "Chronicarum quae dicuntur Fredegarii Scholastici: Continuationes" in
Fredegarii et aliorum chronica. Vitae sanctorum,
pp. 168-193, (MGH, Script. rer. Merov, vol. 2).
Hanover, Hahnsche Buchhandlung, 1888.

"Fredegar's" continuation till 768.

Wallace-Hadrill, John M., ed. and transl.,
The Fourth Book of the Chronicle of Fredegar with
Its Continuations. Fredegarii Chronicorum liber
quartus cum continuationibus ("Medieval Classics").
London: Thomas Nelson and Sons, 1960.

Latin text verso, English translation recto.

GILDAS (ca. 516-ca. 570)

"Gildae Sapientis De excidio Britanniae liber
querulus," in Migne, Patrologia Latina, 69:329-348.

Mommsen, Theodor, ed., "Gildae Sapientis De
excidio et conquestu Britanniae ac flebili casti-
gatione in reges, principes et sacerdotes," in
Chronica minora saec. IV, V, VI, VII, 3:1-85;
3 vols. (MGH, AA, vol. 13). Berlin: Weidmann,
1898, reprint ed., 1961.

Giles, J. A., transl., "The Works of Gildas,
surnamed Sapiens or the Wise," in Six Old English
Chronicles, pp. 293-380 ("Bohn's Antiquarian
Library"). London: Henry G. Bohn, 1848.

Williams, Hugh, ed. and transl., Gildae "De
excidio Britanniae." Gildas "The Ruin of Britain."
2 vols. ("Cymmrodorion Record Series," vol. 3 in
2). London: David Nutt, 1899-1901.

Latin text based on Mommsen's edition, verso,
English translation recto.

Winterbottom, Michael, ed. and transl.,
Gildas "The Ruin of Britain and other works".
("History from the Sources", gen. ed. John Morris).

London and Chichester: Phillimore; Totowa, N.J.:
Rowman and Littlefield, 1978.

Latin text based on Mommsen's edition.

Stevens, C. E., "Gildas Sapiens," in English
Historical Review, 56 (1941):353-373.

NENNIUS (fl. ca. 800)

Lot, Ferdinand, ed., Nennius et l"Historia
Brittonum:" étude critique suivie d'une édition
des diverses versions de ce texte ("Bibliotheque
de l'école des hautes etudes: Sciences historiques et philologiques" vol. 263). Paris:
Librarie ancienne Honoré Champion, 1934.

Mommsen, Theodor, ed., "Historia Brittonum
cum additamentis Nennii," in Chronica minora saec.
IV, V, VI, VII, 3:111-222; 3 vols. (MGH, AA, vol.
13). Berlin: Weidmann, 1898.

Giles, J. A., transl., "Nennius History of
the Britons," in Six Old English Chronicles,
pp. 381-416 ("Bohn's Antiquarian Library").
London: Henry G. Bohn, 1848.

Wade-Evans, Arthur, transl., Nennius's
"History of the Britons" together with "The Annals
of the Britons" and "Court Pedigrees of Hywel the
Good," also "The Story of the Loss of Britain."
London: Society for Promoting Christian Knowledge,
1938.

Liebermann, F., "Nennius the Author of the
Historia Brittonum," in Essays in Medieval His-
tory Presented to Thomas Frederic Tout, ed. A. G.
Little and F. M. Powicke, pp. 25-44. Manchester:
Printed for the Subscribers, 1925.

DIONYSIUS EXIGUUS (died after 525)

"Dionysii Exigui Liber de Paschate," in
Migne, Patrologia Latina, 67:483-508.

Poole, Reginald L., "The Earliest Use of the Easter Cycle of Dionysius," in Austin Lane Poole, ed., <u>Studies in Chronology and History by Reginald Poole</u>, pp. 28-37. Oxford: The Clarendon Press, 1934.

ROYAL FRANKISH ANNALS

"Annales Laurissenses et Eginhardi" ⫽from 741 to 829⫽, in Migne, <u>Patrologia Latina</u>, 104:367-508.

Kurze, Friedrich, ed., <u>Annales regni Francorum inde ab a. 741 usque ad a. 829 qui dicuntur Annales Laurissenses majores et Einhardi</u> (<u>MGH, Script, in usum schol.</u>). Hanover: Hahnsche Buchhandlung, 1895: several reprint eds.

Pertz, Georg H., ed., "Einhardi <u>Annales a. 741-829,</u>" in <u>MGH, SS</u>, 1:135-218. Hanover: Hahnsche Buchhandlung, 1826.

Scholz, Bernard Walter, transl., "Royal Frankish Annals (741-829)," in <u>Carolingian Chronicles</u>, pp. 35-125. ("Ann Arbor Paperback"). Ann Arbor: The Michigan University Press, 1972.

For other English translations of all listed works see <u>Bibliography of English Translations from Medieval Sources</u> (listed above, p.44 under "Early Christian Historians."

HISTORIANS OF THE HIGH MIDDLE AGES
(from the Mid-eleventh Century to ca. 1300)

Towards the middle of the eleventh century in Europe events began to develop in rapid succession that dramatically influenced and in several cases radically changed the political and military set-up of the somewhat stagnating historical stage of the preceding decades. First the Normans came in-to prominence.[1] Since the days of Rollo (911-932) the Viking question had been rather dormant in continental Europe until after 1030 the sons of a Norman knight, Tancred of Hauteville,[2] left for Sicily and southern Italy to conquer new territor-ies for the Norman rule. Scarcely had the Haute-ville brothers made their first military advances when in 1066 the duke of Normandy, William, called the Bastard (1035-1087) conquered England and be-came the first Norman ruler of the Anglo-Saxon kingdom. In modern historiography he is usually referred to as William I, the Conqueror (1066-1087). With the Norman conquest, the Anglo-Saxon period in English history not only came to an end, but also gave way to an epoch of long, bloody and costly wars on the continent between the English and French monarchs.

William was still occupied with pacifying his rebellious Anglo-Saxon subjects when conti-nental Europe was shaken by a new political and military uproar--the Investiture Controversy.[3] By the mid-eleventh century the medieval papacy had also come of age, and the revival of high ecclesiastical zeal under Rome's leadership led to the first real confrontation between the papal or spiritual and the imperial or secular authority over primacy in Europe. The first fierce politi-cal battle was fought during the Investiture Con-troversy between Pope Gregory VII (1073-1085) and Emperor Henry IV (1056-1105) of Germany. However, the climax of papal power was reached in the thir-teenth century, particularly during the pontificate

145.

of Innocent III (1198-1216).

Only the Eastern Roman Empire, commonly known as the Byzantine Empire, had so far been little affected by events in Western Europe. Nevertheless, the Byzantines had their own problems to face and wars to fight. In the mid-eleventh century the Selchükid Turks appeared at the eastern frontier of the Empire, and their victory in 1071 over the Byzantines at Manzikert in Armenia finally forced Emperor Alexius I Comnenus (1081-1118) in the last decade of the century to turn to the West for military help. Alexius' request for western knights led to the preaching of the first crusade by Pope Urban II (1088-1099) in 1095 at Clermont in Aquitaine. Urban's appeal to western knights for reconquest and colonization of the Holy Land did not die with the capture of Jerusalem in 1099, but had set into motion a new religious, military and economic adventure by the Latins,[4] usually called the Crusades (1095-1291, an enterprise that in the end proved to be a failure. Nevertheless, during the two centuries of the high Middle Ages the Crusades captivated the minds, the manpower and the resources of western Europeans and the attention of those who preferred pen to sword.

Moreover, during the high Middle Ages several other important political and cultural developments began to take shape. The uninterrupted wars between the French and the English kingdoms led to the summoning of the first representative assemblies, Parliaments in England and Estates-General in France. These two countries infuriated by papal interference and attempts to dominate the political side of the wars, witnessed a growth of nationalism, which, in turn, led to the origins of national states in the Middle Ages. The intellectuals of the high Middle Ages produced a cultural revival, the so-called Renaissance of the Twelfth Century, an intensified interest in classical learning, literature and education. Perhaps the greatest achievement of the Twelfth Century Renaissance was the rise of universities.

Just as there is no definite date when to begin the high Middle Ages, so there is no binding
year for ending them: in intellectual history it
seems convenient to stop with Dante (1265-1321),
in ecclesiastical history with the pontificate of
Boniface VIII (1294-1303). In political and constitutional history the reigns of Philip IV the
Fair (1285-1314) of France and Edward I (1272-
1307) of England, the great contemporaries to
Boniface VIII, seem a valid landmark for ending
the high and starting the late Middle Ages. As
for military history, there has never been a cessation of wars and hostilities. Perhaps the end
of the Crusades in 1291 can be accepted as a point
of departure for new military enterprises and
ideals of chivalry.

All these events, to be sure, found mention
and frequently even meaningful description in
contemporary chronicles. Historical writing itself
reached a new height during the high Middle Ages.
To begin with, the scanty, laconic monastic and
local annals grew into national, or even universal
chronicles. Thus, early medieval historical writing was brought out of its swaddling clothes.
Next, the gestae, or the descriptions of deeds of
great warriors and military events were expanded
to acquire greater mastery and richness. And finally, the compilation of handbooks of general
knowledge, the medieval encyclopedias, was supplemented by the new learning, derived from the
revival of classical scholarship and medieval
travel.

The people who set the stage for the early
events of the high Middle Ages were the Normans.
Their conquest of Sicily and Southern Italy is
well recorded. The best literary accounts are
written by two Benedictine monks, AMATUS (Amatus
Casinensis, ca. 1020-ca. 1105) and GODFREY MALA-
TERRA (Gaufredus Malaterra, fl. ca. 1097). Amatus, a monk at Monte Cassino,[5] began his work
The History of the Normans with the origins of
the Norman people, then described the period of
their expansion and invasions of England and

147.

Italy, and brought down their rule in the southern part of the Apennine peninsula to 1078. Though Amatus' original Latin text is lost, it is, nevertheless, preserved in a late thirteenth century French translation as L'Ystoire de li Normant par Aimé. Malaterra, after repeating much of what Amatus had said, described the conquest of Sicily by the Hauteville brothers Robert Guiscard and Roger. The work, called the History of Sicily (Historia Sicula), ends with 1099. It makes reference also to the great pillage of the city of Rome by Robert Guiscard and the latter's relations with the Roman papacy.

The Norman invasion of England by William the Conqueror is narrated from two different points of view--Anglo-Saxon and Norman. The Anglo-Saxon attitude is described in the Anglo-Saxon Chronicle, particularly in the version "D", written in northern England. The Norman point of view is best represented by the pen of two continental chroniclers--William of Poitiers and William of Jumièges.[6] WILLIAM OF POITIERS (Guillaume de Poitiers, also Guilelmus Pictaviensis, ca. 1020-before 1101) was Duke William's chaplain, who between 1073 and 1074--thus after the conquest--wrote for his master the Deeds of William, Duke of the Normans and King of the English (Gesta Guillelmi ducis Normannorum et regis Anglorum). Though William of Poitiers, a well-educated and well-read cleric in classical historians, was also acquainted firsthand with contemporary events and had even been present at some of Duke William's battles, he, nevertheless, wrote a highly biased account of the Norman conquest of England. William's chief aim was to glorify his patron William the Conqueror and his Norman achievement, and to blacken the Conqueror's opponent, Harold, the leader of the Anglo-Saxons. Notwithstanding all his favoritism toward the Normans, William of Poitiers' Deeds are the best account of Duke William's conquest of England, though the beginning and the end of the work are no longer extant.

A Norman monk, WILLIAM OF JUMIÈGES (Guillaume

de Jumièges, died ca. 1090), wrote, a year or so before William of Poitiers, a work called the Deeds of the Dukes of the Normans (Gesta Normannorum ducum) in which he described Norman history beginning with the early dukes and brought it down to William the Conqueror. William of Jumièges' work is less prejudiced than William of Poitiers'; therefore, it is regarded as a rather truthful biography of William the Conqueror. Both William of Poitiers and William of Jumièges were used extensively by later chroniclers Orderic Vitalis, William of Malmesbury and Wace.

Of the Investiture Controversy the most dramatic part is the events which led to the Canossa incident in early 1077. Oddly enough, this stage of the controversy is well documented in official papal and imperial correspondence, but purely described in narrative sources. A Benedictine monk LAMBERT OF HERSFELD[7] (Lampertus Hersfeldenis, died after 1080) wrote a chronicle called the Annals of Hersfeld (Annales). This chronicle begins with a sketchy summary of world history from the Creation to 1040, then follows a more detailed account of events during Lambert's own manhood, climaxing with the Investiture struggle and the emperor's and pope's confrontation at Canossa.[8] Lambert and Herman of Reichenau are regarded as the best historians of the eleventh century, though Lambert's truthfulness has been seriously questioned by modern German historians, and his strong bias in favor of the papacy proven. Nevertheless, Lambert wrote in good Latin, imitating the style of the classical Roman historians Livy and Sallust and describing contemporary history on a much wider basis than anyone else. His Annals even include scenes from town and peasant life. More hostile to Henry IV than Lambert was a Saxon priest BRUNO (fl. ca. 1100), who wrote about the Saxon Revolt (Saxonicum bellum) during the time of Henry IV, covering the events from 1073 to 1081. From the imperial side Henry IV's struggles are described by an anonymous author in the LIFE OF EMPEROR HENRY IV (Vita Henrici IV imperatoris). Whether or not the author was Bishop Erlung of

Würzburg, he was a well-educated man, learned in
the classics and the church fathers, who wrote
the Life right after Henry's death, still being
under the influence of the sorrow over a deceased
emperor, as a eulogy to a lost protector and idol.
The author wanted to remain unknown, lest he arouse
the anger of the papal party. Even his work, it
seems, was kept in concealment in a monastery at
Regensburg.[9] Nevertheless, the Life was written
to glorify the emperor, to extol his virtues, to
describe his deeds, to keep his memory in high
esteem, and--to rehabilitate the emperor's fail-
ures and blame Lady Fortune[10] for a man's lack of
success. To achieve all this the author used his
skill in rhetoric and his knowledge of classical
and biblical literary models.

The first half of the eleventh century, down
to 1077, found also a talented historian in the
Byzantine Empire. After the death of Emperor
Justinian I (died 565), the Byzantine Empire ex-
perienced a long period of decline in power and
size, until its greatness again was partially re-
stored by Emperor Basil II Bulgaroctonus (the
Bulgarslayer, 976-1025). The prominent historian
of the reign of Basil and his successors was
MICHAEL PSELLUS (Constantinus Psellus, 1018-ca.
1078), a nobleman and professor of rhetoric in the
University of Constantinople (founded 1045) and
later first minister and leading politician and
statesman of the Empire. Extremely well-read in
classical Greek authors and eastern church fathers
Michael Psellus revived and continued the old
Greek tradition of writing history, not just mere
annals or chronicles of the sort that had become
commonplace in the West. Besides some five hundred letters and several treatises, Psellus wrote
a history of his own times, called Chronography[11]
(Chronographia) from the beginning of the reign
of Basil II (976) to the overthrow of Michael VII
in 1078. Psellus had spent almost all of his ma-
ture life at the imperial court; therefore court
intrigue and imperial lives were his main concern.
Being an eloquent narrator, he has left to posterity a vivid and rather accurate picture, mostly

based on his own observations, of the internal history of the Empire during its height under Basil II and its gradual decline under the Macedonian (867-1056) and Ducas' (1059-1081) dynasties. Michael paid little attention to wars and foreign policy; even some important internal events, not directly connected with the court, escaped Michael's attention. Since Psellus arranged the history according to the reigns of fourteen emperors between 976 and 1077, his work could be compared to Tacitus' Annals and Histories and Suetonius' Lives of the Twelve Caesars. Both of the Romans, like Michael Psellus, had been court historians. Modern scholars regard Psellus as the best Byzantine historian after Procopius.

The turbulent second half of the eleventh century came to a close with the preaching of the first crusade. The crusading movement produced also its own typical form of historiography, the gestae or the deeds of the crusaders. For the sake of conformity the great number of narratives about the Crusades will be considered as one topical complex, arranged according to individual crusades.

Chronologically, the earliest account of the Crusades was written by an unknown author about the first crusade, the Deeds of the Franks and the Other Pilgrims to Jerusalem (Gesta Francorum et aliorum Hierosolimitanorum). In modern historiography the work is usually referred to as the /ANONYMOUS/ GESTA FRANCORUM. The author probably came from southern Italy. He had participated in the first crusade, perhaps as a knight with modest education, for his Latin is rather poor. The most important aspect of his narrative is the fact that he was an eyewitness of the events he described. Though not being present at Clermont,[12] where in 1095 Pope Urban II preached the first crusade, he began his story with Urban's appeal for a holy war, and then described in great detail the deeds and battles of the crusaders down to the capture of Jerusalem in July, 1099, with additional information about the defeat of the Egyptian Fatimid army at Ascalon[13] a month later. There the narrative ends. As a narrator the anonymous author is fairly good; he even has achieved some drama in his story. However, what really establishes his work as a good source is the author's realistic description of the deeds of the crusaders, his impartiality towards the leaders of the crusade, and even towards the Muslims, and the truthfulness of the given facts. It is assumed that the author wrote the chronicle from time to time while he was with the crusader army and completed it soon after the last event described, the battle at Ascalon in August, 1099. For certain, this work was completed by 1101.

Because of its thoroughness this chronicle was used as a primary source by all chroniclers-- by some less, by others more extensively--who wrote about the first crusade after the composition of the Gesta Francorum. Even his contemporaries and participants in the first crusade, such as Raymond of Aguilers and Fulcher of Chartres relied on the Gesta heavily.

The next account, in chronological sequence, was written by RAYMOND OF AGUILERS (Raimundus de Aguilers, fl. ca. 1100), the chaplain to Count Raymond IV of Toulouse. Raymond of Aguilers[14] accompanied his lord on the crusade; thus he was, like the anonymous author, an eyewitness of events and wrote his account, the History of the Frankish Conquerors of Jerusalem (Historia Francorum qui ceperunt Iherusalem), about a year after the Gesta Francorum. Raymond's work was completed by 1102. The author, though using extensively the Gesta, is particularly valuable for his account of the Provencal contingent in the first crusade. Raymond is also explicit about the alleged discovery of the holy lance which, according to biblical tradition, pierced the side of Jesus Christ.

Another French priest, PETER TUDEBODE (Petrus Tudebodus, fl. ca. 1110) of Civray,[15] who has visited the Holy Land in the early twelfth century, wrote his version of the crusade before 1111, called The History of the Journey to Jerusalem

(<u>Historia de Hierosolymitano itinere</u>), by merely
plagiarizing the anonymous <u>Gesta Francorum</u> and
adding some information from Raymond of Aguilers.

The most popular history of the first crusade,
however, is written by FULCHER OF CHARTRES (Ful-
cherius Cartonensis, 1058 or 1059--after 1127),
<u>A History of the Expedition to Jerusalem, 1095-1127</u>
(<u>Historia Hierosolymitana, 1095-1127</u>). Fulcher was
a priest and chaplain to Baldwin I, the first king
(1100-1118) of the Latin Kingdom of Jerusalem.
Probably Fulcher was present at Clermont in November 1095; for certain from 1096 he accompanied the
French crusading army led by Duke Robert II of
Normandy (1087-1106) and Stephen, count of Blois and
Chartres[16] (1089-1102). In 1097 Fulcher became
the chaplain to Count Baldwin of Edessa[17] (1098-
1100), the later king of Jerusalem. Fulcher is
the first crusader historian who stayed in the
East and spent his remaining days in the Holy City;
after 1127 he is no longer traceable in historical
documents. Fulcher is the main source of information about the Council of Clermont, and an eyewitness of the deeds of the Franks till late 1097,
and the first historian of the Latin Kingdom of
Jerusalem (1100-1291) from 1100 till 1127. His
<u>History</u> is an independent narrative for the peri-
ods mentioned; only for the time he was in Edessa
(October 1097-November 1099) Fulcher had to rely
on the anonymous <u>Gesta Francorum</u> and Raymond of
Aguilers. It is assumed that Fulcher occasionally
used letters of the crusaders and information sup-
plied by participants in events he did not witness.
Presumably he began composing the <u>History</u> shortly
after settling down in Jerusalem, continued it in
installments and ended abruptly with the year 1127.
It is also established that he was fairly well read
in classical and early Christian authors and occasionally used their works as models for his own
<u>History</u>. Fulcher of Chartres is also a more tal-
ented narrator than his predecessors, but above
all, he is regarded as the most reliable and accurate historian (particularly in dates) of the
first crusade and the early Kingdom of Jerusalem.

With Fulcher of Chartres the line of chroniclers who participated in person in the first
crusade ends; not so the line of men who wrote
valuable narratives. A well-educated Frenchman,
GUIBERT OF NOGENT (Guibertus Novigentus, ca.
1064-ca. 1125), abbot of a monastery of the same
name in northern France, wrote a work called the
History of the Deeds of God through the Franks
(Historia quae dicitur gesta Dei per Francos).
Guibert never participated in a crusade, but was
a careful observer and diligent listener to stories of those who had taken the Cross[18] and returned to France. Guibert also made use of earlier chronicles of the first crusade, and combin-
ing his information with rational way of thinking,
he produced a fairly truthful narrative of the
holy war. Guibert also thoughtfully arranged the
social and economic conditions in France prior to
the Crusades, and made these conditions partly
responsible for the rather enthusiastic French
response to Urban's appeal. As a rational thinker
he also tried to minimize the significance of the
various miraculous happenings during the crusade,
as narrated by previous chroniclers. Guibert's
chronicle was written from 1108 to 1112. Besides
the History Guibert also wrote a memorable autobiography, called the Memoirs (De vita sua sive
monodiarum suarum libri tres), which contain ample
evidence about medieval French society, intellectual life and monasticism.

Of the French chroniclers who wrote on the
first crusade mention may be made also of ROBERT
THE MONK (Robertus Monachus, also Robertus
Remensis, fl. ca. 1105) from St. Remi of Reims,
who wrote a History of the Expedition to Jerusalem
(Historia Hierosolymitana). This work is fre-
quently mentioned because of Robert's version of
Pope Urban II's address at Clermont in 1095.
ALBERT OF AIX, also, Albert of Aachen (Albertus,
also Abericus Aquensis, died after 1120), prob-
ably a canon at the cathedral of Aix-la-Chapelle
(Aachen), wrote his account of the crusade,
History of the Expedition to Jerusalem (Historia

<u>Hierosolymitana</u>), after 1120 from the information he had obtained from those who had participated in the crusade. Neither Robert the Monk nor Albert of Aix had taken the Cross.

A unique position in crusader historiography belongs to ANNA COMNENA (Anna e Komnena, 1083-after 1148). Anna was a Byzantine princess, the daughter of Emperor Alexius I Comnenus. Her father was the Byzantine ruler whose appeal to Pope Urban II for Western mercenaries instigated the preaching of the first crusade. Anna neither participated in the crusade nor wrote a chronicle of the crusade; she wrote a history of her father's reign in fifteen books, called the <u>Alexiad</u> (<u>Alexias</u>) several years after her father's death. However, she was in Constantinople at the time when the crusaders with their ambitious and rivalrous leaders passed through the imperial city on their way to the Holy Land. Being a sharp observer, Anna had wonderfully sketched the characters and behavior of some of the crusader leaders whom she simply regarded as western barbarians. Likewise, Anna had viewed the crusade from a different angle than the Latin chroniclers, from the Byzantine point of view. In this way she sheds fresh light and offers different interpretation of the crusading movement. Anna wrote the <u>Alexiad</u> in excellent, almost classical Greek, thus attesting her high intelligence and truly remarkable education in ancient Greek culture, at that time available only in Constantinople.

The second crusade, the crusade of Louis VII (1137-1180) of France is well described by ODO OF DEUIL[19] (odo de Deogilo, died ca. 1162). Odo was chaplain to Louis VII and he accompanied the king to the Holy Land. Odo's account, the <u>Journey of Louis VII to the East</u> (De Ludovici VII <u>profectione in orientem</u>) is a vivid, though biased, narrative of the events and participants of the crusade.

The most complete, though not the most original account of the Crusades to 1184 is William of Tyre's <u>History of Deeds Done Beyond the Sea</u> (<u>Historia rerum in partibus transmarini gestarum</u>).

WILLIAM OF TYRE[20] (Guilelmus Tyrensis, ca. 1130–
before 1185) was born in the Kingdom of Jerusalem,
probably of French extraction, and received good
education in the East, including proficiency in
Greek and Arabic. He went to France to complete
his education, and after returning to the Holy
Land he became archdeacon of Tyre in about 1160,
was made chancellor of the kingdom from 1170 to
1174, and a year later, archbishop of Tyre.
William used as sources for the early period of
the Crusades the works of Albert of Aix, Raymond
of Aguilers and Fulcher of Chartres, but from
1127, when Fulcher broke off, to 1184, when William's work ends, his History is our primary
source of information about life and events in the
crusader kingdoms. William of Tyre is regarded as
a dependable historian, with a good understanding
of events in the Holy Land and a broad outlook.
And yet, his chronology often is at fault, and not
infrequently he is biased in favour of the Church.
William of Tyre had several continuators and trans-
lators, the most important being by Ernoul to 1229,
and the so-called History of the Deeds (Estoire
d'Eracles), of which each version ends with a
different year; they all are written in old French.

On the third crusade the best known narratives are written about the English and French
phase of the war. The most interesting account
comes from the pen of a jongleur AMBROSE[21] (fl.
ca. 1196), a Norman who wrote a verse chronicle in
old French towards the close of the twelfth century in England, known as the History of the Holy
War (L'Estoire de la guerre sainte). Unique about
this chronicle is the fact that it is not written
in prose, but in verse. The metrical or verse
chronicles, also called rhymed chronicles became
rather popular during the Crusades. They were
composed by minstrels or wandering poets in the
vernacular so that their compositions could be
recited before a non-Latin speaking audience, before the poorly educated laity, the knights,
princely courts and women. Closely connected
with Ambrose's verse chronicle is the Latin prose
chronicle composed by RICHARD (Ricardus, fl. ca.

1220), canon of Holy Trinity priory in London.
Richard between 1216 and 1222 wrote the <u>Itinerary</u>
<u>of the Pilgrims and the Deeds of King Richard</u>
(<u>Itinerarium peregrinorum et gesta regis Ricardi</u>).
Both chroniclers wrote about the third crusade and
its Anglo-Norman hero King Richard the Lionhearted
(1189-1199). It seems that canon Richard either
borrowed much information from Ambrose, or both
authors used a common source, now lost.

The French again made up the bulk of the contingent in the fourth crusade, which conquered
Constantinople instead of the Holy City. Consequently, the French wrote also the best accounts
of this crusade. A French nobleman GEOFFREY OF
VILLEHARDOUIN (Geoffroy de Villehardouin, ca.
1150-ca. 1213) who in 1185 was made marshal of
Champagne,[22] an officer similar to the minister of
war, took the Cross in 1199 in company with his
lord Count Theobald III of Champagne (1197-1201).
Geoffrey became one of the organizers and later
leaders of the fourth crusade, and after the crusaders in 1204 took the imperial city and founded
the Latin Empire of Constantinople (1204-1261),
he became its marshal. In 1207 or shortly afterwards he wrote his memoirs of the crusade, called
<u>The Conquest of Constantinople</u> (<u>La conquête de</u>
<u>Constantinople</u>), as an apology for diverting the
crusaders from the Holy Land to the Byzantine Empire. Nevertheless, Villehardouin being an eyewitness and one of the leading officers of the
crusade, wrote a factual and true account of the
events that led to the diversion of the crusade
as well as of the actual warfare, the capture of
Constantinople, the founding of the Latin Empire
and its adminstration. Villehardouin's chronicle
ends with 1207, with the death of Marquis Boniface
II of Montferrat[23] (1192-1207), the nominal leader
of the crusade. Villehardouin defended well the
deeds and decisions of the participants of the
crusade, and from this point of view Geoffrey's
story is biased by the author's stand and feelings.
He also omitted some of the causes for the actions
of the crusaders. However, what Villehardouin
described, he narrated accurately and in good faith.

The other chronicler of the fourth crusade
was an ordinary French knight from Picardy,[24]
ROBERT OF CLARI (Robert de Clari, died after 1216).
About his life little is known, but it is presumed
that he had returned from the East to Picardy in
about 1205 and there wrote his chronicle The Conquest of Constantinople (La conquête de Constantinople). Robert's chronicle deals with the same
time period and events as Villehardouin's, but
Robert saw some of the causes and deeds in slightly different light: he was a simple knight who
actively participated in battles but had no part
in decision making as his companion-in-arms Villehardouin had. Therefore, his narrative pays more
attention to warfare than to politics. Likewise,
Robert's style as a narrator is simpler than Villehardouin's. However, Robert of Clari has given
a very vivid description of Constantinople and
its marvels. Robert's account of the crusade also
could be used for checking Villehardouin's accu-
racy. Both Robert of Clari and Geoffrey of Villehardouin wrote their chronicles in old French.

About the fifth crusade the chief source is
OLIVER OF PADERBORN[25] (Oliverus Paderbornensis,
died 1227), who was the secretary to Cardinal
Pelagius (1205-1230), the papal legate on the
fifth crusade. This crusade was directed against
Muslim strongholds in Egypt, and it culminated
with the capture and brief Christian dominance of
Damietta, a port in the delta of the Nile river.
Oliver's chronicle, The Capture of Damietta (Historia Damiatina) is an eyewitness' account of the
events and covers the entire crusade from 1217 to
1222. It is a rather brief work, written during
the crusade, containing only eighty-nine chapters,
or actually paragraphs. Nevertheless, Oliver had
managed to sketch clearly and impartially the
events of the crusade.

The much-publicized crusade of Emperor
Frederick II (1211-1250), sometimes called the
sixth crusade, attracted the attention of no
great chronicler. It is, however, in some detail
referred to by several general chroniclers of the

Crusades, as well as by numerous universal historians. The most explicit account of Frederick's political maneuverings in the Holy Land may be found in Philip of Novara's Memoires (Les Mémoires). PHILIP OF NOVARA[26] (Philippe de Novarre, ca. 1195-ca. 1265), a Lombard who before 1218 had gone to the East as a crusader, in the mid-twenties settled down in Cyprus, and later on became adviser to his feudal lord, John of Ibelin (ca. 1198-1236), lord of Beirut, and to King of Cyprus Henry I of Lusignan (1218-1253). Probably Philip wrote his memoirs on the war of Emperor Frederick II against the Ibelins between 1243 and 1247; they cover Frederick's crusade in the Holy Land from 1228 to 1229, with an extention of the war between the Ibelins and Frederick's adherents in the "Outremer" till 1247. Naturally, Philip, being in the service of the Ibelins, defended their cause against the "imperialists."[27] The actual text of Philip's memoires is lost, but since his work was interpolated into another chronicle, the Deeds of the Cypriots (Gestes de Chiprois), it was reconstructed as close to the original as possible by a French medievalist Charles Kohler in 1913.

Of the later crusades an interesting account may be found in the biography of St. Louis by JOHN OF JOINVILLE[28] (Jean sire de Joinville, 1224-1317); his work bears the simple title Life of St. Louis (Vie de St. Louis). The French king Louis IX or St. Louis (1226-1270) participated in two crusades, the seventh crusade in 1248 and again in 1270. Both of these crusades were a failure for the Latins, and even more so for St. Louis: the first ended with the capture of the king by the Egyptians at Mansurah;[29] the second, with Louis' death in Tunis, near Carthage. Joinville has left a rather detailed description of St. Louis' first crusade and a masterly written biography of the saintly king. Joinville was St. Louis' seneshal, something similar to a marshal of ceremonies, but above all, he was an admirer and devotee to his master; therefore, the Life of St. Louis, though

honestly and truthfully written, sounds more like
a eulogy than a critical evaluation of the king,
his character and deeds. Nevertheless, Joinville's
biography sheds light on many aspects of the French
royal court in the thirteenth century and on religious and feudal life and royal administration in
particular. Joinville's Life of St. Louis is written in old French.

To evaluate the impact of the Crusades on
western medieval historiography, several aspects
need be scrutinized. To begin with, for the first
time non-Christian peoples were encountered and
described on a larger scale than ever before. Not
that they were now more respected or better liked:
they still were the cursed infidels, the enemies
of the Faith, the ones condemned to eternal perdition. And yet, the Latins in the crusader kingdoms had to live side by side with Islamic people;
they learned Muslim medical skills, the Westerners
even needed their help for building castles and
fortresses, cultivating fields, and--rather sur-
prisingly--as allies and fighting men. In short,
the Muslims had gained a status in crusader historiography. Secondly, as seriously as the contemporaries looked upon the Crusades as a holy war
against the Infidel, elements of adventure, pub-
licity, material gain and personal greed played a
prominent role in every crusade. Many leaders of
the Crusades found adherents eager enough to put
in writing their deeds and ventures, thus preserving to posterity the memory of a western enterprise that already from the mid-twelfth century had
been doomed to failure. Nevertheless, it was an
adventure that fascinated and kept captive the
minds of western Europeans for two centuries and
attracted the attention and active participation
not only of ordinary knights and clerics but also
of the most powerful popes (though no pope had
ever taken the Cross), bishops, emperors, kings
and princes. Even the peasants and children were
aroused to depart for the Holy Land and fight the
infidels barehanded. Thus, the historians of the
Crusades had an opportunity to record a Europe-
wide military-religious adventure during the

height of Latin Christianity. Thirdly, a new
genre in history writing, the "deeds" or the <u>gesta</u>
not only partially replaced the flourishing hagiography of the early Middle Ages but also produced
the first western historians of high repute who
either wrote in the vernacular (Villehardouin,
Robert of Clari, Joinville) instead of the traditional Latin, or who had settled down or were born
in and had become permanent residents of Latin
colonies overseas, or as the French termed them--
<u>Outremer</u>. It is worth noting that the two out-
standing crusader chroniclers - Fulcher of Chartres
and William of Tyre, both easterners - had written
the best contemporary histories of their new fatherland (<u>patria</u>). In this connection, mention
should be made of the fact that French historiography of the high Middle Ages reached its zenith
with the many chronicles of the Crusades and the
<u>Life of St. Louis</u>. One should be little surprised
about it: the Crusades were mostly a French enterprise; the French were the most successful Latins in the <u>Outremer</u>. And finally, due to the participation of kings and princes and bishops, the
Crusades captured the attention also of national
and universal chroniclers; for some, such as Otto
of Freising had taken the Cross in person; others,
such as Matthew Paris felt the impact of the Crusades even in the monastic scriptorium. Consequently, there is hardly a chronicle of any repute
in the high Middle Ages which has not touched upon
the Crusades either in passing, or in some detail.

One of the earliest universal chroniclers who
achieved mastery and paid great attention to the
Crusades, was EKKEHARD OF AURA (Ekkehardus Uraugiensis, ca. 1080-after 1126), a German, perhaps of
noble lineage, and abbot in the monastery of Aura,
near Würzburg. Ekkehard actually wrote a continuation to the <u>Chronicle</u> (<u>Chronica</u>) of Frutolf of
Michelsberg (died 1103), who had composed his work
from the Creation to 1101. Since Frutolf's information about the last couple of years was extremely
limited, Ekkehard began his narrative with 1096.
However, his independent information starts with
1099, with the description of the first crusade.

In 1101 Ekkehard took the Cross and departed for
the Holy Land with the German contingent of Duke
Welf IV of Bavaria (ca. 1030-1101). In Jerusalem
Ekkehard read an account of the first crusade,
probably the anonymous Gesta Francorum, which influenced him to put in writing his own observations
of the new military-religious movement. The most
valuable part of Ekkehard's story is his grasping
of the crusading spirit in Germany and the narrative of the crusade of 1101 of which he was an eyewitness. However, Ekkehard's interest in literary
work did not die with the account of the crusade;
he continued to describe events, with intervals,
down to 1125, to the death of his beloved Emperor
Henry V (1105-1125). Being a truly religious and
highly pious man, Ekkehard took a stand in support
of the Church and papacy. This point of view de-
cisively influenced his negative attitude towards
the old Emperor Henry IV, the great adversary of
papal power. Nevertheless, Ekkehard tried to avoid
abusive narrative. He was also well informed, because of his connections with the imperial court,
about events in Germany, France, Italy, and Spain
and even about happenings in England; thus, Ekkehard has achieved a high reputation as a universal
chronicler. Modern historians regard Ekkehard as
one of the most accurate and reliable German chroniclers of the high Middle Ages.

However, the greatest of all German chroniclers - some even say, the greatest medieval chronicler - was OTTO OF FREISING[30] (Otto Frisigensis,
ca. 1114-1158). Otto was of noble blood; his
father was Margrave Leopold III of Austria (ca.
1073-1136), his mother - daughter of Emperor
Henry IV of Germany. Otto was half-brother to
Emperor Conrad III, uncle to Henry V and nephew
to Emperor Frederick I Barbarossa (1152-1190).
From about 1128 to 1133 Otto studied in the University of Paris, then joined the Cistercian Order
and in 1138 was made bishop of Freising, near
Salzburg in Austria. Though he remained bishop of
that city for the rest of his life, he joined the
entourage of Emperor Frederick I Barbarossa and
accompanied the emperor on his many journeys.

Otto also had taken the Cross, and in 1147 with
his half-brother Emperor Conrad III went on the
second crusade. Otto died in the monastery of
Morimond in Champagne, where he had gone to at-
tend the chapter-general of the Cistercian Order;
he was laid to rest in the abbey's chapel.

Otto wrote two remarkable works: the Chronicle or History of the Two Cities (Chronica sive
historia de duabus civitatibus) and The Deeds of
Emperor Frederick Barbarossa (Gesta Frederici seu
rectius Chronica). The History of the Two Cities
is written as a world chronicle, beginning with
the Creation, and is brought down to the year 1146;
it was completed in 1147. The entire work is divided into eight books, of which the first three
treat ancient history, the next three books the
Middle Ages, the seventh book, events of his own
day, and the last book visualizes the Last Judgment and times thereafter. Otto's main source of
information was the Chronicle of Frutolf of Michelsberg. For the ancient period he also drew
upon Eusebius' History of the Church as translated
and continued by Rufinus of Aquileia, then Orosius'
Seven Books of History, Cassiodorus' Tripartite
History and some classical writers and philosophers.
For the Middle Ages Otto had used extensively Jordanes' History of the Goths, Paul the Lombard's
History of the Lombards, several German chronicles
and descriptions of saints' lives, and the works
of the Christian church fathers. For the period
of his own day, from 1106 to 1146, Otto relied on
oral information and on his own observation and
knowledge of facts. However, Otto's spiritual and
philosophical guide was St. Augustine's work The
City of God. Otto had conceived his Chronicle in
the pattern of St. Augustine as a universal history of mankind which has a beginning and an end,
and an everlasting life in bliss for the saved
after the Day of the Second Coming. Both authors
were aiming toward that goal, with the distinction
that St. Augustine tended to write a history of
the true Christians only, while on pilgrimage in
this earthly life, whereas Otto fully acknowledged
the real existence of two cities in this world--the

one being represented by the Church, or the holy
community, the other by the secular state or the
worldly society. The other distinction that separates the two philosophies of history is St.
Augustine's uncompromising stand towards the secular state as against Otto's more conciliatory attitude. As a high-ranking member of the hierarchy
of the Church he certainly was in favor of undis-
puted papal authority. But Otto also was a relative of the imperial family, even a close adviser
and member of the household of the emperor; therefore, he just could not take a stand against the
secular state. Otto found a safe path to follow
in dealing with the struggle between the two powers: he did not take sides in settling the issue;
he simply described the combat. The third aspect
that separates the philosophies of the two bishops
is their scheme of periodization. St. Augustine
had divided the entire history of mankind into six
ages; Orosius had emphasized the idea of four world
monarchies. Otto, though mentioning the four monarchies, paid little attention to their role in
history. He also substituted St. Augustine's six
ages with a tripartition of the history of mankind: the first age Otto ended with Constantine's
recognition of Christianity as a legal religion,
the second age will come to a close with Christ's
Second Coming, and the third age is eternal life
for the faithful in heavenly Paradise. Apart from
these differences Otto and St. Augustine basically
follow a common path in developing their ideas on
history. Both of them also were looking towards a
Domesday, near at hand. Otto's outlook of the remaining days for mankind was, however, gloomier
than St. Augustine's: Otto has had more chance to
observe and realize the fact that Christianity has
not changed the nature of man nor could it solve
the contest for power between the Church and the
state.

Thus, for some six hundred years the idea of
two cities, as developed by St. Augustine, had
been kept alive in medieval historiography, but
never prior to Otto of Freising was it so dramatically restated and made again a point of

departure. Though all medieval chroniclers had written their narratives as histories of the Christian people, none, however, had attempted to polarize, or set apart the secular government from the ecclesiastical hierarchy, for all subjects of a secular ruler were also members of the Church. No doubt, even Otto of Freising had not made such an attempt without a precedent, the Investiture Controversy, set in motion by Emperor Henry IV and Pope Gregory VII, and still raging during Otto's own day. At least, the Concordat of Worms of 1122, which was to settle the Investiture Dispute, was neither tolerated, nor highly respected by Otto's emperor Frederick I Barbarossa.

Otto of Freising wrote another historical work of great importance, The Deeds of Frederick Barbarossa. Upon Frederick's request Otto had presented a copy of the History of the Two Cities to the emperor in the spring of 1157. Evidently the emperor was very much impressed by Otto's work, for he asked Otto to compose a history of his own day. It seems that Otto had a similar intention, and after receiving an official commission from the emperor, he wasted no time (and lucky he was!) to set to work. Already in late summer of 1157 he began The Deeds of Frederick, in a year's time he had finished the first two books of the Deeds, and then he died on September 22, 1158, at the age of about forty-five. Although in the Deeds Otto began the description of events with the Investiture Controversy, thus partially repeating the narrative of the seventh book of the History of the Two Cities, the Deeds are, nevertheless, basically contemporary history, treating persons and events he had met and witnessed. The first book deals mainly with the reign of Conrad III. It also pays much attention to the second crusade, in which Otto and Conrad participated. The second book opens with the election in 1152 of Frederick Barbarossa as the king of Germany and continues his life to 1156, to the creation of the Duchy of Austria. Had Otto completed his task of narrating a life story of the Emperor Frederick, he undoubtedly would have written the best uniform biography of the great

Hohenstaufen emperor. In its present state Otto's
Deeds is the best available account about the rise
of the Hohenstaufens and the early reign of Frederick Barbarossa. Furthermore, in this work again
Otto faced the old dilemna of impartiality: he
certainly defended the imperial policy toward the
Italian city-states, but when he confronted the
papacy, he avoided taking sides in favor of the
emperor or the Church.

On his deathbed Otto designated his chaplain
and canon at Freising, RAHEWIN (Rahewinus, also
Radewicus, died ca. 1170) to complete the Deeds of
Frederick Barbarossa. The emperor gave his approval to Otto's choice. As a historian Rahewin
is regarded inferior to Otto. Nevertheless, Rahewin tried to retain Otto's style, but with no great
success, and without Otto's impartial stand.
Though Rahewin was not a member of the emperor's
entourage, he had access to official documents as
well as to some information from court circles.
However, it seems that by and large Rahewin had to
rely on his own initiative in getting information;
it appears that many of the events which he described he had witnessed himself. Rahewin continued Frederick's life to mid-1160; then his chronicle was presented to the emperor.

Interesting is Rahewin's attitude towards history writing in comparison to Otto's: Rahewin was
more a recorder than a historian, and certainly he
was not a philosophical historian. Rahewin's idea
of history was to narrate events and describe persons he had met. To this end he included verbatim
some thirty documents to support his narrative,
sometimes even without an introduction to the circumstances; Rahewin also lacked the theological
background of Otto. Being inferior to Otto as a
stylist and narrator, Rahewin tried to make up his
deficiency by introducing long direct speeches,
quotations from ancient authors, even using their
descriptions of persons and situations as true
stories of his own men and circumstances. Rahewin's favorite ancient authorities were the Roman
historian Sallust (83-34 B.C.) and the Jewish

historian Josephus (37-100).

   Otto of Freising raised the medieval chronicle to the rank of universal history, even for
contemporary events, for in both of his works persons of prominence came not only from Germany and
its various provinces, but also from Italy and
Sicily, France and Poland, Hungary and Bohemia,
Denmark and England, the Byzantine Empire and the
Holy Land, and from the Roman Church. Popes and
cardinals, bishops and abbots, scholars and saints,
warriors and adventurers, even Jews and women –
they all have a role in Otto's story, they all are
of international repute. And so are the wars, the
councils, the meetings and the journeys, all so
carefully described. It is a true world picture
which Otto reconstructed on the stage of history.
But with Otto of Freising the height of German
medieval historical school came to an end. Later
German historians contributed but little to the
advance of chronicle as a genre of universal history. They also added nothing new to the medieval
philosophy of history. An interesting aspect of
later German historiography is the growth of town
chronicles which in part replaced the declining
importance of universal chronicle. Increasing by
dozens, they recorded well the rising town life
with its social and intellectual movements and, in
addition, frequently also described great political
and military events of general European history.

   The German eastward expansion during the
Hohenstaufen period is well narrated by two chroniclers: HELMOLD OF BOSAU[31] (Helmoldus Bosoviensis,
died ca. 1177) and ARNOLD OF LÜBECK (Arnoldus
Lubecensis, died ca. 1212). Helmold, a priest who
had worked for many years as a missionary amongst
the western Slavs, wrote a Chronicle of the Slavs
(Chronica Slavorum) in two books and sympathetically
described Slavic resistance to German colonization
and exploitation during the twelfth century. Helmold is also our best narrative source about the
early period of the Margravate of Brandenburg.
Arnold of Lubeck could be regarded as continuator
to Helmold. Arnold wrote his Chronicle of the

Slavs (<u>Chronica Slavorum</u>) in seven books, describing events where Helmold left off, from 1171 to
1209. Arnold's main concern was the German eastward drive and the colonization of Mecklenburg,
Brandenburg and Pomerania.[32] The farthest northern German expansion into medieval Livonia[33] and
early contacts with the heathen Baltic and Esto-
nian tribes at the Gulfs of Riga and Finland are
described by HENRY OF LIVONIA (Henricus, died
after 1259) in <u>Livonian Chronicle</u> (<u>Chronicon
Livoniae</u>); it covers the period of German expansion in the Baltic region till 1227. Henry was
priest in the service of the bishop of Riga and
later worked among the neophite Latvians. It is
appropriate to regard the German eastward drive
and colonization attempts along the southeastern
coast of the Baltic Sea as a northern extension
of the Crusades.

Besides the Crusades and the Investiture
Controversy, still being contested during the
twelfth century, another movement came to prominence, by far more intellectual than the previous
ones, also more secular than religious, though
the Church, capitalizing on her rising power and
prestige, tried to interfere and even regulate
certain aspects of the new development. It was
the rise of universities. And again, it is much
easier to catch the flavor of the expanding interest in scholarship and reconstruct the course
of events from university charters and student
poetry than from narrative history, for contemporary chroniclers have touched upon the intellectual revival only in passing, only now and then
interrupting their narratives of political and
military history to insert an episode of academic
life or a student uproar. The only literary work
which stands out as a unique composition in the
field of intellectual history, shedding much light
on the origins of the University of Paris, is
Peter Abelard's autobiography <u>Story of My Adver-
sities</u> (<u>Historia calamitatum</u>). PETER ABELARD
(Petrus Abaelardus, 1079-1142), a French nobleman
who exchanged chivalry and warfare for pen and
teaching, usually is regarded as the founder of

the University of Paris, for during his lifetime, mostly due to his talent, charm and popularity, the former cathedral school of Notre Dame of Paris became recognized as a <u>studium generale</u>, as a university. By writing a life story about his controversies and fights with other professors and intellectuals of the day, Abelard, a scholar and professor in the University has vividly depicted also the rise of the university and the theological and philosophical disputes of twelfth century scholastics.[34] Besides that, Abelard's autobiography is spiced with erotic sentiment, an inalienable part of student and university life.

Apart from the religious and intellectual revival in twelfth-century Europe a new sentiment began to take root in two countries which previously were not regarded as first-rate political and military powers, in France and England. It was the rudimentary consciousness of nationalism which raised its head above the feudal or personal relationship. In France this consciousness originated as a reaction against feudal disunity; in Norman England, as a result of controlled feudalism, and in both countries the new sentiment gained momentum as a counterbalance to the growing power of the Universal Church. Both in England and in France—contrary to events in the Empire—the prolonged struggle with the papacy led to the rise of strong national monarchies, and—strangely enough—to the origins of parliaments. These developments took shape in the thirteenth and fourteenth centuries. It is also an odd coincidence that with the decline of the Empire, the excellence of German historiography decreased. Likewise, with the coming to prominence of French, and particularly of English political and military power, history writing also grew and flourished in these countries; and again, especially in England. The Universal Church, which had governed German international politics during the twelfth century, reached its greatest power in England a century later.

The first Anglo-Norman chronicler of repute

ORDERIC VITALIS (Ordericus Vitalis, 1075-1142), a
contemporary to Peter Abelard (though Orderic does
not mention him). Orderic was of mixed English
and Norman parentage: born in England, he regarded
himself an Englishman but spent almost all his life
in Normandy, in the monastery of St. Evroul; therefore, the French consider him a Frenchman. Being
aware of his English extraction, Orderic had a
nostalgic sentiment for his native country. He
also paid much attention to English affairs in his
life work, the Ecclesiastical History (Historia
ecclesiastica), composed between 1114 and 1141 in
thirteen books. Though begun as a history of Normandy and the Norman conquest of England, it was
expanded into a world chronicle from the days of
Christ to the early reign of King Stephen (1135-
1154) of England. Orderic used as his sources
the works of Eusebius, Gildas, Paul the Lombard,
Bede, William of Poitiers, William of Jumièges,
and William of Malmesbury, as well as saints'
lives, his monastery's archives, the library and
the annals of St. Evroult. For contemporary history Orderic also relied on oral reports and personal knowledge. Orderic compiled almost an encyclopedic treasure of knowledge about medieval
ecclesiastical, political, institutional and social history. He discusses events and persons
from the entire known world, thus elevating his
narrative to a first-rate universal chronicle.
He is also very explicit on the first crusade, an
international movement in its own right. Orderic
is also a good and interesting narrator; he is
claimed as their historian by the French and the
English alike. Though Orderic has no specific
philosophy of history, he is, nevertheless, the
best Norman monastic chronicler and, together
with the crusader chroniclers, makes up the best
of French historiography during the high Middle
Ages.

Orderic's contemporary, also of mixed Norman
and English parentage, was WILLIAM OF MALMESBURY
(Willelmus Malmesberiensis, ca. 1095-1143) who,
unlike Orderic, spent his life in England, in the
monastery of Malmesbury in southern England.

William began his association with the monastery
as a child, first helping out the abbot in the
library, later becoming the librarian himself.
Being curious to acquire knowledge, he sat down to
study the books in the library, becoming particularly fascinated with history. Not being satis-
fied with the histories he had read, he began to
write his own and produced three important works.
The Deeds of the Kings of England (Gesta regum
Anglorum) covers the period from 449 to 1127.
This work was continued under a separate title--
Modern History (Historia novella), which brought
events to 1142, thus right down to his death.
William's third work, The Deeds of the Bishops and
Abbots of England (Gesta pontificum Anglorum)
treats English ecclesiastical history from 601 to
1125.

William of Malmesbury is regarded as the best
English chronicler after Bede: he had an understanding of the chronological sequence of events,
he tried to be accurate and detailed, and he also
attempted to be honest in relating events and
lives of English kings. In the works of William
of Malmesbury one can begin to notice the author's
pride when talking about English affairs. It
would be too strong to call it a national consciousness; it is just a feeling that the English
are different from the peoples of the continent.
However, while telling true historical facts,
William also now and then includes miracles, and
not infrequently interrupts his story about En-
land by inserting tales of historical content from
continental Europe, often interwoven with legends.
Thus, talking about King Ethelwulf of Wessex35
(839-858), William finds it necessary to insert a
vision of Charlemagne; writing about Ethelred,
King of England (979-1016), William narrates a
story about Pope Sylvester II (999-1003), also
known as Gerbert, and a legend about Sylvester's
miraculous skill as a magician and treasure-
discoverer. As his source of information, William
of Malmesbury used Bede, the Anglo-Saxon Chronicle,
Asser's Life of Alfred and other minor Anglo-Saxon
narratives. From the ancients, Suetonius was his

favorite. William also included some documents,
since he has had access to material in monastic
archives. When William approaches his own times,
the narrative becomes fuller, more detailed and
more accurate. It appears that William had carefully noted, collected and recorded all the important events in England. This is particularly
true about book five of the Deeds of the Kings of
England and the Modern History, in which the reigns
of King Henry I (1100-1135) and King Stephen (1135-
1154) are described. The best treatment of King
Stephen's reign is by an anonymous contemporary
chronicler who wrote THE DEEDS OF STEPHEN (Gesta
Stephani). William of Malmesbury, in addition,
records in some detail the preaching of the Crusades by Pope Urban II, as well as the progress of
the crusaders to Jerusalem.

With William of Malmesbury began a very prolific period in English historiography, during
which not only were many histories written, but
also they were written in good historical sense.
William's contemporary was HENRY OF HUNTINGDON
(Henricus Huntendunensis, ca. 1084-1157), a cleric
who first served in the household of the bishop of
Lincoln but later became the archdeacon of Huntingdon.[36] Henry had turned to writing, encouraged by
the bishop of Lincoln, and completed his History
of the English (Historia Anglorum) in 1130 in seven
books. But Henry liked writing; therefore, he continued his work and revised it several times, till
the final version in ten books was produced in
1154. Henry's narrative begins with the invasion
of England by Julius Caesar (ca. 100-44 B.C.) in
54 B.C. and ends with the beginning of the reign
of King Henry II (1154-1189). The most independent
and valuable part of Henry of Huntingdon's work
covers the period of his own lifetime, the reigns
of Henry I and Stephen. Henry of Huntingdon is
less a universal chronicler than some of his predecessors and contemporaries; however, such great
international event as the Crusades did not escape
his attention. It would be fair to say that the
Crusades had become activities celebrated beyond
national boundaries to be recorded by all English

chroniclers of the high Middle Ages. Describing
events in England, Henry of Huntingdon carefully
documented and depicted the building up of the
friction between the several baronial parties
within the realm and against the king. Such tur-
bulence fermented for over half a century, till
it led to open revolt by the barons in 1215.

Of some interest, though little historic
value, is the work by GEOFFREY OF MONMOUTH[37]
(Gaufridus Monemutensis, ca. 1084-ca. 1154),
A History of the Kings of Britain (Historia regum
Britanniae), written probably in 1136. Geoffrey,
it seems, has had a long association with Oxford,
and he was appointed bishop of St. Asaph in 1152.
Geoffrey's work supposedly covers British history
from the arrival of Brutus, the first legendary
king of the Britons, in ca. 1100 B.C. to the death
of another legendary ruler, Cadwallader, in 689 A.D.
Geoffrey's history is full of tales; it also contains the legends about King Arthur, King Lear,
Brut and the Holy Grail.[38] He drew his inspiration
about the legendary kings from the fictitious elements in Gildas, Nennius, Bede, William of Malmesbury, Henry of Huntingdon, old Welsh oral traditions, Latin classics and the Old Testament. After reading these authorities, Geoffrey made use
of his immense power of imagination and talent for
story telling. As a result he produced an amusing
and very readable piece of literature which was
well received by the literate people of his day,
was intensively copied (almost two hundred manuscript copies are still extant from England as
well as the continent) and read. Geoffrey of Monmouth's work not only became a "bestseller" but
was also translated into the vernacular and used
as a source-book by later historians and men of
letters. As a factual history Geoffrey's work has
no significance, but it demonstrates the growing
English national consciousness and pride in its
past, brought to a point of pure chauvinism.

The close of the twelfth century produced
quite a few chroniclers in England. They all
dwelt, with varying success, on the reigns of

Kings Henry II (1154-1189) and Richard the Lionhearted (1189-1199). The most exciting event of
Richard's reign was his crusade to the Holy Land,
already dealt with. From Henry II's reign the
great event was the so-called Becket Controversy
between the king and his Archbishop of Canterbury
THOMAS BECKET (Thomas à Becket, ca. 1118-1170)
which strained the relationship of the royal government towards the English church and the papacy
and finally resulted in Becket's murder in 1170 in
the cathedral. These developments are well treated
by WILLIAM OF NEWBURGH (Guilelmus Neubrigensis,
ca. 1135-ca. 1198), an Augustinian canon at Neu-
burgh, Yorkshire, in the History of English Affairs
(Historia rerum Anglicarum), GERVASE OF CANTERBURY
(Gervasius Dorobornensis, died ca. 1210), a monk
at Christ Church, Canterbury, in his Chronicle
(Chronica), and RALPH OF DICETO (Radulfus de
Diceto, died 1202), archdeacon of St. Paul's in
London, who wrote Impressions of History (Ymagines
historiarum). All three works stop recording
events with the close of the century. Another
chronicle describing church-state relations from
the same period, though with heavy emphasis on con-
ventual life, was written by JOCELIN OF BRAKELOND
(Jocelinus de Brakelonda, died ca. 1203), a monk
at the monastery of St. Edmund in West Suffolk.
His Chronicle (Chronica) depicts as the central
person St. Edmund's abbot Samson (1182-1211) and
his endless quarrels with the brothers and outside
adversaries. The actual time span discussed in
the Chronicle covers the years 1173 to 1202. The
most important of the late twelfth century chroniclers, however, is ROGER OF HOWDEN[39] (also
Hoveden, Rogerus de Houedene, died ca.1201). He
was a clerk in the employ of Henry II, serving the
king as an emissary and as an itinerant justice.
In 1191 Roger participated in the third crusade,
and it seems, after returning home, wrote his
Chronicle (Chronica), treating events from 732 to
1201. Thus, Roger regarded his work as a continuation to Bede's Ecclesiastical History. For information to 1148 he relied on earlier chronicles,
among others on Henry of Huntingdon's History of
the English; the years 1148 to 1164 are treated

extremely briefly. From 1164 to 1169 he seems to be an independent source, describing the main event for these years, the Becket's Controversy, mostly through twenty-eight official letters. For the years 1170 to 1192 Roger either wrote his own version, or interpolated in his work an anonymous chronicle, called The Chronicle of the Reigns of Henry II and Richard I, A.D. 1169-1192, Known Commonly under the Name of Benedict of Peterborough (Gesta regis Henrici Secundi Benedicti abbatis). From 1192 to the end of the Chronicle Roger again is an independent source of information. It seems that Roger was very fond of supporting his narrative with official documents, for he copied them verbatim in great numbers; particularly in abundance are papal letters sent to England. Likewise, he paid attention to the king's government and Henry II's contest with Archbishop Becket, though without taking sides. But Roger not only described the course of affairs in the British Isles but also gave a good account of Richard I's adventurous participation in the third crusade. He tells about several events in the German Empire and the French Kingdom, in Italy, Spain, the Holy Land and Constantinople. Thus, Roger of Howden continued the line of universal chroniclers, already begun by William of Malmesbury.

The thirteenth century produced the two greatest English medieval historians: Roger of Wendover and Matthew Paris. Both were monks and historiographers at the monastery of St. Albans, located on a much trafficked highway twenty miles north of London. The monastery and its scriptorium came to prominence in the late twelfth century, when after 1180 a monk or monks wrote a chronicle of England which in the following years was expanded by several anonymous authors into a world chronicle. In the early thirteenth century ROGER OF WENDOVER[40] (Rogerus de Wendover, died 1236) used the information of the existing chronicle, revised it thoroughly and continued it, describing events to 1235. Roger's work, entitled Flowers of History (Flores historiarum), is a world chronicle beginning with the Creation. For the early part

of his work, to 447 A.D., Roger has gathered information from ancient writers, and as a source
of historical information this portion has no
value. With 447 A.D. Roger began to describe
events of English history, and it appears that besides some original documents his main authorities
for the period to 1193 were Bede, the <u>Anglo-Saxon</u>
<u>Chronicle</u>, William of Malmesbury, Henry of Hunting-
don and also some continental chroniclers, such as
Herman of Reichenau (Hermannus Contractus). With
the Norman invasion Roger's chronicle becomes
richer in English history, and for the last decade
of the twelfth century, for which his chief sources
were Roger of Howden and Ralph of Diceto, he is
rather explicit (Roger of Howden's chronicle ends
with 1201, Ralph of Diceto's--1202). After 1201
Roger of Wendover is original and our best source
for the reign of King John and the early rule of
Henry III (1216-1272). Roger described with particular care events during John's reign that led
to the signing of Magna Carta[41] in 1215: John's
perversity and greediness and his interference in
English ecclesiastical affairs which resulted in
John's excommunication and in placing England under
interdict.[42] Further, Roger describes the king's
submission as vassal to Pope Innocent III, John's
loss of English possessions in France, baronial
opposition to the king's money exactions, and finally the open revolt in arms by the barons
against the king. True, Roger tended to underline
the dark side or the shortcomings of John's rule,
but even taking that into consideration, the real
picture of baronial disapproval of the king's
autocratic rule has come through very clearly.
The friction between the king and barons continued
well into the reign of Henry III, and Roger of
Wendover has successfully--though he himself was
for certain unaware of it--described and documented
the polarization of English political thought during the thirteenth century. The barons more rapid-
ly than the king, developed their awareness of
belonging to an English nation whose interests
often differed from those of the king and the
Roman papacy. Such national consciousness led to
the origins of the medieval national state and

royal government by consent. On the whole, Roger has included in the <u>Flowers of History</u> unusually rich and valuable material, frequently by copying original papal and royal charters and letters verbatim or by adding detailed information about ecclesiastical, political, constitutional and military events in England as well as occasional news from the continent of importance to England and the affairs in the Holy Land relative to the great international movement, the Crusades. Although Roger does not reveal his sources of information about the contemporary events, there is little doubt that he was a careful observer and skillful gatherer of material on the developments of his day. He was extremely well-informed and aware of what was taking place in his own country. Besides having access to official documents, he easily could muster other sources of authentic information, such as narratives of royal progresses and the movements of the members of the ecclesiastical hierarchy and baronial leaders. One may believe that Roger has had trustworthy informers from amongst the royal retinue and the high dignitaries of the English church. In this respect it is worth remembering that his abbey was located on a busy road, and the monastery was regularly frequented by all kinds of wayfarers; even kings used it for stopovers.

Roger of Wendover did not develop his own philosophy of history, but trustfully followed the pattern of earlier chroniclers who described events in strict chronological sequence. However, Roger could be regarded as an honest historian who tried to write an objective narrative of his time, though slightly biased in favor of the English church. This, nevertheless, does not hold true in regard to papal extortions from English clergy under King Henry III.

After Roger of Wendover's death in 1236 MATTHEW PARIS (Matthaeus Parisiensis, ca. 1200-1259), a monk at St. Albans, became his successor as chronicler. Matthew probably had studied at the University of Paris; hence his acquired name

"Paris." Though a Benedictine monk since 1217,
he, nevertheless, often travelled around, visited
the court of Henry III rather frequently, attended
the king's wedding in 1236, and called himself the
king's "constant companion in the palace, at table,
and in his bedchamber"[43] and the "most particular
friend."[44] In 1248 Matthew served as Pope Innocent IV's (1243-1253) representative to look into
the disorderly affairs of the monastery of St.
Benedict of Holm in Norway. Thus, Matthew was well
acquainted with many of the great men of England
whose patronage he enjoyed, and his intimacy with
the court, the Anglo-Norman aristocracy and the
higher ecclesiastical hierarchy was responsible
for his extraordinarily rich and sound information
about events of his day. Matthew also had access
to a great variety of official documents, quite a
number of which he included verbatim in his chronicle. Matthew's main work, begun in 1240, is the
Greater Chronicle (Chronica majora). Its part to
1235 is nothing more than a slavish copy of Roger
of Wendover's Flowers of History, with occasional
short omissions or brief additions of new information. Matthew continued Roger's chronicle after
1235 without a separate introduction or a transi-
tional paragraph; even the mentioning of an earlier
author is missing. Thus, Matthew gave his Greater
Chronicle the appearance of one authorship. From
this point of view Matthew Paris' work may be regarded as the masterpiece of medieval literary
piracy and plagiarism. However, from 1236 Matthew's chronicle is an independent and original
source of information for the middle years of King
Henry III's reign.

And an excellent chronicle Matthew wrote!
With unprecedented richness of information Matthew
narrated affairs in England and continental Europe,
in Scotland and the Latin Empire of Constantinople,
in Wales, Norway, Denmark, Flanders, France, Spain,
Germany, Venice, Hungary, the Papal States, the
Holy Land and Egypt; even Russia, the Saracens and
the Mongols are mentioned. Monks and friars,
Knights Templar and Knights Hospitaller,[45] scholars,
merchants, bishops, papal legates, justices and

adulterers--they all march in the pages of Matthew's chronicle. The battle cry between France and England and England Wales echoes in many paragraphs; the loss of English territory is lamented. Crusaders depart, fight, fall and are taken prisoner; some return. Reigning popes die and new ones are elected; emperors wage wars and are excommunicated; ambassadors travel, Jews are massacred; councils are convoked and decrees passed; churches are consecrated; grievances at the unversities of Paris and Oxford are discussed; royal marriages are concluded; knightly tournaments are held. In short, reading Matthew's chronicle, one gets the feeling as of looking through world news in a modern newspaper.

Through such conglomerate of information, however, clearly discernible is Matthew's real grief about his king and country. Henry III vainly attempted to place his son Edmund on the Sicilian throne and to establish his brother Richard as the king of Germany. To substantiate such vague hopes Henry III taxed his subjects heavily and sent thousands of pounds of silver to Rome in order to gain papal support. Matthew vividly described baronial and clerical opposition to these heavy pecuniary contributions to Rome and called them Roman "oppressions."[46] He also described the exhaustion of England's wealth, as "wretched conditions of the kingdom."[47] Papal extortions, coupled with King Henry III's unsuccessful diplomatic maneuvers and military defeat resulted in baronial revolt, led by Simon de Montfort, the earl of Leicester, and the summoning of the first Parliament of England in 1265. Although Matthew Paris did not live long enough to see the convocation of the first Parliament, the word itself is continuously used throughout Matthew's work to describe the king's meeting with his Small and Great Councils.

Papal extortions also consolidated English national consciousness against the internationalism of the Universal Church, or the Christian Commonwealth, dominated by the Roman Pontiff.

179.

Under Henry III's successor, his son Edward I
(1272-1307), this sentiment finally manifested
itself in open royal refusal to recognize papal
demands and papal leadership in national politics.
Edward's unwillingness to comply with Roman politics ultimately led to the origin of the medieval
English national state. However, the ingredients
and symptoms for oppostion to papal dominance already were clearly noticeable during the reign of
Henry III, and Matthew Paris in his chronicle had
masterfully, though most probably still unwittingly,
grasped these new forces at work; for certain, he
has demonstrated their existence.

From Matthew's narrative in the <u>Greater
Chronicle</u> it becomes clear that he was unusually
well-versed in both political and ecclesiastical
history, and he is regarded as a trustworthy historian who has not only preserved correct facts to
posterity, but also has described them in neutral
light, though his antipathy against papal extortions from England cannot be denied. Matthew is
also unsympathetic towards the great influence that
the king's foreign relatives and adherents exercised
in England; therefore, it seems just to call Matthew a true English national historian. However,
Matthew did not try to develop his own philosophy
of history; he is scarcely touched by St. Augustine's and Otto of Freising's visions of the two
cities. Matthew is a business-like chronicler,
who avoids excessive inclusion of miracles and
legends, who pays little attention to the importance of Divine Providence in human history.
Matthew deals mainly with concrete facts and political and secular history. Therefore, Matthew's
<u>Greater Chronicle</u> can be looked upon as the most
scholarly and rational history the English Middle
Ages produced, and Matthew himself as the ablest
English historian since the Venerable Bede. For
certain, Matthew brought the unversality of contemporary world chronicle to its highest pinnacle.
It should be added that Matthew wrote in comparatively good Latin; his style is clear; his message
honest. To support his narrative, Matthew, following the tradition of Roger of Wendover, has

transcribed verbatim an abundance of historical documents in the text. They could be regarded, if one so wishes, as Matthew's way of footnoting his statements. But Matthew's love for documents was so great that he compiled a whole collection of them, called the Book of Supplements (Liber additamentorum, or Additamenta) and affixed it as an appendix to the Greater Chronicle.

Another pecularity of Matthew's work needs mentioning. He added numerous illustrations to the narrative, usually with captions describing the depicted scene, sometimes even adding words as coming out of a person's mouth. Illustrations in medieval chronicles was not at all unusual, but Matthew's Greater Chronicle probably is one of the most amply illustrated of historical narratives. Matthew's artistic talent is revealed by the fact that the autograph or Matthew's original manuscript of the Greater Chronicle has survived to our day. Several of his illustrations have recently been published in separate books.

Matthew Paris has written several other works, of which probably the most significant is the Lesser Chronicle, called also the History of the English (Historia Anglorum). It was composed after 1250 as an epitome of his Greater Chronicle. The History of the English covers the period from William's conquest of England in 1066 to 1253, and is restricted mainly to England's history. In this work Matthew has softened some of his expressions and modified some opinions from the Greater Chronicle, has rewritten certain parts completely and added other material which was not found in the Greater Chronicle. Therefore, the History of the English can be regarded, in some respects, as an independent compilation, and certainly both chronicles are of great value for medieval English history.

With Matthew Paris the height of English medieval historiography was reached. After Matthew in England, as after Otto of Freising in Germany, the quality of history writing sharply declined. The period from 1260 to the end of the century is documented in a variety of local chronicles of which three may be choses as examples: the Flowers of History, the Chronicle of Bury St. Edmunds and Peter Langtoft's Chronicle.

It is now believed that Matthew Paris compiled a short version of his Greater Chronicle, called the Flowers of History (Flores historiarum); this epitome ends with 1259. Matthew's compilation was continued, as Flowers of History, first at St. Albans abbey from 1259 to 1265, but afterwards at several monasteries, of which the most significant continuation (till 1327) was produced at Westminster Abbey,[48] London. The continuators are not known, but the Westminster version of the continuation for a long time was accepted as the Flowers of History by a Matthew of Westminster. The entries of importance are for the years from 1259 to 1327; these are written down in the traditional annalistic form with little originality. Nevertheless, they are an excellent source of information for the last decade of the reign of Henry III and the rule of Edward I.

Another annalistic compilation by several authors is the CHRONICLE OF BURY ST. EDMUNDS (Chronica Buriensis), which covers world history from the Creation to 1301. It was compiled by several chroniclers at the monastery of St. Edmunds,[49] and the valuable part of the Chronicle falls between 1265 and 1301, when the annals are contemporaneous to the recorders.

Of some value to historiography is also a verse chronicle in old French to 1307 by Peter Langtoft of Bridlington,[50] simply called the Chronicle. PETER LANGTOFT (Pierre de Langtoft, died ca. 1307) was a canon at Bridlington, and in the early fourteenth century he composed the Chronicle in verse from Brutus' legendary arrival in England to the death of King Edward I. The only valuable part as a source of information covers the reign of Edward I, and it deals mostly with English-Scottish relations. What seems interesting is the fact that verse chronicles of the high Middle Ages mostly are written in the vernacular, in old French or old German, but not in old English or Latin.

To conclude the survey of history writing during the high Middle Ages, one other chronicler from Italy deserves mentioning, SALIMBENE (Salimbene di Guido di Adam, 1221-1288) from Parma.[51] Salimbene was a Franciscan friar who travelled widely in northern Italy and southern France. While on his errands he kept his eyes and ears wide open, and between 1283 and 1288 he wrote down his observations, feelings and experiences in the form of autobiography and memoirs. Since Salimbene was contemporary to many great men whom he had either met in person, or heard stories about, he has depicted quite a gallery of notables in the Chronicle (Chronica). There we meet Emperor Frederick II (1211-1250) and his successors in Italy Conrad IV (1250-1254), Conradin (1254-1268), Manfred (1258-1266) and Charles of Anjou (1266-1282). The King of France St. Louis (1226-1270) is discussed, as are also the great thirteenth century popes: Innocent IV (1243-1254), Alexander IV (1254-1261), Urban IV (1261-1264), Clement IV (1265-1268), Gregory X (1271-1276) and Martin IV (1281-1285). Scholars of his own day are immortalized: Rober Bacon (ca. 1214-ca. 1294), Thomas Aquinas (1225-1274), Bonaventure (1221-1274), Grosseteste (ca. 1175-1253) and the young Dante (1265-1321). But Salimbene also has successfully grasped the minds of friars and clerics, townspeople and soldiers; even women have a role to play in Salimbene's Chronicle.

Notes

[1] Normans - Danish Norsemen or Vikings who in early tenth century settled down in the northern part of Neustria, round the estuary of the River Seine, in the north bordering the English Channel. In 911 their leader Hrolf or Rollo, became a vassal

to the Frankish king Charles III the Simple (898–929); Rolo was made a duke, and the Norman occupied territory became known as the Duchy of Normandy, with Rouen as its capital. Its territory was gradually expanded by Rollo's successors to Brittany in the west and Flanders in the east.

[2] Hauteville – a fief in northwestern Normandy (in the Cotentin peninsula).

[3] Investiture Controversy – originally a struggle between the Roman papacy and secular rulers over the rights to appoint and invest clergy. The controversy ultimately led to papal challenge of royal power even in secular matters in several European countries. The Investiture struggle was touched off by Pope Gregory VII and Emperor Henry IV in 1075, and though a formal settlement between the papacy and the emperor was reached in 1125 with the Concordat of Worms, in fact the controversy over papal secular power continued until the days of Pope Boniface VIII (1294–1303).

[4] Latins – western or Roman Christians who used Latin as the language of the Church and followed the rites of Rome.

[5] Monte Cassino – a monastery in Italy halfway between Rome and Naples, founded by St. Benedict (died ca. 547). Benedict also wrote a "Rule" for his monks which became the dominant monastic Rule in the West. Monks who live after the Rule of St. Benedict are called Benedictines.

[6] Poitiers – town in Aquitaine, south of Tours; Jumièges – a monastery in Normandy near Rouen.

[7] Hersfeld – a Benedictine monastery in central Germany on the banks of the River Fulda.

[8] Canossa – a castle in northcentral Italy, near Parma and Modena, owned by the Countess Matilda of Tuscany, where Pope Gregory VII in 1077 received and absolved Emperor Henry IV.

9 Würzburg and Regensburg - towns in Bavaria, southcentral Germany.

10 Lady Fortune - Fortuna, Roman goddess of good luck.

11 Chronography - Greek word for annals.

12 Clermont - town in southcentral France.

13 Ascalon - town in southern Palestine.

14 Aguilers - village in southcentral France, near Le Puy; Toulouse - town in southwestern France, near the Pyrenees.

15 Civray - town in westcentral France, south of Poitiers.

16 Blois - town and county in central France; Chartres - town in the county of Blois in central France, south of Paris.

17 Edessa - town and the first crusader county in southern Armenia.

18 To take the Cross - to take the crusader's vow to go on a crusade; to become a crusader.

19 Deuil - a town near Paris.

20 Tyre - old Phoenician city in the Latin Kingdom of Jerusalem (in present-day southern Lebanon).

21 Jongleur - a travelling medieval poet and singer.

22 Villehardouin - castle in central France near Troyes, southeast of Paris; Champagne - county in northeastern France.

23 Montferrat - county in northwestern Italy, east of Turin.

[24] Picardy – region in northwestern France with Amiens as the main city.

[25] Paderborn – town in northcentral Germany.

[26] Novara – town in northcentral Lombardy, west of Milan.

[27] Ibelins – adherents to the Frankish reigning house in the Latin Kingdom of Jerusalem, as opposed to the imperialists, supporters of the German imperial house of Hohenstaufens who both claimed superiority in "Outremer" ("Overseas"-- across the Mediterranean, looking from Western Europe)--the French name for Latin possessions in Syria and Palestine during the Crusades.

[28] Joinville – a town in Lorrain, northeastern France.

[29] Mansurah – a town in the delta region of Egypt.

[30] Freising – a town in southeastern Bavaria.

[31] Bosau – village in Schleswig-Holstein, near Kiel in Germany.

[32] Brandenburg, Mecklenburg, Pomerania – originally regions inhabited by west Slavic peoples along the southern coast of the Baltic Sea; conquered, settled and colonized by the Germans during their eastward expansion between the twelfth and fourteenth centuries. The conquered territories were organized into marches or frontier counties (Germ. Markgrafschaften), i.e. margravates.

[33] Medieval Livonia – central eastern coast of the Baltic Sea, conquered by the Germans during the thirteenth century; medieval name for the territories of modern Latvia and Esthonia.

[34] Scholastic – a medieval scholar; also the head of a medieval chapter school.

35 Wessex – Anglo-Saxon Kingdom in southwestern England.

36 Huntingdon – county and town in east-central England.

37 Monmouth – county in southeastern Wales.

38 Arthur, Lear and Brut – legendary kings of Britain before Anglo-Saxon migrations; Holy Grail – legendary cup used by Christ at the Last Supper.

39 Howden – medieval Hoveden, a town in northern England, near York.

40 Wendover – a town north of London.

41 Magna Carta – The "Great Charter"; a feudal document sealed by King John in June, 1215, in which he granted certain privileges to the English corporate baronage and recognized that the king of England has to rule according to the existing law.

42 Interdict – an ecclesiastical ban within the Catholic Church which deprives a country or a district of the privilege of celebrating the Mass and of administering the sacraments and Christian burial.

43 Matthew Paris, English History from the Year 1235 to 1273, transl. J. A. Giles. 3 vols. ("Bohn's Antiquarian Library"). (London: Henry G. Bohn, 1852-1854, vol. 3, p. 220 (for the year 1257).

44 Matthew Paris, vol. 2, p. 285 (for the year 1248).

45 Monks – religious compelled to live in seclusion (monastery) under the three monastic vows (poverty, chastity, obedience) and follow one of the monastic rules; monks are mostly concerned with the salvation of their own souls.

Friars – religious living under the three monastic vows and members of a mendicant order; friars are not required to live in a monastery, but to walk around living from begging (thus also called "beggar monks") and preaching the Word of God to the people (thus, also called "preacher monks"), mostly in towns to save the souls of others. The three most popular mendicant orders are the Franciscans, the Dominicans and the Jesuits. Knights Templar and Knights Hospitaller – two of the most popular military religious orders founded in the Holy Land at the early days of the Crusades for the protection of pilgrims visiting the holy shrines, for caring for the poor and the sick, and for fighting against the infidels to safeguard Christian conquests in Palestine and Syria. Both Templars and Hospitallers established houses or branches also in Western Europe and during the Crusades were looked upon as the model knights in defense of Christianity.

[46] Matthew Paris, vol. 3, p. 273 (for the year 1258).

[47] Matthew Paris, vol. 3, p. 136 (for the year 1255).

[48] Abbey – a monastery ruled by an abbot; Westminster Abbey – the royal church in London.

[49] Bury St. Edmunds – a monastery and town in eastern England, east of Cambridge.

[50] Bridlington – a town in northeastern England at the North Sea.

[51] Parma – a town in northcentral Italy.

A SELECT BIBLIOGRAPHY

Historiographical Works

See above, pp. 113-114, under "Historians of the Early Middle Ages."

Bibliographical Guides

Altschul, Michael, <u>Anglo-Norman England 1066-1154</u> ("Conference on British Studies Bibliographical Handbooks"). Cambridge: The University Press, 1969.

Wilkinson, Bertie, <u>The High Middle Ages in England 1154-1377</u> ("Conference on British Studies Bibliographical Handbooks"). Cambridge, London, New York, Melbourne: Cambridge University Press, 1978.

Guth, Delloyd J., <u>Late Medieval England 1377-1485</u> ("Conference on British Studies Bibliographical Handbooks"). London, New York and Melbourne: Cambridge University Press, 1976.

For other bibliographical guides, see above, pp. 114-115, under "Historians of the Early Middle Ages."

Source Collections and Serial Editions

<u>Patrologiae cursus completus: series Graeca</u>, ed. Jacques Paul Migne; see above, p. 45, under "Early Christian Historians."

<u>Patrologiae cursus completus: series Latina</u>, ed. Jacques Paul Migne; see above, p. 45, under "Early Christian Historians."

<u>Recueil des historiens des croisades</u>, publié par les soins de l'Academie des inscriptions et belles-lettres. 5 series, totalling 16 vols. Paris: Imprimerie Royale (name of publishers vary), 1841-1906.

This prestigeous collection prints in folio the works of crusade historians as well as law books. There are five series: "Western Historians" (<u>Historiens occidentaux</u>) in 5 vols., 1844-1895, which prints in Latin westerner chronicles; "Eastern Historians" (<u>Historiens orientaux</u>) in 5 vols., 1872-1906, prints in Arabic with free rendering in French Muslim historians; "Byzantine Historians" (<u>Historiens grecs</u>) in 2 vols., 1875-1881, prints in Greek with Latin translation Byzantine chronicles; "Armenian Historians" (<u>Documents arméniens</u>) in 2 vols., 1869-1906, prints Armenian and Western chronicles in Armenian, Latin and French; "The Laws," (<u>Lois</u>) in 2 vols., 1841-1843, prints in Old French the statues and selected charters in Latin of the Kingdom of Jerusalem. For Western historiography the most important series are the <u>Historiens occidentaux</u> (abbr. <u>RHC, Occ.</u>), the <u>Historiens grecs</u> (abbr. <u>RHC, Grecs</u>) and the <u>Documents arméniens</u> (abbr. <u>RHC, Armen.</u>).

For other source collections and serial editions, see above, pp. 116-117, under "Historians of the Early Middle Ages."

Source Collections and Serial Editions in English Translation

<u>English Historical Documents</u>, gen. ed. David C. Douglas, vol. 2: <u>English Historical Documents 1042-1189</u>, eds. David C. Douglas and George W. Greenway. London: Eyre and Spottiswoode, 1968.

<u>English Historical Documents</u>, gen. ed. David C. Douglas, vol. 3: <u>English Historical Documents 1189-1327</u>, ed. Harry Rothwell. London: Eyre and Spottiswoode, 1975.

Both vols. contain translations in excerpts from some of the important chronicles.

<u>Medieval Classics</u>, see below, under "Nelson's Medieval Texts."

Medieval Texts, see below, under "Nelson's
Medieval Texts."

Nelson's Medieval Classics, see below, under
"Nelson's Medieval Texts."

Nelson's Medieval Texts, gen. eds. V. H.
Galbraith and R.A.B. Mynors. 25 vols. London:
Thomas Nelson and Sons, 1949-1965.

This series, began as "Medieval Classics,"
was changed to "Medieval Texts" and commonly known
as "Nelson's Medieval Classics" or "Nelson's Medieval Texts;" it published several important medieval chronicles in Latin (verso) with English
translation (recto), mostly concerning English
history. From 1967 this series was continued as
Oxford Medieval Texts.

Oxford Medieval Texts, gen. eds., V. H.
Galbraith, R.A.B. Mynors and C.N.L. Brooke.
Vols. 1-. Oxford: Clarendon Press, 1967- in
progress.

This series, being the continuation of Nelson's Medieval Texts, reprints earlier editions
as well as publishes new texts of medieval chronicles in Latin (verso) with English translations
(recto).

For other source collections and serial editions in English translation, see above, pp. 118-
119, under "Historians of the Early Middle Ages."

Modern Studies on High
Medieval Historiography

Archambault, Paul, Seven French Chroniclers:
Wittnesses to History. Syracuse: Syracuse University Press, 1974.

Studies of Villehardouin, Joinville, Froissart, Chastellain, La Marche, Basin and Commynes.

Hanning, Robert W., The Vision of History in Early Britain from Gildas to Geoffrey of Monmouth; see above, p.120, under "Historians of the Early Middle Ages."

Jenkins, Claude, The Monastic Chronicler and the Early School of St. Albans. London: Society for Promoting Christian Knowledge, 1922.

Jones, W. Lewis, "Latin Chronicles from the Eleventh to the Thirteenth Centuries," in Cambridge History of English Literature, eds. A. W. Ward and A. R. Waller, 1:173-203 (1907). 15 vols. New York and London: G. P. Putnam's Press, 1907-1933.

Deals with English and Anglo-Norman Chronicles.

Tout, Thomas Fredrick, The Study of Mediaeval Chronicles. Manchester: At the University Press, 1922.

A brief essay on selected chroniclers.

Individual Historians

LAMBERT OF HERSFELD (died after 1080)

Text Editions

"Annals"

"Lamberti Hersfeldensis Annales," in Migne, Patrologia Latina, 146:1053-1248.

Fritz, Wolfgang Dietrich, ed., Lamperti monachi Hersfeldensis "Annales." Lampert von Hersfeld "Annalen." Transl. Adolf Schmidt. ("Ausgewählte Quellen zur deutschen Geschichte des Mittelalters," vol. 13). Darmstadt: Wissenschaftliche Buchgesellschaft, 1957; reprint ed., Berlin: Rütten and Loening, /n.d./.

This edition contains the entire chronicle, from the Creation till 1077 A.D. Latin text verso,

German transl. recto.

Hesse, Ludwig, Friedrich, ed., "Lamberti Hersfeldensis <u>Annales</u>" /1040-1077/, in <u>MGH, SS</u>, 5:134-263. Hanover: Hahnsche Buchhandlung, 1844.

Holder-Egger, Oswald, ed., "Lamperti Hersfeldensis <u>Annales</u>" in <u>Lamperti monachi Hersfeldensis</u> "Opera," pp. 1-304 (<u>MGH, Script. in usum schol.</u>). Hanover and Leipzig: Hahnsche Buchhandlung, 1894; reprint ed., 1956.

Pertz, Georg, Heinrich, ed., "Lamberti Hersfeldensis "<u>Annales</u>" /to 1039/, in <u>MGH, SS</u>, 3:22-29; 3:33-69; 3:90-102. Hanover, Hahnsche Buchhandlung, 1839.

MICHAEL PSELLUS (1018-ca. 1078)

Text Edition

"Chronography"

Renaud, Émile, ed. and transl., <u>Psellos</u> "<u>Chronographie</u>," ou, "<u>Histoire d'un siècle de Byzance (976-1077).</u>" 2 vols. Paris: Société d'édition "Les Belles Lettres," 1926-1928.

Greek text verso, French translation recto.

English Translations

"Chronography"

Sewter, E.R.A., transl., "<u>Chronographia</u>" of <u>Michael Psellus</u> ("Rare Masterpieces of Philosophy and Science," ed. W. Stark). New Haven: Yale University Press, 1953.

Sewter, E.R.A., transl., <u>Fourteen Byzantine Rulers: The "Chronographia" of Michael Psellus;</u> rev. ed. ("Penguin Classics"). Harmondsworth, Eng.: Penguin Books, 1966.

Modern Studies

Gadolin, Anitra, A Theory of History and Society with Special Reference to the "Chronographia" of Michael Psellus; 11th Century Byzantium. ("Acti Universitatis Stockholmiensis. Stockholm Studies in History of Literature," vol. 11). Stockholm: Almquist and Wiksell, 1970.

/Anonymous/ GESTA FRANCORUM

Text Editions

"Gesta Francorum et aliorum Hierosolymitanorum seu Tudebodus abbreviatus," in RHC, Occ., 3:119-163. Paris: Imprimerie Impériale, 1866.

The editors ascribed this anonymous chronicle to Peter Tudebode; see below, p.221.

Brehier, L., ed. and transl., Histoire anonyme de la premiere croisade ("Les Classiques de l'histoire de France au moyen age," vol. 4) Paris: Librairie ancienne Honoré Champion, 1924.

Latin text verso, French translation recto.

Hagenmeyer, Heinrich, ed., Anonymi Gesta Francorum et aliorum Hierosolymitanorum. Heidelberg: Carl Winters Universitätsbuchhandlung, 1890.

English Translations

Hill, Rosalind, ed. and transl., Gesta Francorum et aliorum Hierosolimitanorum. The Deeds of the Franks and the Other Pilgrims to Jerusalem ("Medieval Texts."). London: Thomas Nelson and Sons, 1962.

Latin text verso, English translation recto.

Krey, August, C., transl., "Anonymi Gesta Francorum et aliorum Hierosolymitanorum," in August C. Krey, ed., The First Crusade: The Accounts of Eye-Witnesses and Participants,

printed intermittently with other accounts.
Princeton: Princeton University Press, 1921;
reprint ed., Gloucester, Mass.: Peter Smith, 1958.

   Translation from Hagenmeyer's text edition;
for sequence of pages, see Krey, p. 283.

FULCHER OF CHARTRES (1058-after 1127)

Text Editions

   "A History of the Expedition to Jerusalem"

   "Fulcherii Carnotensis Historia Hierosolymitana ab anno 1055 ad annum usque 1127," in Migne,
Patrologia Latina, 155:821-942.

   "Historia Jherosolymitana gesta Francorum
Jherusalem peregrinantium ab anno Domini MXCV
usque ad annum MCXXVII auctore Domno Fulcherio
Cartonensi," in RHC, Occ., 3:311-485. Paris:
Imprimerie Impériale, 1866.

   Hagenmeyer, Heinrich, ed., Fulcheri Carnotensis "Historia Hierosolymitana, (1095-1127)."
Heidelberg: Carl Winters Universitätsbuchhandlung,
1913.

English Translations

   "A History of the Expedition to Jerusalem"

   McGinty, Martha Evelyn, transl., Fulcher of
Chartres "Chronicles of the First Crusade."
(University of Pennsylvania, Department of History,
"Translations and Reprints from the Original Sources
of History." 3rd series, vol. 1). Philadelphia:
University of Pennsylvania Press, 1941.

   Translation of Fulcher's first book. Re-
printed in The First Crusade: The Chronicle of
Fulcher of Chartres and Other Source Materials,
ed. Edward Peters, pp. 23-90. Philadelphia:
University of Pennsylvania Press, 1971.

Ryan, Frances Rita, transl., Fulcher of
Chartres "A History of the Expedition to Jerusalem,
1095-1127," ed. Harold S. Fink. Knoxville: The
University of Tennessee Press, 1969; reprint ed.
("Records of Civilization" in Norton Paperback
Editions), New York: W. W. Norton and Co., 1973.

A complete translation of Fulcher's work.

ANNA COMNENA (1083-after 1148)

Text Editions

"Alexiad"

"Syntagma Deo juvante rerum ab imp. Alexio
Comneno gestarum ab ejusdem filia domina Anna
porphyrogenita principe elaboratum et Alexius
inscriptum" /i.e. Alexiad/, in Migne, Patrologia
Graeca, 131:79-1212.

Anna Comnena /"Alexiad"/, books 10-14, in
RHC, Grecs, vol. 1, part 2:1-204. Paris:
Imprimerie Nationale, 1875.

Books 10-14 contain Anna's description of
the first crusade.

Parallel columns with Greek original and
Latin translation.

Leib, Bernard, ed. and transl., Anna Comnène
"Alexiade" (Règne de l'empereur Alexis i Comnène,
1081-1118). 3 vols. ("Collection Byzantine").
Paris: Société d'édition "Les Belles Lettres,"
1937-1945.

Greek text recto, French translation verso.

English Translations

"Alexiad"

Dawes, Elizabeth, A. S., transl., The "Alexiad" of the Princess Anna Comnena, being the

<u>History of the Reign of Her Father, Alexius I,</u>
<u>Emperor of the Romans, 1081-1118 A.D.</u> London:
Kegan Paul, Trench, Trubner and Co., 1928; reprint
ed., New York: Barnes and Noble, 1967.

Sewter, E. R. A., transl., <u>The "Alexiad" of</u>
<u>Anna Comnena</u>, ("The Penguin Classics"). Baltimore,
Maryland: Penguin Books, 1969.

Modern Studies

Buckler, Georgina, <u>Anna Comnena: A Study</u>.
London: Oxford University Press, 1929.

Dalven, Rae, <u>Anna Comnena</u> ("Twayne's World
Authors Series," vol. 213). New York: Twayne
Publishers, 1972.

Mitchison, Naomi, <u>Anna Comnena</u> ("Representative Women"). London: Gerald Howe, 1928.

WILLIAM OF TYRE (ca. 1130-before 1185)

Text Editions

"History of the Deeds Done Beyond the Sea"

<u>"Historia rerum in partibus transmarinis</u>
<u>gestarum a tempore successorum Mahumeth usque</u> ad
annum Domini MCLXXXIV edita a venerabili Guillelmo
Tyrensi archiepiscopo," in Migne, <u>Patrologia</u>
<u>Latina</u>, 201:209-892.

"Guilelmi Tyrensis continuata <u>Belli sacri</u>
<u>historia</u>," in Migne, <u>Patrologia Latina</u>, 201:893-
1060.

Continuation of William's <u>Historia rerum...</u>
<u>transmarinis</u> in old French to the days of Gregory X
(pope 1271-1276).

<u>"Historia rerum in partibus transmarinis</u>
<u>gestarum a tempore successorum Mahumeth usque</u> ad
annum Domini MCLXXXIV edita a venerabili Willelmo
Tyrensi archiepiscopo. L'Estoire de eracles

empereur et la conqueste de la Terre d'Outremer;
c'est la translation de l'Estroire de Guillaume
arcevesque de Sur," in <u>RHC, Occ</u>., vol. 1.   Paris:
Imprimerie Royale, 1844.

    Latin text with Old French translation.

    Paris, M. Paulin, ed., <u>Guillaume de Tyr et</u>
<u>ses continuateurs</u>.   2 vols. ("Histoire générale
des croisades par les anteurs contemporains").
Paris: Librairie de Firmin-Didot et cie, 1879-
1880.

    A thirteenth century French translation of
William of Tyre (without continuators).

English Translation

    "History of the Deeds Done Beyond the Sea"

    Babcock, Emily Atwater and Krey, August C.,
transl., <u>"A History of Deeds Done Beyond the Sea"</u>
<u>by William, Archbishop of Tyre</u>. 2 vols. (Columbia
University, Department of History," Records of
Civilization: Sources and Studies," vol. 35 in 2).
New York: Columbia University Press, 1943.

    The translation does not contain William's
continuators, but ends with his original work in
1184.

AMBROSE (fl. ca. 1196)

Text Edition

        "History of the Holy War"

    Paris, Gaston, ed., <u>"L'Estoire de la guerre</u>
<u>sainte: Histoire en vers de la troisième croisade</u>
<u>(1190-1192)" par Ambroise</u> ("Collection de documents
inédits sur l'histoire de France," vol. 11).
Paris: Imprimerie Nationale, 1897.

English Translations

"History of the Holy War"

Hubert, Merton Jerome, transl., "The Crusade of Richard Lion-Heart" by Ambroise. Notes and documentation by John L. LaMonte (Columbia University, Department of History, "Records of Civilization: Sources and Studies," vol. 34). New York: Columbia University Press, 1941.

A verse translation of Ambroise's chronicle from Gaston Paris' edition.

Stone, Edward Noble, transl., "The History of the Holy War (L'Estoire de la guerre sainte), being an Account of the Third Crusade, Composed in Verse by Ambrose," in Three Old French Chronicles of the Crusades, pp. 1-160 (University of Washington, "Publications in the Social Sciences," vol. 10, pp. 1-378). Seattle: The University of Washington, 1939.

A prose translation of Ambroise's verse chronicle from Gaston Paris' edition.

GEOFFREY OF VILLEHARDOUIN (ca. 1150-ca. 1213)

Text Editions

"The Conquest of Constantinople"

Faral, Edmond, ed. and transl., Villehardouin "La Conquête de Constantinople." 2 vols. ("Les Classiques de l'histoire de France au moyen age," vols. 18-19. Paris: Société d'édition "Les Belles Lettres," 1938-1939; 2nd rev. ed. in 1961.

Old French text verso, modern French translation recto.

English Translations

"The Conquest of Constantinople"

Marzials, Frank, transl., "Villehardouin's
Chronicle of the Fourth Crusade and the Conquest
of Constantinople," in Memoirs of the Crusades by
Villehardouin and de Joinville, pp. 1-134.
("Everyman's Library," vol. 333). London: J. M.
Dent and Sons; New York: E. P. Dutton and Co.,
1908; several reprint eds.

Shaw, M. R. B., transl., "Villehardouin The
Conquest of Constantinople," in Joinville and
Villehardouin: Chronicles of the Crusades, pp.
27-160 ("The Penguin Classics"). Baltimore:
Penguin Books, 1963.

Modern Studies

Archambault, Paul, "Villehardouin: History
in Black and White," in Seven French Chroniclers:
Witnesses to History by Paul Archambault, pp. 25-
39. Syracuse: Syracuse University Press, 1974.

Beer, Jeannette, M. A., Villehardouin, Epic
Historian. ("Études de philologie et d'histoire,"
vol. 7). Genèva: Libraire Droz, 1968.

ROBERT OF CLARI (died after 1216)

Text Edition

"The Conquest of Constantinople"

Lauer, Philippe, ed., Robert de Clari "La
Conquête de Constantinople." ("Les Classiques
Francais du moyen age," vol. 40). Paris: Librairie ancienne Honorè Champion, 1924; reprint
ed. 1956.

English Translations

"The Conquest of Constantinople"

McNeal, Edgar Holmes, transl., Robert of
Clari "The Conquest of Constantinople" (Columbia
University, Department of History, "Records of
Civilization: Sources and Studies," vol. 23).

New York: Columbia University Press, 1936; reprint ed.,("Records of Civilization" in Norton Paperback Editions), New York: W. W. Norton and Co., 1969.

Stone, Edward Noble, transl., "The History of them that took Constantinople (Li estoire de chians qui conquisent Constantinoble), being an Account of the Fourth Crusade ⁄by⁄ Robert of Clari in Amiénois, Knight," in Three Old French Chronicles of the Crusades, pp. 161-246 (University of Washington "Publications in the Social Sciences," vol. 10, pp. 1-378). Seattle: The University of Washington, 1939.

JOHN OF JOINVILLE (1224-1317)

Text Edition

"Life of St. Louis"

Wailly, Natalis de, ed., Jean Sire de Joinville "Histoire de Saint Louis." Paris: Librairie de Finmin Didot frères, fils et co., 1874.

Old French text verse, modern French translation recto.

English Translations

"Life of St. Louis"

Evans, Joan, transl., The "History of St. Louis" by Jean, Sire de Joinville. London: Oxford University Press, 1938.

Johnes, Thomas, transl., "Lord de Joinville's Memoirs of Louis IX, King of France, Commonly Called Saint Louis," in Chronicles of the Crusades, pp. 343-500 ("Bohn's Antiquarian Library"). London: Henry G. Bohn, 1848; reprint ed., New York: AMS Press, 1969.

Marzials, Frank, transl., "Joinville's Chronicle of the Crusades of St. Lewis," in

Memoirs of the Crusades by Villehardouin and de Joinville, pp. 135-328 ("Everyman's Library," vol. 333). London: J. M. Dent and Sons; New York: E. P. Dutton and Co., 1908; several reprint eds.

Shaw, M.R.B., transl., "Joinville The Life of Saint Louis," in Joinville and Villehardouin: Chronicles of the Crusades, pp. 161-353 ("Penguin Classics"). Baltimore: Penguin Books, 1963.

Modern Studies

Archambault, Paul, "Joinville: History as Chivalric Code," in Seven French Chroniclers: Witnesses to History by Paul Archambault, pp. 41-57. Syracuse: Syracuse University Press, 1974.

EKKEHARD OF AURA (ca. 1080-after 1126)

Text Editions

"Chronicle"

"Chronicon Wirziburgense auctore, ut videtur, Ekkehardo," in Migne, Patrologia Latina, 154:459-496.

It is a brief chronicle from the Nativity to 1057, ascribed to Ekkehard.

"Ekkehardi Chronicon universale," in Migne, Patrologia Latina, 154:497-998.

A universal chronicle from Moses to 1106.

"Ekkehardi Pars altera anni 1106-1125," in Migne, Patrologia Latina, 154:999-1060.

Continuation of Ekkehard's universal chronicle to 1125.

"Ekkehardi abbatis Uraugiensis Hierosolymita" in RHC, Occ., 5:1-40. Paris: Imprimerie Nationale, 1895.

202.

This text excerpts from Ekkehard's Chronicle
scattered descriptions of the Crusades from 1096
to 1104 and organizes them into a unit.

Schmale, Franz-Josef and Schmale-Ott, Irene,
eds. and transl., "Ekkehardi Chronica; Ekkehard
von Aura," in Frutolfi et Ekkehardi "Chronica"
necnon Anonymi "Chronica imperatorum." Frutolfs
und Ekkehards "Chroniken" und die Anonyme"
Kaiserchronik," pp. 123-209. ("Ausgewählte Quellen zur deutschen Geschichte des Mittelalters,"
vol. 15). Darmstadt: Wissenschaftliche Buchhandlung, 1972.

This editions prints the entire Chronicle
arranged according to different redactions. Latin
text verso, German translation recto.

Waitz, Georg, ed., "Chronicon Wirziburgense
ad a. 1057" in MGH, SS, 6:17-23. Hanover:
Hahnsche Buchhandlung, 1844.

Waitz, Georg, ed., "Ekkehardi Chronicon universale ad a. 1106." Ibid., pp. 33-231.

Waitz, Georg, ed., "Chronici universalis pars
altera, a. 1106-1125," Ibid., pp. 231-265.

Waitz's edition prints the entire Chronicle
in three parts, as in Migne.

English Translation

"Chronicle"

Clarke, Howard W., transl., "Ekkehard of
Aurach The First Crusade," in Gerald M. Straka,
ed., The Medieval World and Its Transformations,
800-1650, pp. 155-177. ("Western Society: Institutions and Ideals," vol. 2). New York: McGraw-
Hill Book Co., 1967.

Translation of Ekkehard's "Hierosolymita"
from RHC, Occ., 5:11-40.

OTTO OF FREISING (ca. 1114-1158)

Text Editions

"Chronicle of the Two Cities"

Hofmeister, Adolph, ed., Ottonis ep. Frisingensis "Chronica sive historia de duabus civitatibus" (MGH, Script in usum schol.). Hanover and
Leipzig: Hahnsche Buchhandlung, 1912.

Lammers, Walther, ed., Ottonsis episcopi
Frisingensis "Chronica sive historia de duabus
civitatibus." Otto Bischof von Freising "Chronik
oder Die Geschichte der zwei Staaten;" transl.
Adolf Schmidt. ("Ausgewählte Quellen zur deutschen
Geschichte des Mittelalters," vol. 16). Berlin:
Rütten and Loening, 1960.

Latin text verso, German translation recto.

Wilmans, Roger, ed., "Ottonis episcopi Frisingensis Chronicon," in MGH, SS, 20:83-301.
Hanover: Hahnsche Buchhandlung, 1868.

"The Deeds of Emperor Frederick Barbarossa"

Schmale, Franz-Josef, ed., Ottonis episcopi
Frisingensis et Rahewini "Gesta Frederici seu
rectius cronica." Bischof Otto von Freising und
Rahewin "Die Taten Friedrichs oder richtiger
Cronica;" transl. Adolf Schmidt. ("Ausgewählte
Quellen zur deutschen Geschichte des Mittelal-
ters," vol. 17). Berlin: Deutscher Verlag der
Wissenschaften, 1965.

Latin text verso, German translation recto.

Simson, B., H., ed., Ottonis et Rahewini
"Gesta Friderici I imperatoris." (MGH, Script. in
usum schol.). Hanover and Leipzig: Hahnsche
Buchhandlung, 1912.

Wilmans, Roger, ed., "Gesta Friderici I
imperatoris auctoribus Ottone episcopo et

Ragewino praeposito Frisingensibus," in <u>MGH, SS</u>, 20:338-493. Hanover: Hahnsche Buchhandlung, 1868.

English Translations

"Chronicle of the Two Cities"

Mierow, Charles Christopher, transl., "<u>The Two Cities: A Chronicle of Universal History to the Year 1146 A.D.</u>," by Otto Bishop of Freising; ed Austin P. Evans and Charles Knapp. (Columbia University, Department of History, "Records of Civilization: Sources and Studies," vol. 9) New York: Columbia University Press, 1928; reprint ed., New York: Octagon Books, 1966.

"The Deeds of Frederick Barbarossa"

Mierow, Charles Christopher and Emery, Richard, transl., "<u>The Deeds of Frederick Barbarossa</u>" by Otto of <u>Freising and His Continuator, Rahewin</u> (Columbia University, Department of History, "Records of Civilization: Sources and Studies," vol. 49). New York: Columbia University Press, 1953.

Modern Studies

Mierow, Charles Christopher, "Bishop Otto of Freising, Historian and Man," in <u>Proceedings of the American Philological Association</u>, 80(1949): 393-401.

Mierow, Charles Christopher, "Otto of Freising: A Medieval Historian at Work," in <u>Philological Quarterly</u>, 14(1935):344-362.

Mierow, Charles Christopher, "Otto of Freising and His Two Cities Theory," in <u>Philological Quarterly</u>, 24(1945):97-105.

HELMOLD OF BOSAU (died ca. 1177)

Text Editions

"Chronicle of the Slavs"

Lappenberg, Johann, M., ed., "Helmoldi presbyteri Chronica Slavorum," in MGH, SS. 21:1-99.
Hanover; Hahnsche Buchhandlung, 1869.

Schmidler, Bernhard, ed., Helmoldi presbyteri
Bozoviensis "Chronica Slavorum." 3rd ed. (MGH,
Script. in usum schol.) Hanover: Hahnsche Buch-
handlung, 1937.

Stoob, Heinz, ed. and transl., Helmoldi
presbyteri Bozoviensis "Chronica Slavorum."
Helmold von Bosau "Slawenchronik." ("Ausgewählte
Quellen zur deutschen Geschichte des Mittelalters,"
vol. 19). Berlin: Rütten and Loening, 1969.

Latin text verso, German translation recto.

English Translation

"Chronicle of the Slavs"

Tschan, Francis Joseph, transl., "The Chronicle of the Slavs" by Helmold, Priest of Bosau.
(Columbia University, Department of History.
"Records of Civilization: Sources and Studies,"
vol. 21). New York: Columbia University Press,
1935.

ARNOLD OF LÜBECK (died ca. 1212)

Text Editions

"Chronicle of the Slavs"

Lappenberg, Johann M., ed., "Arnoldi abbatis
Lubecensis Chronica" /i.e. Chronica Slavorum/, in
MGH, SS, 21:101-250. Hanover: Hahnsche Buchhand-
lung, 1869.

206.

Pertz, Georg Heinrich, ed., <u>Arnoldi</u> "Chronica Slavorum" (<u>MGH, Script. in usum schol.</u>).
Hanover: Hahnsche Buchhandlung, 1868; reprint
ed. 1930.

ORDERIC VITALIS (1075-1142)

Text Editions

"Ecclesiastical History"

"Orderici Vitalis Angligenae, coenobii
Uticensis monachi, <u>Historiae ecclesiasticae libri
XII in partes tres divisi</u>," in Migne, <u>Patrologia
Latina</u>, 188:9-984.

Le Prevost, Augustus, ed., <u>Orderici Vitalis
Angligenae, coenobii Uticensis monachi "Historiae
ecclesiasticae libri tredecim</u>." 5 vols. ("Société de l'histoire de France," vol. 2 in 5).
Paris: Julius Renouard and co., 1838-1855;
reprint ed. 1965.

English Translations

"Ecclesiastical History"

Chibnall, Marjorie, ed. and transl., "<u>The
Ecclesiastical History of Orderic Vitalis</u>, vol.
2-5 (in progress) "Oxford Medieval Texts"). Oxford: The Clarendon Press, 1969- in progress.

Latin text verso, English translation recto.
Vol. 1 in preparation.

Forester, Thomas, transl., "<u>The Ecclesiasti-
cal History of England and Normandy</u>" by Ordericus
Vitalis. 4 vols. (Bohn's Antiquarian Library").
London: Henry G. Bohn, 1853-1856; reprint ed.,
New York: AMS Press, 1968.

WILLIAM OF MALMESBURY (ca. 1095-1143)

Text Editions

"The Deeds of the Kings of England"

"Willelmi Malmesburiensis monachi De gestis regum Anglorum libri quinque," in Migne, Patrologia Latina, 179:945-1392.

Stubbs, William, ed., Willelmi Malmesbiriensis monachi "De gestis regum Anglorum libri quinque." 2 vols. (RS, vol. 90 in 2). London: Her Majesty's Stationery Office, 1887-1889.

"Modern History"

"Willelmi Malmesburiensis monachi Historiae novellae libri tres," in Migne, Patrologia Latina, 179:1391-1440.

Stubbs, William, ed., Willelmi Malmesbiriensis monachi "Historiae novellae libri tres" (RS, vol. 90, pt. 2:525-596). London: Her Majesty's Stationery Office, 1889.

"The Deeds of the Bishops
and Abbots of England"

"Willelmi Malmesburiensis monachi De gestis pontificum Anglorum libri quinque," in Migne, Patrologia Latina, 179:1441-1680.

Hamilton, N.E.S.A., ed., Willelmi Malmesbiriensis monachi "De gestis pontificum Anglorum libri quinque" (RS, vol. 52). London: Longman and Co. and Trübner and Co., 1870.

English Translations

"The Deeds of the Kings of England"

Sharpe, John, transl., William of Malmesbury "Chronicle of the Kings of England from the Earliest Period to the Reign of King Stephen;" ed. John Allen Giles ("Bohn's Antiquarian Library"). London: Henry G. Bohn, 1847.

Sharpe, John, transl., "William of Malmesbury's History of the Kings of England;" transl. revised by Joseph Stevenson, in The Church Historians of England, vol. 3, part 1:1-381. London: Seeleys, 1854.

"Modern History"

Potter, K.R., ed. and transl., The "Historia Novella" by William of Malmesbury ("Medieval Texts"). London: Thomas Nelson and Sons, 1955.

Latin text verso, English translation recto.

Sharpe, John, transl., "William of Malmesbury's History of His Own Times;" transl. revised by Joseph Stevenson, in The Church Historians of England, vol. 3, part 1:381-422. London: Seeleys, 1854.

Modern Studies

Farmer, Hugh, "William of Malmesbury's Life and Work," in Journal of Ecclesiastical History, 13 (1962): 39-54.

Farmer, D. H., "Two Biographies by William of Malmesbury," in T. A. Dorey, ed., Latin Biography, pp. 157-176 ("Studies in Latin Literature and Its Influence," ed. D. R. Dudley and T. A. Dorey). New York: Basic Books, 1967.

James, M. R., Two Ancient English Scholars: St. Aldhelm and William of Malmesbury ("Glasgow University Publications," vol. 22). Glasgow: Jackson, Wylie and Co., 1931.

A brief essay on several works at the former library at Malmesbury, once held by Aldhelm and William of Malmesbury.

HENRY OF HUNTINGDON (ca. 1084-1157)

Text Editions

"History of the English"

"Henrici archidiaconi Huntingdonensis Historiarum libri octo," in Migne, Patrologia Latina,
195:799-978.

Arnold, Thomas W., Henrici archidiaconi
Huntendunensis "Historia Anglorum." "The History
of the English" by Henry, Archdeacon of Hunting-
don, from B.C. 55 to A.D. 1154, in Eight Books
(RS, vol. 74). London: Longman and Co. and
Trübner and Co., 1879.

English Translations

"History of the English"

Forester, Thomas, transl., "History of the
English," in The Chronicle of Henry of Hunting-
don, comprising the History of England from the
Invasion of Julius Caesar to the Accession of
Henry II; also "The Acts of Stephen, King of
England and Duke of Normandy." ed. Thomas Fores-
ter, pp. 1-297 ("Bohn's Antiquarian Library").
London: Henry G. Bohn, 1853; reprint ed.,
New York: AMS Press, 1968.

Douglas, David C. and Greenway, George W.,
transl., "Henry of Huntingdon: Some Events in
the Reign of Stephen described, in The History of
the English," in English Historical Documents
2:305-313. London: Eyre and Spottiswoode, 1968.

ROGER OF HOWDEN (died ca. 1201)

Text Editions

"Chronicle"

Stubbs, William, ed., "Chronica" magistri
Rogeri de Houedene. 4 vols. (RS, vol. 51 in 4).
London: Her Majesty's Stationery Office, 1868-
1871; reprint ed., New York: Kraus Reprint Corp.,
1964.

This edition covers the years from 732 to
1201.

Stubbs, William, ed., "Gesta regis Henrici
Secundi" Benedicti abbatis. "The Chronicle of
the Reigns of Henry II and Richard I. A.D. 1169-
1192," Known Commonly under the Name of Benedict
of Peterborough. 2 vols. (RS, vol. 49 in 2).
London: Longmans, Green, Reader, and Ayer, 1867.

This chronicle apparently is Roger of Howden's first draft for his Chronicle 732-1201,
containing the years 1169-1192; see below, under
"Modern Studies:" Doris M. Stenton, "Roger of
Hoveden and Benedict;" see also below, p. 233
under "Benedict of Peterborough."

English Translations

"Chronicle"

Riley, Henry T., transl., The "Annals" of
Roger de Hoveden, comprising the History of England and of other Countries of Europe from A.D.
732 to A.D. 1201. 2 vols. ("Bohn's Antiquarian
Library"). London: Henry G. Bohn, 1853; reprint
ed., New York: AMS Press, 1968.

Riley, H. T., transl., "The Chronicle of
Mr. Roger of Howden: Selected Passages from the
Years 1190-2," in English Historical Documents,
3:63-81. London: Eyre and Spottiswoode, 1975.

Modern Studies

Barlow, Frank, "Roger of Howden," in English
Historical Review, 65(1950):352-360.

Stenton, Doris M., "Roger of Hoveden and
Benedict," in English Historical Review, 68(1953):
574-582.

Stubbs, William, "The Chronicle of Roger of
Hoveden, vol. 2, 3, 4," in Historical Introductions to the Rolls Series by William Stubbs, ed.

Arthur Hassall, pp. 178-309. London: Longmans,
Green and Co., 1902.

Stubbs, William, "The Chronicle of the
Reigns of Henry II and Richard I, A.D. 1169-1192,
known commonly under the name of Benedict of
Peterborough, vol. 2," in Historical Introductions
to the Rolls Series by William Stubbs, ed. Arthur
Hassall, pp. 89-172. London: Longmans, Green and
Co., 1902.

ROGER OF WENDOVER (died 1236)

Text Editions

"Flowers of History"

Coxe, Henry Octavius, ed., Rogeri de Wendover "Chronica," sive "Flores historiarum." 5
vols. ("English Historical Society Publications,"
vols. 14-18). London: English Historical Society,
1841-1845.

This edition prints only the portion from
447 to 1235.

Hewlett, Henry G., ed., Rogeri de Wendover
liber qui dicitur "Flores historiarum," ab anno
Domini MCLIV annoque Henrici Anglorum regis
secundi primo. The "Flowers of History" by Roger
de Wendover from the Year of Our Lord 1154, and
the First Year of Henry the Second, King of the
English. 3 vols. (RS, vol. 84 in 3). London:
Longman and Co., 1886-1889.

This edition prints the years 1154-1235.

For a complete edition of the Flores, with
Matthew Paris' interpolations, see below, under
"Matthew Paris."

English Translations

"Flowers of History"

Giles, J. A. transl., Roger of Wendover's
"Flowers of History," comprising the History of
England from the Descent of the Saxons to A.D.
1235, formerly ascribed to Matthew Paris. 2 vols.
("Bohn's Antiquarian Library"). London: Henry G.
Bohn, 1849; reprint ed., New York: AMS Press,
1968.

The translation contains the years 447-1235
from H. O. Coxe's edition.

Modern Studies

Galbraith, Vivian Hunter, Roger Wendover
and Matthew Paris. ("Glasgow University Publications," vol. 61). Glasgow: Jackson, Son and
Co., 1944.

Holt, J. C., "The St. Albans Chroniclers and
Magna Carta," in Transactions of the Royal Historical Society, 5th series, 14 (1964):67-88.

Kay, Richard, "Wendover's Last Annal," in
English Historical Review, 84(1969):779-785.

MATTHEW PARIS (ca. 1200-1259)

Text Editions

"Greater Chronicle"

Luard, H. R., ed., Matthaei Parisiensis,
monachi Sancti Albani, "Chronica majora." 7 vols.
(RS, vol. 57 in 7). London: Longman's and Co.
and Trübner and Co., 1872-1883.

The Chronicle, from the Creation to 1259, is
printed in vols. 1-5; book 6 contains the "Supplements" (Additamenta); book 7 contains the
"Index," a "Glossary," the "Erratum" and the
"Addenda." This edition also prints in small
type the complete text of Roger of Wendover's
"Flowers of History."

213.

"History of the English" or
"The Lesser Chronicle"

Madden, Frederic, ed., <u>Matthaei Parisiensis</u>, <u>monachi Sancti Albani</u>, "Histo<u>ria Anglorum</u>," sive, <u>ut vulgo dicitur, "Historia minor</u>." 3 vols. (<u>RS</u>, vol. 44 in 3). London: Longmans, Green, Reader and Ryer, (publishers vary), 1866-1869.

"Flowers of History"

Luard, Henry Richard, ed. <u>Flores historiarum</u>. 3 vols. (<u>RS</u>, vol. 95 in 3). London: Her Majesty's Stationery Office, 1890.

Matthew's authorship can be proven only for vol. 1 of the <u>Flores</u> and to the year 1259 for vol. 2. From 1259 to the end of vol. 2 (1264) the <u>Flores</u> were continued at St. Albans by an unknown scribe, but from 1265 to 1326 (i.e. vol. 3) they were compiled at Westminster. Previously the <u>Flores historiarum</u> were wrongly attributed to a Matthew of Westminster.

"Drawings"

James, M. R., ed., "The Drawings of Matthew Paris," in <u>The Fourteenth Volume of the Walpole Society 1925-1926</u>, pp. 1-26. Oxford: The Walpole Society, 1926.

Dr. James' introduction and description of the drawings is preceded by the frontis-piece to the volume and followed by 30 plates containing 143 more facsimile drawings attributed to Matthew Paris and his school of drawings, taken from nine manuscripts, incl. the <u>Historia majora</u> and the <u>Historia Anglorum</u>.

Wormald, Francis, ed., "More Matthew Paris Drawings," in <u>The Thirty-First Volume of the Walpole Society 1942-1943</u>, pp. 109-112. London: The Walpole Society, 1946.

Wormald's brief introduction is followed by

three plates containing four facsimile drawings attributed to the school of Matthew Paris.

English Translations

"Greater Chronicle"

Giles, J. A., transl., Matthew Paris's "English History" from the Year 1235 to 1273. 3 vols. ("Bohn's Antiquarian Library"). London: Henry G. Bohn, 1852-1854; reprint ed., New York: AMS Press, 1968.

Giles' translation is prepared from William Wats' 2nd ed. of Matthaei Paris monachi Albanensis angli "Historia Major," London, 1684.

The third vol. contains a "Continuation of Matthew Paris" from 1259 to 1273, ascribed to William Rishanger, monk of St. Albans, as well as selections from Matthew Paris's Additamenta for the years 1239 to 1257.

Giles, J. A., transl., "The Greater Chronicle (Chronica Majora) of Matthew Paris of St. Albans for the Years 1258-9" (transl. revised by Harry Rothwell), in English Historical Documents, 3: 103-153. London: Eyre and Spottiswoode, 1975.

"Flowers of History"

Yonge, C. D., transl., Matthew of Westminster "Flowers of History," especially such as Relate to the Affairs of Britain. From the Beginning of the World to A.D. 1307. 2 vols. (Bohn's Antiquarian Library). London: Henry G. Bohn, 1853.

Yonge's translation was made from an earlier printing of the Flowers of History, ed. by Matthew Parker, Flores historiarum Matthaei Westmonasteriensis monachi, London, 1567; therefore Yonge's translation does not quite agree with Luard's text.

Modern Studies

Galbraith, Vivian Hunter, <u>Roger Wendover and
Matthew Paris</u>; see above, under Roger of Wendover.

Powicke, F. M. "The Compilation of the <u>Chron-
ica majora</u> of Matthew Paris," in <u>Proceedings of
the British Academy</u>, vol. 30 (1944):147-160.

Vaughan, Richard, <u>Matthew Paris</u> ("Cambridge
Studies in Medieval Life and Thought," New Series,
vol. 6). Cambridge: The University Press, 1958.

The best biography of Matthew Paris.

Vaughan, Richard, "The Handwriting of Matthew Paris," in <u>Transactions of the Cambridge
Bibliographical Society</u>, 1(1949-1953):376-394.

SALIMBENE (1221-1288)

Text Editions

"Chronicle"

Holder-Eggers, Oswald, ed., "<u>Chronica</u>
fratris Salimbene de Adam, Ordinis Minorum," in
<u>MGH, SS</u>, vol. 32. Hanover and Leipzig: Hahnsche
Buchhandlung. 1905-1913.

Scalia, Giuseppe, ed., <u>Salimbene di Adam</u>
"Cronica." 2 vols. ("Scrittori d'Italia," vols.
232-233). Bari: Gius, Laterza and Figli, 1966.

English Translations

"Chronicle"

Coulton, G. G., transl., <u>From St. Francis to
Dante: Translations from the "Chronicle" of the
Franciscan Salimbene (1221-1288)</u>; 2nd rev. and
enlarged ed. by Edward Peters. Philadelphia:
University of Pennsylvania Press, 1972.

This work actually is a paraphrase of

216.

Salimbene's Chronicle in English with extensive
direct quotations.

Hermann, Placid, transl., "The Chronicle of
Brother Salimbene degli Adami: Selections" in,
XIIIth Century Chronicles: Jordan of Giano,
Thomas of Eccleston, Salimbene degli Adami,
pp. 193-290. Chicago: Franciscan Herald Press,
1961.

Minor Historians

Text Editions, English Translations, Modern
Studies

AMATUS (ca. 1020-ca. 1105)

Champollion-Figeac, Jacques Joseph, ed.,
"L'Ystoire de li Normant," et "La Chronique de
Robert Viscart," par Aime, moine du Mont-Cassin.
Paris: Chez Jules Renouard, 1835.

De Bartholomaeis, Vincenzo, ed., "Storia de'
Normani" di Amato di Montecassino volgarizzata in
antico Francese ("Fonti per la storia d'Italia,"
vol. 76). Roma: Instituto storico Italiano per
il Medio evo, 1935.

Dalarc, O., ed., "Ystoire de li Normant" par
Aimé, évèque et moine au Mont-Cassin ("Societé de
l'histoire de Normandie"). Rouen: A. Lestringant, 1892.

GODFREY MALATERRA (fl. ca. 1097)

"Gaufredi Malaterrae Historia Sicula," in
Migne, Patrologia Latina, 149:1087-1216.

Pontieri, Ernesto, ed., "De rebus gestis
Rogerii Calabriae et Siciliae comitis et Roberti
Guiscardi ducis fratris eius auctore Gaufredo
Malaterra, monacho Benedictino," in Muratori,
Rerum Italicarum scriptores, new ed., vol. 5,
part 1. Bologna: Nicola Zanichelli, 1927.

This is a new and revised edition of "Historia Sicula," in Muratori, Rerum Italicarum scriptores, 5:537-602. Milan: Typographia societatis palatinae, 1724.

WILLIAM OF POITIERS (ca. 1020-before 1101)

"Willelmi Conquestoris gesta a Willelmo Pictavensi Lexoviorum archidiacono, cotemporaneo scripta," in Migne, Patrologia Latina, 149:1217-1270.

Foreville, Raymonde, ed. and transl., Guillaume de Poitiers "Histoire de Guillaume de Conquirant" ("Les Classiques de l'histoire de France du moyen age," vol. 23). Paris: Societe d'édition "Les Belles Lettres," 1952.

Latin text verso, French translation recto.

Giles, J. A., ed. "/William of Poitiers/ Gesta Willelmi ducis Normannorum," in Scriptores rerum gestarum Willelmi Conquestoris, pp. 77-159. London: D. Nutt, 1845.

Douglas, David C. and Greenway, George W., transl., "William of Poitiers The Deeds of William, Duke of the Normans and King of the English," in English Historical Documents, 2:217-231. London: Eyre and Spottiswoode, 1968.

Partial translation of William's work.

Dorey, T. A., "William of Poitiers: "Gesta Guillelmi Ducis," in T. A. Dorey, ed., Latin Biography, pp. 139-155 ("Studies in Latin Literature and Its Influence," ed. D. R. Dudley and T. A. Dorey). New York: Basic Books, 1967.

Analysis of William's work.

WILLIAM OF JUMIÈGES (died ca. 1090)

"Willelmi Calculi Gemmeticensis monachi Historiae Northmannorum libri octo," in Migne,

<u>Patrologia Latina</u>, 149:779-910.

This edition contains an interpolated text.

Marx, Jean, ed., <u>Guillaume de Jumièges "Gesta Normannorum ducum."</u> ("Societe de l'histoire de Normandie"). Rouen: A. Lestringant (also Paris: Auguste Picard), 1914.

A critical edition of William's text.

Douglas, David C. and Greenway, George W., transl., "William of Jumièges: Description of the Invasion of England by William the Conqueror," in <u>English Historical Documents</u>, 2:215-216. London: Eyre and Spottiswoode, 1968.

A brief excerpt from William's work.

Stevenson, Joseph, transl., "<u>History of King Henry the First</u>, by Robert de Monte," in <u>The Church Historians of England</u>, vol. 5, part 1:1-39. London: Seeleys, 1858.

This composition sometimes is regarded as the seventh book of the <u>History</u> of William of Jumiege.

BRUNO (fl. ca. 1100)

"Brunonis clerici Magdeburgensis <u>Liber de bello Saxonico</u>," in Migne, <u>Patrologia Latina</u>, 147:489-586.

Pertz, Georg Heinrich, ed., "Brunonis <u>Liber de bello Saxonico</u>," in <u>MGH</u>, <u>SS</u>, 5:327-384. Hanover: Hahnsche Buchhandlung, 1844.

Schmale, Franz-Josef, ed., and transl., "Brunonis <u>Saxonicum bellum</u>. Brunos <u>Sachsenkrieg</u>," in <u>Quellen zur Geschichte Kaiser Heinrichs IV</u>, pp. 191-405 ("Ausgewählte Quellen zur deutschen Geschichte des Mittelalters," vol. 12). Berlin: Rütten and Loening, 1963.

Wattenbach, W., ed., Brunonis "De bello Saxonico liber" (MGH, Script. in usum schol.). Hanover: Hahnsche Buchhandlung, 1880.

LIFE OF EMPEROR HENRY IV

Eberhard, W., ed., Vita Heinrici IV imperatoris (MGH, Scrip. in usum schol.). Hanover: Hahnsche Buchhandlung, 1899; reprint eds. 1925-1949.

Schmale, Franz-Josef, ed., "Vita Heinrici IV imperatoris. Das Leben Kaiser Heinrichs IV;" transl. Irene Schmale-Ott, in Quellen zur Geschichite Kaiser Heinrichs IV, pp. 407-467 ("Ausgewählte Quellen zur deutschen Geschichte des Mittelalters," vol. 12). Berlin: Rütten and Loening, 1963.

Wattenbach, W., ed., "Vita Heinrici IV imperatoris," in MGH, SS, 12:268-283. Hanover: Hahnsche Buchhandlung, 1856.

RAYMOND OF AGUILERS (fl. ca. 1120)

"Raimundi de Agiles canonici Podiensis Historia Francorum qui ceperunt Jerusalem," in Migne, Patrologia Latina, 155:591-668.

"Raimundi de Aguilers canonici Podiensis Historia Francorum qui ceperunt Jherusalem," in RHC, Occ., 3:231-309. Paris: Imprimerie Impériale, 1866.

Hill, John Hugh and Hill, Laurita L., eds. Le Liber de Raymond d'Aguilers ("Documents relatifs à l'histoire des croisades" publiés par l'Académie des inscriptions et belles-lettres). Paris: Librairie orientaliste Paul Geuthner, 1969.

Hill, John Hugh and Hill, Laurita L., transl., Raymond d'Aguilers "Historia Francorum qui ceperunt Jherusalem" ("Memoirs of the American Philosophical Society," vol. 71).

Philadelphia: The American Philosophical
Society, 1968.

Krey, August, C., transl., "Historia Francorum qui ceperunt Jerusalem by Raymond of Aguilers,"
in The First Crusade: The Accounts of Eye-Witnesses and Participants, ed. August C. Krey, printed
intermittently with other accounts. Princeton:
Princeton University Press, 1921; reprint ed.,
Gloucester, Mass.: Peter Smith, 1958.

Translation from RHC, Occ,; for sequence of
pages, see Krey, p. 283.

PETER TUDEBODE (fl. ca. 1110)

"Petri Tudebodi sacerdotis Siuracensis Historia de Hierosolymitano itinere," in Migne,
Patrologia Latina, 155:763-822.

"Petri Tudebodi seu Tudebovis sacerdotis
Sivracensis Historia de Hierosolymitano itinere,"
in RHC, Occ., 3:1-117. Paris: Imprimerie
Impériale, 1866.

Hill, John Hugh and Hill, Laurita L., transl.,
Peter Tudebode "Historia de Hierosolymitano
itinere" ("Memoirs of the American Philosophical
Society," vol. 101). Philadelphia: The American
Philosophical Society, 1974.

GUIBERT OF NOGENT (ca. 1064-ca. 1125)

"Historia quae dicitur gesta Dei per Francos
edita a ven. Guiberto abbate monasterii Sanctae
Mariae Novigenti" /also Historia Hierosolymitana/,
in Migne, Patrologia Latina, 156:679-838.

"Historia quae dicitur gesta Dei per Francos
edita a venerabili domno Guiberto, abbate monasterii Sanctae Mariae Novigenti," in RHC, Occ.,
4:113-263. Paris: Imprimerie Nationale, 1879.

Krey, August C., transl., "Gesta Dei per
Francos by Guibert, abbot of Nogent," in The First

Crusade: The Accounts of Eye-Witnesses and Participants, ed., August C. Krey, pp. 36-40; 47-48. Princeton: Princeton University Press, 1921, reprint ed., Gloucester, Mass.: Peter Smith, 1958.

Only the events at the Council of Clermont, 1095, and the account of the role of Peter the Hermit are translated.

"Ven. Guiberti De vita sua sive monodiarium libri tres," in Migne, Patrologia Latina, 156: 837-962.

Bourgin, Georges, ed., Guibert de Nogent "Histoire de sa vie" (1053-1124) ("Collection de textes pour servir à l'étude et à l'enseignement de l'histoire"). Paris: Librairie Alphonse Picard et fils, 1907.

Bland, C. C. Swinton, transl., The "Autobiography" of Guibert, Abbot of Nogent-sous-Coucy. ("Broadway Translations"). New York: E. P. Dutton and Co., 1925; rev. ed. by John F. Benton, Self and Society in Medieval France: The "Memoirs" of Abbot Guibert of Nogent (1064?-c. 1125). ("Harper Torchbooks" TB 1471). New York: Harper and Row, 1970.

ROBERT THE MONK (fl. ca. 1105)

"Roberti monachi s. Remigii in diocesi Remensi Historia Hierosolymitana," in Migne, Patrologia Latina, 155:667-758.

"Roberti monachi Historia Jherosolimitana," in RHC, Occ., 3:717-882. Paris: Imprimerie Imperiale, 1866.

Krey, August C., transl., "Hierosolymitana expeditio by Robert the Monk," in The First Crusade: The Account of Eye-Witnesses and Participants, ed. August C. Krey, pp. 30-33; see above, under "Guibert of Nogent."

Events at the Council of Clermont, 1095, alone translated.

ALBERT OF AIX (died after 1120)

"Alberici Aquensis Historia Hierosolymitanae expeditionis," in Migne, Patrologia Latina, 166:389-716.

"Alberti Aquensis Historia Hierosolymitana," in RHC, Occ., 4:265-713. Paris: Imprimerie Nationale, 1879.

Krey, August C., transl., "Liber Christianae expeditionis pro ereptione, emundatione, restitutione Sanctae Hierosolymitanae by Albert of Aix," in The First Crusade: The Accounts of Eye-Witnesses and Participants, ed. August C. Krey, printed intermittently with other accounts; see above, under "Guibert of Nogent."

Translation of several passages from RHC, Occ., for sequence of pages, see Krey, p. 283.

ODO OF DEUIL (died ca. 1162)

"Odonis de Deogilo De Ludovici VII Francorum regis cognomento junioris, profectione in Orientem, in Migne, Patrologia Latina, 185:1201-1246.

Waquet, Henri, ed., Eudes de Deuil "La Croisade de Louis VII roi de France." ("Documents relatifs a l'histoire des croisades" publiés par l'Académie des inscriptions et belles-lettres," vol. 3). Paris: Librairie orientaliste Paul Geuthner, 1949.

Berry, Virginia Gingerick, ed. and transl., Odo of Deuil "De profectione Ludovici VII in Orientem." "The Journey of Louis VII to the East." (Columbia University, Department of History, "Records of Civilization: Sources and Studies," vol. 42). New York: Columbia University Press, 1948; reprint ed. ("Records of Civilization" in Norton paperback editions), New York: W. W. Norton and Co., 1965.

Latin text verso, English translation recto.

CONTINUATORS TO WILLIAM OF TYRE

"Continuatur Historia rerum in partibus transmarinis gestarum ab anno Domini MCLXXXIII usque ad annum MCCLXXVII, edita a venerabili Willermo Tyrensi archiepiscopi." "L'Estoire de eracles empereur et la conqueste de la Terre d'Outremer; c'est la continuation de l'estoire de Guillaume arcevesque de Sur" in RHC, Occ., vol. 2. Paris: Imprimerie Impériale, 1859.

Mas Latrie, Jacques Marie Joseph Louis, de, ed., Chronique d'Ernoul et de Bernard le Trésorier. ("Société de l'histoire de France"). Paris: Jules Renouard, 1871.

Morgan, Margaret R., The Chronicle of Ernoul and the Continuations of William of Tyre. ("Oxford Historical Monographs"). London: Oxford University Press, 1973.

A scholarly analysis of the Old French continuations of William of Tyre (without texts).

ITINERARIUM PEREGRINORUM (Richard, fl. ca. 1220)

Stubbs, William ed., "Itinerarium peregrinorum et gesta regis Ricardi: auctore, ut videtur, Ricardo, canonico Sanctae Trinitatis Londoniensis," in Chronicles and Memorials of the Reign of Richard I, 1:1-450. 2 vols. (RS, vol. 38 in 2). London: Longman, Green Longman, Roberts, and Green, 1864.

Itinerarium peregrinorum is a Latin prose adaption of Ambrose; see above, p. 198.

Fenwick, Kenneth, transl., The Third Crusade: An Eye Witness Account of the Campaigns of Richard Coeur-de-Lion in Cyprus and the Holy Land. London: Folio Society, 1958.

Translation based on Bohn's edition; see below.

Giles, John Allen and Johnes, T., transl., "Geoffrey de Vinsauf's Itinerary of Richard I and Others to the Holy Land," in Chronicles of the Crusaders, pp. 65-339 ("Bohn's Antiquarian Library"). London: Henry G. Bohn, 1848; reprint ed., New York: AMS Press, 1969.

Edwards, J. G., "The Itinerarium Regis Ricardi and the Estoire de la Guerre Sainte," in Historical Essays in Honor of James Tait, pp. 59-77, ed. J. G. Edwards, V. H. Galbraith and E. F. Jacob. Manchester: Printed for the Subscribers, 1935.

Landon, Lionel, comp., The Itinerary of King Richard I ("The Publications of the Pipe Roll Society," vol. 51; New Series, vol. 13). London: Pipe Roll Society, 1935.

A calendar of Richard I's travels.

OLIVER OF PADERBORN (died 1227)

Hoogeweg, H., ed., "Historia Damiatina," in Die Schriften des Kölner Domscholasters, späteren Bischofs von Paderborn und Kardinal - Bischofs von S. Sabina Oliverus, pp. 159-282 ("Bibliothek des litterarischen Vereins in Stuttgart," vol. 202). Tübingen: Litterarischer Verein in Stuttgart, 1894.

Garigan, Joseph J., transl., "The Capture of Damietta" by Oliver of Paderborn (University of Pennsylvania, Department of History, "Translations and Reprints from the Original Sources of History," 3rd series, vol. 2). Philadelphia: University of Pennsylvania Press, 1948; reprint ed. in Christian Society and the Crusades 1198-1229, ed. Edward Peters, pp. 49-139. Philadelphia: University of Pennsylvania Press, 1971.

225.

PHILIP OF NOVARA (ca. 1195-ca. 1265)

"Estoire de la guerre qui fu entre l'empereor Frederic et Johan d'Ibelin" in <u>Les Gestes des Chiprois</u>, pp. 670-736 (<u>RHC, Armen</u>, vol. 2). Paris: Imprimerie Nationale, 1906.

<u>Les Gestes</u> are made up of three books: 1st - "Chronique de Terre Sante (1132-1224)", pp. 653-689; 2nd - "Estoire de la guerre" (1228-1243) by Philip of Novara; 3rd - "Livre III" (1243-14th cent.), attributed to Templar of Tyre, pp. 737-872.

Kohler, Charles, ed., <u>Philippe de Novare</u> "Mémoires 1218-1243" (Les Classiques francais du moyen age" vol. 10). Paris: Librairie ancienne Honoré Champion, 1913.

Best edition of the <u>Mémoires</u>.

Raynaud, Gaston, ed., "Philippe de Novarre Mémoirs," in <u>Les Gestes des Chiprois</u>, pp. 25-138 ("Publications de la Société de l'orient latin: serie historique," vol. 5). Paris and Geneva: J. G. Fick, 1887; reprint ed., Osnabrück: Otto Zeller, 1968.

In this edition of the <u>Gestes</u> the "Chronique de Terre-Sainte" (1131-1224) is printed on pp. 1-24; Philip's "Mémoires" (1212-1242), occupy pp. 25-138 and the "Chronique" (1242-1309) by Templar of Tyre appears on pp. 139-334.

La Monte, John L. and Hubert, Merton Jerome, transl., <u>The Wars of Frederick II against the Ibelins in Syria and Cyprus</u> (Columbia University, Department of History, "Records of Civilization: Sources and Studies," vol. 25). New York: Columbia University Press, 1936.

Translation of Philip of Novara's <u>Mémoires</u> from Charles Kohler's edition.

HENRY OF LIVONIA (died after 1259)

Arbusow, Leonid and Bauer, Albert, eds., Heinrichs "Livländische Chronik," 2nd ed. (MGH, Script. in usum schol.). Hanover: Hahnsche Buchhandlung, 1955.

Arndt, Wilhelm, ed., "Heinrici Chronicon Lyvoniae," in MGH, SS, 23:231-332. Hanover: Hahnsche Buchhandlung, 1874.

Brundage, James A., transl., The "Chronicle" of Henry of Livonia ("Documents from Medieval Latin"). Madison: University of Wisconsin Press, 1961.

PETER ABELARD (1079-1142)

"Petri Abaelardi operum pars prima: epistulae," in Migne, Patrologia Latina, 178:113-182.

The first of the Epistulae containing Abelard's Historia calamitatum.

Monfrin, Jacques, ed., Abélard "Historia calamitatum" ("Bibliothèque des textes philosophiques," ed., Henri Gouhier). Paris: Librairie philosophique J. Vrin, 1959; 3rd ed., Paris: J. Vrin, 1967.

Bellows, Henry Adams, transl., "Historia calamitatum, The Story of My Misfortunes." An Autobiography by Peter Abelard. Saint Paul: T. A. Boyd, 1922.

Moncrieff, C. K. Scott, transl., The Letters of Abelard and Heloise. London: G. Chapman, 1925; there are several reprint eds.

Radice, Betty, transl., The Letters of Abelard and Heloise ("The Penguin Classics"). Harmondsworth, Engl.: Penguin Books, 1974.

The first "Letter" in Moncrieff's and Radice's transl. is the Historia calamitatum.

Muckle, J. T., transl., The Story of Abelard's Adversities. Toronto: The Pontifical Institute of Mediaeval Studies, 1954; reprint ed., 1964.

A translation of Abelard's Historia calamitatum.

Benton, John Frederick and Ercoli, Fiorella Prosperetti, "The Style of the Historia calamitatum: A Preliminary Text of the Authenticity of the Correspondence Attributed to Abelard and Heloise," in Viator 6(1975):59-86.

In the article the authors question the authenticity of the Historia calamitatum.

Luscombe, David, E., The School of Peter Abelard: The Influence of Abelard's Thought in the Early Scholastic Period. ("Cambridge Studies in Medieval Life and Thought," N.S., vol. 14). Cambridge: The University Press, 1969.

McCabe, Joseph, Peter Abelard. New York and London: G. P. Putnam's Sons, 1901; reprint ed. (Burt Franklin, "Research and Source Works Series: Philosophy and Religious History Monographs," vol. 110), New York: Burt Franklin, 1972.

Sikes, J. G., Peter Abailard. Cambridge: The University Press, 1932; reprint ed., New York: Russel and Russel, 1965.

THE DEEDS OF STEPHEN

Howlett, Richard, ed., "Gesta Stephani regis Anglorum," in Chronicles of the Reigns of Stephen, Henry II, and Richard I, 3:3-136. (RS., vol. 82, part 3). London: Her Majesty's Stationery Office, 1886; reprint ed., New York: Kraus Reprint Corp., 1964.

Forester, Thomas, transl., "The Acts of Stephen, King of England and Duke of Normandy, by an Unknown but Contemporaneous Author," in

The Chronicle of Henry of Huntingdon, comprising
the History of England from the Invasion of Julius
Caesar to the Accession of Henry II; also The Acts
of Stephen, King of England and Duke of Normandy,
ed. Thomas Forester, pp. 321-430. ("Bohn's Antiquarian Library"). London: Henry G. Bohn, 1853;
reprint ed., New York: AMS Press, 1968.

Potter, K. R., ed. and transl., Gesta Stephani. The Deeds of Stephen ("Nelson's Medieval
Texts"). London: Thomas Nelson and Sons, 1955;
new ed. ("Oxford Medieval Texts"), Oxford:
Clarendon Press, 1976.

Latin text verso, English translation recto.

Stevenson, Joseph, transl., "The Acts of
Stephen, King of England and Duke of Normandy,"
in The Church Historians of England, vol. 5,
part 1:41-129. London: Seeleys, 1858.

Davis, R. H. C., "The Authorship of the
Gesta Stephani," in English Historical Review,
77(1962):209-232.

GEOFFREY OF MONMOUTH (ca. 1084-ca. 1154)

Faral, Edmond, ed., "Geoffray de Monmouth
Historia regum Britanniae" in La Legénde arthur-
ienne, études et documents. Premiere partie:
les plus anciens textes. Tome III: Documents,
pp. 74-303 ("Bibliothéque de l'école des hautes
études: Sciences historiques et philologiques,"
vol. 257). Paris: Librairie ancienne Honoré
Champion, 1929.

Griscom, Acton, ed., and Jones, Robert Ellis,
transl., The "Historia regum Britanniae" of Geoffrey of Monmouth. London and New York: Longmans,
Green and Co., 1929.

This edition contains the Latin text with an
English translation of a Welsh manuscript, of
which the text is not given.

Thompson, Aaron, transl., "Geoffrey of Monmouth's British History," in Six Old English Chronicles, ed. J. A. Giles, pp. 87-292 ("Bohn's Antiquarian Library"). London: Henry G. Bohn 1848; reprint ed., New York: AMS Press, 1968.

Thorpe, Lewis, transl., Geoffrey of Monmouth "The History of the Kings of Britain." ("The Penguin Classics"). Harmondsworth, England: Penguin Books, 1966; reprint ed., 1968.

Fletcher, Robert Huntingdon, The Arthurian Material in the Chronicles, Especially Those of Great Britain and France ("Burt Franklin Bibliographicas Series," vol. 10). New York: Burt Franklin, 1958.

This work was originally published in 1906 in "Harvard Studies and Notes in Philology and Literature," vol. 10.

Jones, Thomas, "The Early Evolution of the Legend of Arthur," in Nottingham Mediaeval Studies, 8(1964), 3-21.

Keeler, Laura, "The Historia regum Britanniae and Four Mediaeval Chroniclers," in Speculum, 21 (1946):24-37.

Keeler, Laura, Geoffrey of Monmouth and the Late Latin Chroniclers 1300-1500. (University of California, "Publications in English," vol. 17). Berkeley and Los Angeles: University of California Press, 1946; reprint ed., New York: Kraus Reprint Co., 1977.

Lloyd, J. E., "Geoffrey of Monmouth," in The English Historical Review, 57(1942):460-468.

Parry, John J. and Caldwell, Robert A., "Geoffrey of Monmouth," in Arthurian Literature in the Middle Ages: A Collaborative History, ed. Roger S. Loomis, pp. 72-93. London: Oxford University Press, 1959.

Tatlock, J. S. P., The Legendary History of Britain: Geoffrey of Monmouth's "Historia regum Britanniae" and Its Early Vernacular Versions. Berkeley and Los Angeles: University of California Press, 1950.

A thorough scholarly study of Geoffrey of Monmouth's work.

WILLIAM OF NEWBURGH (ca. 1135-ca. 1198)

Howlett, Richard, ed., "The First Four Books of the Historia rerum Anglicarum of William of Newburgh," in Chronicles of the Reigns of Stephen, Henry II, and Richard I, 1:3-408(1884); 4 vols. "The Fifth Book of the Historia rerum Anglicarum of William of Newburgh," in Ibidem, 2:409-583 (1885). (RS, vol. 82 in 4). London: Her Majesty's Stationery Office, 1884-1889.

Douglas, David C. and Greenway, George W., transl., "William of Newburgh The History of England," in English Historical Documents, 2:322-373. London: Eyre and Spottiswoode, 1968.

Translation contains books 2-3.

Stevenson, Joseph, transl., "The History of William of Newburgh," in The Church Historians of England, vol. 4, part 2: 395-672. London: Seeleys, 1856.

GERVASE OF CANTERBURY (died ca. 1210)

Stubbs, William, ed., "The Chronicle of the Reigns of Stephen, Henry II, and Richard I, by Gervase, the Monk of Canterbury," vol. 1. 2 vols. (RS, vol. 73 in 2). London: Her Majesty's Stationery Office, 1879; reprint ed., New York: Kraus Reprint Corp., 1965.

RALPH OF DICETO (died 1202)

Stubbs, W., ed., "Ymagines historiarum" in Radulfi de Diceto decani Lundoniensis opera

PETER LANGTOFT OF BRIDLINGTON (died ca. 1307)

Wright, Thomas ed., "The Chronicle of Pierre de Langtoft" in French Verse, from the Earliest Period to the Death of King Edward I. 2 vols. (RS, vol. 47 in 2). London: Longmans, Green, Reader, and Dyer, 1866-1868.

Old French verse verso, English verse translation recto. The present translation is based on a translation by Robert of Brunne, a later contemporary of Peter Langtoft.

Wright, Thomas, transl., "The Chronicle of Peter Langtoft of Bridlington for the Years 1297 to 1307," in English Historical Documents, 3:230-265. London: Eyre and Spottiswoode, 1975.

For other English translations of all listed works see Bibliography of English Translations from Medieval Sources (listed above, p. 47, under "Early Christian Historians").

Bohn's Ecclesiastical
  Library, 49
Bonser, Romano-British
  Bibliography, 114;
  Anglo-Saxon and
  Celtic Bibliography,
  114
Book of Supplements,
  see Matthew Paris
Brandt, The Shape of
  Medieval History,
  120
Bruno, 149, 219, 220;
  Saxon Revolt, 149,
  eds., 219-220
Buckler, Anna Comnena,
  197

Caldwell, see Parry
  and Caldwell
Cambridge Medieval
  History, 41
Capture of Damietta,
  see Oliver of
  Paderborn
Carolingian Chronicles,
  106
Carolingian Renaissance,
  94, 95, 97, 98, 105
Cassiodorus, 12, 67,
  70, 140, 163; Chron-
  icle, 12, eds., 67-
  68; Tripartite His-
  tory, 12, 70, 163,
  eds., 67; History of
  the Goths, 70; Let-
  ters, 70, eds., 140,
  transls., 140
Cavanaugh, see Gay and
  Cavanaugh
Chevalier, Répertoire
  ...: bio-bibliogra-
  phie and Répertoire
  ...: topo-bibliogra-
  phie, 42

Christ, Nativity, 4,
  7, 22, 29, 70, 79,
  84, 86, 87, 88;
  death, 4; Second
  Coming, 4, 5, 15,
  18, 19, 21, 22, 79,
  87, 163
Christian era, 11, 18,
  21, 29, 70, 86, 87,
  88
Chronicle, medieval,
  70, 99, 100-102,
  161; development
  from annals, 100,
  147; distinction
  from history, 101-
  102; authorship,
  102; commissioned,
  102, 105; universal,
  147, 167
Chronicle, see Euse-
  bius, Cassiodorus,
  Sextus Julius Africa-
  nus, Sulpicius Seve-
  rus, Thietmar, Herman
  the Cripple, Ekke-
  hard, Trutolf, Roger
  of Howden, Jocelin
  of Brakelond, Ger-
  vase, Peter Lang-
  toft, Salimbene
Chronicle of Bury St.
  Edmunds, 182, 186,
  233, eds., 233,
  transls., 233
Chronicle of the
  Reigns of Henry II
  and Richard I, 175,
  212, 233, eds., 233
Chronicle of the
  Slavs, see Helmold
  of Bosau, Arnold of
  Lübeck
Chronography, see Sex-
  tus Julius Africanus,

Psellus

Chronological Tables,
see Eusebius, Je-
rome, Prosper of
Aquitaine, Isidore
of Seville

Chronology, see Peri-
odization of history

Church Historians of
England, 118

city of devil, see
Augustine, and 33

City of God, see
Augustine

city of man, see
Augustine, and 33

Classiques de l'his-
toire de France au
moyen age, 118

Cognasso, Avviamento
agli studi di storia
medievale, 114

Columbia University,
Department of His-
tory, see Records of
Civilization

Commentary on the
Psalms, see Gregory
of Tours

Comnena, Anna, 155,
196, 197; modern
studies, 197;
Alexiad, 155, eds.,
196, transls., 196-
197

Confessions, see
Augustine

Conquest of Constan-
tinople, see Geof-
frey of Villehard-
ouin, Robert of
Clari

Constantine, emperor,
5, 6, 8, 9

Corpus Christianorum:
series Latina, 46

Corpus scriptorum ec-
clesiasticorum
Latinorum, 46

Course of the Stars,
see Gregory of Tours

Creation, see Adam

Crusades, 146, 147,
151-163, 165, 168,
170, 172, 174, 175,
177, 179, 189-190,
202-203, 220-223,
224, 225; historio-
graphy of first cru-
sade, 151-155, 156,
161, 162, 170, 202-
203, 220-223; of
second, 155, 165,
223; of third, 156-
157, 174, 175, 224;
of fourth, 157-158;
of fifth, 158, 225;
of Frederick II,
158-159, 220; of
St. Louis, 159-160;
impact, 160-161;
northern expansion,
168, 206, 227

Cyprian, 5, 60-61;
modern studies, 61;
The Lapsed, 5, eds.,
61, transls., 61;
Letters, 5, eds.,
60, transls., 61

Cyril, patriarch of
Alexandria, 85-86,
87

Dahlmann-Waitz, Quel-
lenkunde der deut-
schen Geschichte,
114-115

Dalven, Anna Comnena,
197

Gesta Francorum, 151–
152, 153, 162; au-
thorship, 151;
sources, 151; sig-
nificance, 152;
eds., 194, transls.,
194–195
Gildas, 81–82, 91, 92,
142, 143, 170, 173;
On the Destruction
and Conquest of
Britain, 82, 91,
eds., 142, transls.,
142–143
Gothic History, see
Jordanes
Gransden, Historical
Writing in England,
113
Graves, A Bibliography
of English History
to 1485, 115
Greater Chronicle, see
Matthew Paris
Greek Ecclesiastical
Historians, 48
Gregory of Tours, 77–
81, 89, 93, 94, 108,
109, 124, 125; life,
77; sources, 78–79,
80; periodization
of history, 79; phi-
losophy of history,
79–80, belief in
miracles, saints,
relics, providence,
80; significance,
80–81; language,
81; modern studies
125; Miracles, 77,
eds., 124, transls.,
125; The Course of
the Stars, 77–78;
A Commentary on the
Psalms, 78; History
of the Kings of the
Franks, 78–81, 109,
eds., 124, transls.,
125
Griechischen christ-
lichen Schriftstel-
ler, 46–47
Guibert of Nogent,
154, 221, 222; His-
tory of the Deeds of
God, 154, eds., 221,
transls., 221–222;
Memoirs, 154, eds.,
222, transls., 222
Guth, Late Medieval
England 1377–1485,
189

Hanning, The Vision of
History, 120, 192
heavenly city, see
Augustine, and 33
Helmold of Bosau,
167, 168, 186, 206;
Chronicle of the
Slavs, 167, eds.,
206, transls., 206
Henry of Huntingdon,
172, 173, 174, 176,
187, 209, 210;
History of the En-
glish, 172, 174,
eds., 210, transls.,
210
Henry of Livonia, 168,
186, 227; Livonian
Chronicle, 168, eds.,
227, transls., 227
Herman of Reichenau,
107, 111, 138, 139,
149, 176; Chronicle,
107, 108, eds., 138–
139

Herman the Cripple,
see Herman of
Reichenau
Historia Arcana, see
Procopius
Historiographical works,
41–42, 113–114, 189
History in Eight Books,
see Procopius
History journals, 44–
45
History of English
Affairs, see Wil-
liam of Newburgh
History of English
Church and People,
see Bede
History of Sicily,
see Malaterra
History of the Arch-
bishops of Hamburg-
Bremen, see Adam
of Bremen
History of the Bishops
of Metz, see Paul
the Lombard
History of the Britons,
see Nennius
History of the Church,
see Ecclesiastical
History
History of the Deeds
of God, see Guibert
of Nogent
History of the English,
see Henry of Hunt-
ingdon, Matthew Paris
History of the Expedi-
tion to Jerusalem,
see Fulcher of
Chartres, Robert
the Monk, Albert
of Aix
History of the Goths,
see Cassiodorus

History of the Goths,
Vandals and Suevi,
see Isidore of
Seville
History of the Holy
War, see Ambrose
History of the Kings
of Britain, see
Geoffrey of Monmouth
History of the Kings
of the Franks, see
Gregory of Tours
History of the Lom-
bards, see Paul the
Lombard
History of the Normans,
see Amatus
History of the Wars,
see Procopius
Holt, "The St. Albans
Chroniclers", 213
Hunter Blair, The
World of Bede, 129

Impressions of History,
see Ralph of Diceto
International Bibliog-
raphy of Historical
Sciences, 42
International Guide to
Medieval Studies, 42
International Medieval
Bibliography, 43
Investiture Controver-
sy, 145, 149, 165,
168, 184; historiog-
raphy of, 192–193,
219–220
Isidore of Seville, 8,
71–72, 83, 87, 93,
100, 140, Etymolo-
gies, 8, 72, 83,
eds., 64, transls.,
64; History of the
Goths, Vandals and

247.

215; Lesser Chronicle, 181, eds., 214; History of the English, see Lesser Chronicle; Flowers of History, 182, eds., 214, transls., 215; Drawings, 181, eds., 214

Parks and Temple, The Greek and Latin Literatures, 44

Parry and Caldwell, "Geoffrey of Monmouth", 230

Patrologia cursus completus: series Graeca, 45, 115, 189, indices, 45

Patrologia cursus completus: series Latina, 45, 115, 189, supplement, 46

Paul the Deacon, see Paul the Lombard

Paul the Lombard, 92–94, 107, 129, 130, 163, 170; life, 92–93; sources, 93; Carolingian Renaissance, 94; History of the Bishops of Metz, 93, eds., 130; History of the Lombards, 93–94, 163, eds., 129–130, transls., 130

Pelagianism, 13, 27, 32

Periodization of history, see Sextus Julius Africanus, Eusebius, Augustine, Orosius, Bede, Otto of Freising, and

70, 84–86, 120

Persecutions of Christians, 5, 8, 86

Philip of Novara, 159, 186, 226; Memoires, 159, eds., 226, transls., 226; Deeds of the Cypriots, 159, eds., 226

Philosophy of history, see Eusebius, Augustine, Orosius, Gregory of Tours, Otto of Freising, Rahewin

Poole, Chronicles and Annals, 111, 121; "The Earliest Use of the Easter Cycle of Dionysius", 144

Potthast, Bibliotheca historica, 43

Powicke, "The Compilation of the Chronica majora of Matthew Paris", 216

Procopius of Caesarea, 72–76, 96, 122, 123; life, 72–73; significance, 76; modern studies, 123; History in Eight Books, 73–74, 75, eds., 122, transls., 123; History of the Wars and Wars, see History in Eight Books; Secret History, 74–75, 76, 96, eds., 122, transls., 123; Anecdota and Historia Arcana, see Secret History; On Buildings, 75, 76, eds., 122, transls., 123

Profane history, see
Augustine, and 37,
71
Prosper of Aquitaine,
8, 63; Chronicle, 8,
eds., 63-64
Providence, divine,
see Eusebius, Augus-
tine, Gregory of
Tours, Gildas,
Matthew Paris
Psellus, Michael, 150-
151, 193, 194; life,
150; Greek histori-
ographical tradi-
tion, 150; sources,
151; significance,
151; modern studies,
194; Chronography,
150, 151, eds., 193,
transls., 193

Quasten, Patrology, 50

Rahewin, 166-167; con-
tinuator to Otto,
166; sources, 166-
167; idea of his-
tory, 166; see also
Otto of Freising
Ralph of Diceto, 174,
176, 231, 232; Im-
pressions of His-
tory, 174, eds.,
231-232
Raymond of Aguilers,
152, 153, 156, 185,
220, 221; History
of the Frankish
Conquerors, 152,
eds., 220, transls.,
220-221
Records of Civiliza-
tion: Sources and
Studies, 118-119

Recueil des historiens
des croisades, 189-
190
Reference Works, see
General Reference
Works
Relics, 23-24, 80
Repertorium fontium
historiae medii
aevi, 43
Reply to Faustus the
Manichaen, see
Augustine
Rerum Britannicarum
Medii Aevi scrip-
tores, 117, 120
Richard, canon, 156-
157, 224-225; Itin-
erary of the Pil-
grims, 157, eds.,
224, transls., 224-
225
Richer, 106-107, 136,
137; Four Books of
History, 106, eds.,
136-137
Robert of Clari, 158,
161, 200, 201; com-
parison with Ville-
hardouin, 158; The
Conquest of Con-
stantinople, 158,
eds., 200, transls.,
200-201
Robert the Monk, 154-
155, 222, 223; His-
tory of the Expedi-
tion to Jerusalem,
154, eds., 222,
transls., 222-223
Roger of Howden, 174-
175, 176, 187, 210,
211, 212; life, 174;
continuator to Bede,
174; sources,

174-175, modern studies, 211-212; Chronicle, 174, 175, eds., 210-211, 213, transls., 211

Roger of Wendover, 175-177, 180, 181, 187, 212, 213; life, 175; sources, 176-177; Magna Carta, 176; reign of King John, 176; significance, 177; modern studies, 213; Flowers of History, 175, 176, eds., 212, transls., 213

Rolls Series, see Rerum Britannicarum...

Rome, founding of, 7, 22, 28, 29

Rouse, Serial Bibliographies for Medieval Studies, 43

Royal Frankish Annals, 95, 97, 99, 101, 104-105, 106, 144; compilation, 105; authorship, 105; written in Latin, 105; Carolingian Renaissance, 105; sources, 105; relationship to chronicle, 105; continuation, 106; eds., 144, transls., 144

Rufinus of Aquileia, 11, 64-65, 78, 163; Ecclesiastical History, 11, 78, eds., 64-65

Sacred History, see Sextus Julius Africanus, Eusebius, Augustine, Gregory of Tours, Otto of Freising

Saints, 23-24, 80, 91, 108

Salimbene, 183, 216, 217; Chronicle, 183, eds., 216, transls., 216-217

Sallust, 2, 24, 27, 28, 149, 166

Saxon Revolt, see Bruno

Second Coming, see Christ

Secret History, see Procopius

Secular history, see Sextus Julius Africanus, Augustine, Orosius, Jordanes, Bede, Matthew Paris

Secular state, see Sextus Julius Africanus, Augustine, Orosius, Otto ot Freising

Select Library of the Nicene and Post-Nicene Fathers, see Nicene and Post-Nicene Fathers

Seven Books of History, see Orosius

Sextus Julius Africanus, 4, 5, 6, 7, 10, 14, 15, 30, 60, 84; periodization of history, 4; Chronography, 4, 5, eds., 60, transls., 60; Chronicle, see Chronography

Sikes, Peter Abailard, 228

Smalley, Historians in the Middle Ages, 41